World Without Secrets

World Without Secrets

BUSINESS, CRIME, AND PRIVACY IN THE AGE OF UBIQUITOUS COMPUTING

Richard Hunter

Gartner Press
A Division of Gartner, Inc.

John Wiley & Sons, Inc.

Published by John Wiley & Sons, Inc., New York.
Published simultaneously in Canada.

Library of Congress Cataloging-in-Publication Data:

Hunter, Richard, 1952–
    World without secrets: business, crime, and privacy in the age of ubiquitous computing / Richard Hunter.
        p. cm.
Includes bibliographical references and index.
    ISBN 0-471-21816-2 (cloth: alk. paper)
    1. Information technology—Social aspects. 2. Telematics—Social aspects. 3. Electronic commerce—Social aspects. 4. Electronic surveillance—Social aspects. 5. Digital media—Social aspects. 6. Privacy, Right of. 7. Computer crimes. I. Title.
    HM851.H86   2002
    303.48′33—dc21
                2001008167

Printed in the United States of America.

10 9 8 7 6 5 4 3 2 1

*This is for my wife Patty
and my children, Dean and Susan.*

CONTENTS

PREFACE

This book begins with the basic assumption that we're moving rapidly into a *World Without Secrets,* a world in which very little of consequence can't and won't be known about anyone or anything. To create a vision of the World Without Secrets and its workings, I've drawn heavily on the work of my colleagues at Gartner, Inc., the world's premier information technology advisory services company. I've also learned from the individuals who are making and applying the technologies that will be found in this world, and from other professionals, journalists, and researchers who have an interest in the subject.

I've been guided throughout by my belief that, regardless of the changes that occur in our environment, man made or otherwise, the nature of human beings doesn't change much. People generally seek to optimize their environments and circumstances in ways that serve their own immediate needs and desires first. They're inherently resistant to change to a far greater extent than the technologies they deploy. They have limited attention spans and limited capacities for the absorption of new information, especially information that challenges the established ways of thinking.

They tend to act first and think later. This has been especially true where tools and technologies are concerned, and it's more true now than ever. Years after the fact, we still don't understand the full implications of the introduction of now-common technologies such as the internal combustion engine, television, and nuclear power. Yet we continue to introduce new technologies at a blinding rate. The power of our technologies is arguably beyond our ability to control them, but the rate of introduction won't decline while there's money to be made and opportunities to be seized.

It's tempting to assume that the advance of technology through markets and cultures is inevitable, but of course it's not. As Alvin Toffler said years ago, the future arrives at the wrong time and in the wrong order, and no straight-line extrapolation is ever accurate. (One of the big breakthroughs in Clayton Christensen's writings is his insistence that we should *stop trying* to predict the trajectories of disruptive technologies, because predictions just won't work.) It's also tempting to veer toward the most heavenly or hellish scenarios. Both are essentially straight-line extrapolations using different basic assumptions, and neither is likely. It's true that we have enough resources at our disposal now to ensure that no one in the world goes naked or hungry, and yet we've made only sporadic and feeble attempts to do so. It's also true that we hold in our hands the power to destroy all life on the planet, yet we haven't done so, and may never.

Above all, I'm certain that the era of ubiquitous computing won't make life simpler or easier for most humans. The likeliest scenarios are ultimately about how people deploy every ounce of their strength, their intelligence, and their will to deal with a man-made environment that becomes more complex with every passing moment. There's no doubt that some segments of society, worldwide, will crack under the pressure. There's also little doubt that the rest of us will find ways to survive and succeed somehow. This book suggests some of the strategies that will allow us to do so.

If the nature of human beings doesn't change much while all this is going on, perhaps that's okay. A friend of mine, a woman who has been a champion of advanced technology research and development in this country since the mid-1980s, is the child of a Russian mother who was imprisoned, during the Stalin era, in the Gulag Archipelago prison system. Her imprisonment lasted throughout my friend's adolescence. My friend continued to live under the Soviet system, undoubtedly one of the most brutally repressive of the past century, until the late 1970s, when she was allowed to emigrate to America. I met her not long after; she was hired as a trainee programmer at the large insurance company where I was employed, in Boston, Massachusetts. One sunlit day in the spring of 1989, as we walked through Boston's Copley Square on our lunch break, this woman told me, in so many words, that she believed people are essentially *good*.

I was completely astonished. Surely she, as much as anyone I knew, had suffered at the hands of a cruel, impersonal political system. Surely she, as much as anyone, was entitled to a dismal view of human nature.

Surely that was *my* view of human nature, and I had suffered much less at the hands of others than she. Yet this complex person whose past was filled with raw oppression believed simply that human beings are good.

Who was I—who am I now—to claim that she was wrong?

The World Without Secrets is a complex, demanding, and dangerous place for the wary and unwary alike. It's not Hell. Those who populate it are only people, not demons. And people—so I must believe, based on the testimony of those who should know—are basically good.

RICHARD HUNTER

ACKNOWLEDGMENTS

This book has been a while in the making, and a lot of people have helped along the way. I'll start by thanking Carol Wallace, my colleague at Gartner, Inc. Her response, early in 2001, to a sheet of paper with a Global Business Network-style quadrant on it, one corner of which contained the words "World Without Secrets," told me that I had an idea worth pursuing. Bob Knapp made it possible for me to devote all my time to the project, for which I'm grateful.

Marianne Broadbent, the leader of Gartner's Executive Programs Group, gave the earliest, most detailed, and best feedback on this book. Zach Morowitz took the time to read the first few chapters and comment extensively as well. Both helped produce a much better book, one that was more enjoyable to write and, I hope, to read. Bill Kirwin's efforts as my editor and soundboard at Gartner were critically important to my sanity, let alone the project.

In the early stages of the book, some of the most important analysis was done by a team that included French Caldwell, Susan Anderson, and Bill Kirwin. Their efforts in defining the social structure of the World Without Secrets helped enormously in analyzing the impact of such phenomena as the Open Source Movement.

At Gartner, I'm surrounded by extraordinary analysts, and it would take a long time to thank every member of that community who contributed in some way to this book. I'll single out Bill Malik, the leader of the Security Research Community at Gartner, and John Pescatore, one of the best analysts on Bill's strong team, for constantly providing thought-provoking analyses that helped shape my own thoughts on these complex topics, and direct support in defining the future of cyber-crime. Jackie

Fenn's work on advanced technologies was a critical factor in defining the time line for technologies that govern the World Without Secrets.

I am grateful to every interviewee who offered time and insight to me, including Eric Raymond, Susan Anderson, Alicia Peck, Bill Bodin, Chris Amenita, Chris Sagalyn, David Bernstein, Ken Watman, Tom Koloski, Len Hynds, Steve Millstein, Gary Wallace, Mary Jo Deering, Cynthia Baur, Marco Alpert, Max Brunswick, Nicos Peonides, Patty Casey, Victor Kovner, Terry Danner, Ron Sobel, Miles Copeland, Bill Todd, Frances Zelazny, Don Simmonds, David Reid, Neil Scott, Egil Juliussen, Richard Stallman, and Amy Ray.

I've been assisted throughout by Sandra Lahtinen, Dora Salm, and other members of Gartner's Information Resource Center, surely a world-class research team.

Michelle Henderson of Gartner Press assisted, in many ways, with smoothing over the bumps that tend to slow authors down.

Finally, thanks to my wife, Patty, for her support, excitement in the work as it developed, and steely-eyed management of my time for the past six months.

The World Without Secrets is a dynamic place, to say the least. For the latest updates and research, check the World Without Secrets Web site at http:/www.worldwithoutsecrets.com.

R.H.

EVERYTHING YOU NEED
TO KNOW BEFORE WE START

Let's cut to the chase.

—Meg Ryan in *Presidio*

Starting just before yesterday and accelerating over the next 10 years, almost everything that people and the machines around them do will be continuously recorded and stored in databases. We can argue about whether "almost everything" really means "almost *everything*." For the stuff that really matters, it does.

Bulletproof security for information systems doesn't exist now, and it won't exist 10 years from now. People who want to know *anything* badly enough will be able to find out whatever they want to know. We can argue about whether "anything" really means "*anything*." It does.

There's way too much information—about everything—out there now, and it's going to get a lot worse, not least because everything is and will be recorded. We can argue about whether that means *a whole lot* worse. Of course it does.

Those are the basics of the *World Without Secrets*. We're already in it, and its impact is accumulating and accelerating. Within 10 years, the effects will be very strong and widespread, and a lot of the rules for people, businesses, and governments will be very, very different.

If you want the details, read on.

Hunter's First Law:
The network is an amplifier.

Formula:
The power of a network in a given context equals the square of the number of people on the network, times the intrinsic power of those people in that context.

First Corollary:
The instability of a Network Army is directly proportional to the number of Communities in the Army.

Second Corollary:
Relationships matter.

Hunter's Second Law:
When everything is known, no one knows everything.

First Corollary:
Over time the proportion of all knowledge that's known to any individual decreases.

Second Corollary:
People see only what they want to see, and that's usually what lies on the path of least resistance.

Third Corollary:
People mostly see the exceptions: those things at the very bottom, or very top, of any scale.

Fourth Corollary:
Information only matters when someone is looking.

Fifth Corollary:
It's impossible to calculate the full value of a given piece of information to all the people who might possess it.

A Brief History of the Next 10 Years

Technologies arrive at different times, and their impacts are cumulative. Data mining—large-scale statistical analysis of highly structured factual data—is here now, in powerful form. We can process, in a matter of hours, a stack of facts equal in weight to all the transactions done in every Wal-Mart in the United States in a day. In the next three to five years, the size of the databases we can analyze, and the speed of the analysis, will increase by an order of magnitude at least.

High-bandwidth wireless communications will be widely available in the next two to three years. High-bandwidth wireless is important because it makes it much easier to communicate frequently and at length with intelligent devices planted anywhere and everywhere: on moving platforms, in cars, in people's pockets, and at inaccessible locations like the tops of buildings.

Couple some smart machines and embedded computers—tiny, highly functional, communicative devices that are constantly aware of themselves and their surroundings—with high-bandwidth wireless communications and you'll have alert, aware, intelligent devices everywhere. They'll be talking to each other at speeds high enough to transmit streams of numbers, sounds, and images. That will happen between 2005 and 2008.

Add in pattern recognition, natural language processing, and content-based retrieval, all of which vastly increase the ability of machines to understand complex, unstructured information like narrative text, sounds, and pictures. The embedded machines will then not only record and transmit complex information; they will understand it well enough to make accurate decisions about what it represents. That technology will be in place by 2010.

Put it all together and, by the end of the current decade, we'll be living in a man-made environment of intelligent machines that are capable of seeing, hearing, and understanding most of what we do. Everything's recorded. Nothing's forgotten.

That's the technology of a World Without Secrets.

CHAPTER ONE

Why Won't They Leave Me Alone?

When you read a description of a book online at Amazon.com, Amazon helpfully informs you that many people who bought that book bought certain others, too. This little trick is a simple example of how a rapid, large-scale quantitative analysis of facts like names and numbers can tell us a lot about what people do and how they behave.

Given the state of the art in data mining, there are a few different ways that Amazon might handle the task. However the process unfolds, it must begin with a concise fact: a unique identifier, which Amazon can supply, for the book you're reading about at Amazon's site. The hard way—in terms of computer resource consumption, meaning time and money—is to use that identifier to search Amazon's entire purchase database, right then and there, and find all the customers who bought that book. Amazon sold $2.5 billion worth of books in 2000. Even with powerful computers and the identifier in hand, it will take a while to find them all (probably more than most customers care to wait online). Assuming the look-up is done, Amazon can then look up all the *other* books those customers bought, sort and rank them by various factors (such as total purchases across all customers for each book), and present a short list of candidates for your review (and ideally—from their point of view—your purchase). To make it all really slick, Amazon might eliminate titles it knows you have already bought from Amazon. That's something they apparently don't do now, at least if my experience is any proof.

There's a less time- and computer resource-consuming, more likely approach. Amazon could do a full-scale read-through of their transaction database nightly, weekly, monthly, or however often they like. They would see what was purchased and do the same look-up described of all the other products those people bought as well. They would use that information to build a database of books-affiliated-by-purchase that they could reference quickly whenever a new purchase is made. That approach would save them the trouble of building such a database on the fly whenever a customer looks at a book description. It would explain why they don't pick up on the fact that you have already bought one or more of the books on their list. And it could be made to work, for every online customer, in less time than it took to read this paragraph.

Anyone who has shopped at Amazon probably remembers being surprised the first time Amazon presented such a list. The thing that surprises many people is that the list Amazon shows them is often immediately credible, because it includes books that they've already read and enjoyed.

How does Amazon know so much about you? You never told them what you *liked.*

You didn't have to. They knew it almost as soon as you selected your purchases, even before you gave them your money.

THE POWER OF NAMES AND NUMBERS

Facts like names and numbers are precise, quantitative, and unequivocal. They're about what people and machines *do,* not what people *think.* *Customer (John Smith) bought product (X) in quantity (Q) at price (P) from vendor (V) using channel (C) at time (T) in location (latitude, longitude) with credit card number (NNNN).* The purchase is compact and meaningful. We don't have to know *why* it happened to predict with some accuracy when and under what circumstances it will happen again.

What people do often says more about who they are and what they think than what they think they think, and what people *say* they think doesn't necessarily tell you what they'll *do* next. Lots of people who say they care about privacy hand out detailed personal information to anyone who offers them a piece of free software, for example. Even before they've seen the software, even before they know (or think to ask) the uses to which the information will be put, they've shared their personal data.

Amazon isn't telling you what other buyers *think* about the books Amazon is recommending. Reviews are available, if you want them, but that's not how Amazon came up with the recommendations. It's not about what people *liked*. Amazon is telling you what other people *bought*. That information is easy to collect because it's an intrinsic part of every purchase transaction, and it's easy to analyze compared to any ratings that a diverse set of customers might apply to a book that they've all read. (Every customer has his or her own rating system, and Amazon doesn't know what it is. But a purchase is a purchase is a purchase.)

If given a wider universe of data to work with, Amazon might also find that people who bought certain books tended to rent certain videos, or drink certain coffees, or travel more frequently than others to particular locations. Knowing those preferences could open up entirely new avenues for Amazon's recommendations. *Can I add a double latte with cinnamon to your order? Would you like to drink it in Rio de Janeiro? Wearing a scarf in a certain shade of red?* It's neither possible nor necessary to predict all the associations that might turn up. *The power of large-scale analysis of simple facts is precisely that it reveals such patterns.* The technology that makes the analysis possible, *data mining,* is available now in a very robust form, and it's getting stronger.

Amazon doesn't have an infinite universe of data. It has the stuff it can generate from its own sales, plus whatever else it can buy or rent from third parties. (If Amazon were less ethical, we could add: plus whatever it could *steal* from third parties to that list.) Amazon doesn't have everything.

But the universe gets bigger all the time.

WHAT DOES IT TAKE TO CREATE A UNIVERSE?

Databases essentially consist of *attributes*—pieces of data—and *relationships*—the rules that describe how the attributes relate to each other. A *key* is an attribute that uniquely identifies an instance of a certain set of related attributes. A good key is unique, and the data that depend on a good key depend on all of it, not just a part of it. (I'm trying to make this simple, and it'll end soon, I promise.)

Your name is a good *attribute* for referring to you in a message, but it's a poor *key* for correlating information about you—your address, weight, height, and spending habits—because any number of other people might also have your name. Your address is a good *key* for referring to a location, so long as the whole key—street address, city, state, and country—is present.

ABOUT DATA MINING

Data mining—intensive statistical analysis of large masses of structured, factual data—is one of the most important technologies in the World Without Secrets, and it's already mature. Data mining makes *patterns*—patterns of spending, patterns of fraud, patterns of movement of all kinds—buried in huge masses of data immediately obvious. Once a pattern is visible, people can *act*.

In 2001, there are commercial data-mining operations under way that can crunch dozens of *terabytes* (trillions of bytes, each one a thousand times the size of the *gigabytes* that now denominate hard drives on personal computers) of data in a day. The capacity of those systems is driven by Moore's Law, so the numbers will go up rapidly. At Gartner, we've already been briefed on plans for data-mining systems that will crunch hundreds of terabytes daily, starting less than two years from now.

Data mining on big masses of data demands lots of processing power, and so far it's mostly been in the hands of large businesses and governments that can afford the big specialized machines needed to crunch all the data. That's changing. *Big businesses and governments are no longer the only sources that can mine mountains of data for meaningful patterns.* Already, technical solutions that put data-mining capabilities into the hands of much less well-funded organizations are available. Grid computing approaches that break big processing problems down into tiny units and distribute them to thousands of personal computers are being used by projects like *SETI@Home* (which enlists individuals and their computers in the Search for Extra-Terrestrial Intelligence). *SETI@Home* ties thousands of privately owned personal computers into a network of machines that can process and analyze massive amounts of data, in parallel, one piece at a time. It's data mining *for* the masses, using computing power supplied *by* the masses.

By 2010, well over two billion Pentium-class-and-above personal computers will have been sold worldwide. Many more may have been distributed for free; by that time, a Pentium-class processor will cost less than a dollar to manufacture. That's a lot of processing power, and grid computing technologies will make much of it available to nonbusiness, nongovernment players. *Data mining will be available to anyone who can convince enough people that the purpose of the mining is important.* It's an important contributor to multiple trends in the World Without Secrets, including the Exception Economy and the Network Army (as discussed in Chapters Nine and Five).

Drop the state and country and there's room for confusion. (If you live in greater Boston, Massachusetts, where there are five streets named "Arlington," you need a zip code too.)

Here's the most important thing. Databases can be linked, or *related*, when a *key* value is common to both structures. It doesn't really matter whether information is stored in separate physical databases. *All that matters is the keys.* If the same keys are present in two different databases, any information in one can be correlated to any information in the other, *as if they were a single database,* at least in a *logical* sense.

It's pretty easy from here on out. If you want to pull a universe of data together, the first thing you need is a *really good key* that ties the data to something in particular. That something is usually a person, but the person's name alone is not good enough. You need something unique, something that's usable in lots of different places—ideally, something that's already used in lots of places. In this age of global business, you also need something that's unique worldwide.

CROSSING OVER

Database designers talk about *logical* databases—databases that exist in an ideal sense, unfettered by the considerations of available technology, and constrained in structure only by the nature of the information itself—and *physical* databases—logical designs that are restructured and constrained by the needs of particular applications and the technology they use. A logical database is like an artist's drawing of a piece of architecture. A physical database is like the building people live in after all the construction is done.

In a *logical* sense, the ideal identifier is an arbitrary number that's big enough to include a unique value for everyone who might need to be identified. In the *physical* world, the closest thing anyone has to a worldwide *key* for lots of data that matter—concise, factual data that link people to their purchases—is a credit card number.

Visa has issued more than one billion of its various credit and debit cards worldwide. Visa has 60 percent of the worldwide market, so we can figure that another 700 million or so credit cards from other vendors are also out there. Visa says that its cards "are accepted at more than 21 million locations in 300 countries and territories, making Visa the closest thing there is to a universal currency."[1] Every transaction done anywhere in the world using a given credit card can be positively correlated to every other transaction made with the same credit card.

The purchase data don't tell me everything about you, but they give me a good start. I know where you've gone and when you were there. I know where you shopped and how you "paid" for your purchases. Do I need to know much more about you? If I do, I can always ask the people who work at the place where you shopped. If necessary, I can pay them (or coerce them) to tell me. If utterly necessary, I can buy the company they work for.

Arguably, an even better key than a credit card number, assuming that you have the technology to process it efficiently in all the situations where it might be needed, is something that's both unique and intrinsic to your person, like a digitized replica of your face, your voice, or your DNA. In Chapter Two, "Streets Without Secrets," I discuss the potential for widespread use of biometrics like facial scans as keys to a universe of personal information.

But facial scans aren't essential; they are merely useful, convenient, and likely to be deployed in many situations. To anyone who's willing to pay the going price or has a list that can be swapped, credit card numbers give access to a wide range of very useful and highly predictive information about card owners' behavior and habits. We resist a single identifier when it might be in the hands of a government, but we welcome it when we can use the same credit card in Jakarta, Denver, and Bonn without any more effort than it takes to present it.

The demand for common identifiers to support secure global commerce is accomplishing what no government could: the worldwide implementation of what is effectively a unique international personal identifier.

MORE DATA, MORE POWER, FEW CONTROLS

A worldwide identifier enables a wider universe of data, a market where businesses can buy, sell, and combine information about individuals, subject only to what they can afford (information is precious), what is legal in the nation(s) in which they do business, and what they believe the public will tolerate.

As an example of U.S. businesses' freedom to manage and trade information as they see fit, let's look again at Amazon.com. In September 2000, Amazon informed its entire customer base that, contrary to a previously announced policy, Amazon would begin sharing information about its customers with selected third parties. Customers could choose to end their relationship with Amazon, but customer data already gathered by Amazon would be subject to any uses that Amazon deemed appropriate. Amazon described one of those potential uses as follows:

> *Business Transfers:* As we continue to develop our business, we might sell or buy stores or assets. In such transactions, customer information generally is one of the transferred business assets. Also, in the unlikely event that Amazon.com, Inc., or substantially all of its assets are acquired, customer information will of course be one of the transferred assets.[2]

This passage apparently contradicted Amazon's statement, earlier in the Notice, that "Information about our customers is an important part of our business, and we are not in the business of selling it to others." In other words, Amazon reserved the right to change its mind, anytime, about how it uses customers' information. (The statement to customers was issued on the occasion of such a change.) Nothing in current U.S. law or regulatory policy prevents Amazon from doing so.

In the European Union (EU), where laws demand customers' approval of the uses to which their data are put, Amazon might not have been able to change its policy so easily. Criminal, as well as civil, penalties apply, in the EU, to companies that permit sensitive information (like an identifier or a credit card number) to be used in ways that aren't specifically authorized by the original owner of the information—the person the information *describes.* But there's little evidence that the United States will follow Europe's lead soon. And in a global economy, where a company taking an order via a phone or the Internet might be located almost anywhere, information can easily migrate to a place where restrictions are even less stringent than those imposed by public opinion in the United States.

I interviewed Victor A. Kovner, a First Amendment authority and former Corporation Counsel of the City of New York, in October 2001, and I mentioned Amazon's policy change to him. "That's why I don't buy on the Internet," he said drily, and I laughed.[3] But Kovner missed the point. It's not about the Internet, and it's not about Amazon. It's about anyone who uses a credit card, and it's about any company that accepts one.

Amazon didn't do anything that any other company couldn't do. Data arrived via the Internet, but had they come over the phone or in the mail, it wouldn't have made any difference.

UNSTOPPABLE MOMENTUM

In the aggregate, the amount of electronically stored data about individual behavior is massive, detailed, and growing. It includes what we buy, where we buy it, where we go to eat and to entertain or educate ourselves, the people we call on the telephone and how long we talk to them, the correspondence we receive and send via e-mail, the names of businesses and individuals we correspond with, the content of the correspondence, the addresses of Web pages we visit, and the amount of time we spend at each address.

The stored data will continue to grow. Intelligent devices and electronic communications provide too much apparent value for most people to ignore. We want to be as productive and comfortable as our machines can possibly make us, and no one wants to be left behind or left out. (I shuddered when a friend told me recently that her attorney, in prosperous Fairfield County, Connecticut, had neither a fax machine nor e-mail. Who among professionals—except total losers—has no *fax?*)

Commercial initiatives like Microsoft's .NET, by promising even greater convenience at the cost of massive consolidation of the keys to one's personal information, will raise the risks and rewards even higher. Are you willing to put all of the keys anyone needs to do business in your name in the hands of Microsoft? Are you willing to let Microsoft touch every transaction you do? What about someone else? *Anyone* else? Is the *convenience* of being known everywhere worth the *risk* of being known everywhere?

The demand-side alternative is to restrict the information rights and privileges of enterprises, probably via legislation or regulation. For much of the world, that's even less likely. The trend in the industrialized world is toward *less* regulation, not more (regulation related to national security excepted). Public opinion in developed nations is also not fully mobilized against widespread data collection and profiling, and, in the absence of a full-blown disaster, it may never be.

Cultural values in newly industrializing nations make such restrictions even less likely there. Many such societies have tended to be authoritarian and male-dominated. They're not likely to force heavy restrictions on new businesses, especially if those businesses are competing with American companies that can do anything they like where information is concerned. They'll consider information to be the rightful property of the people in charge in both the public and private sectors. There will be few legal or regulatory restrictions on information ownership and use in developing nations during the next 10 years.

BY THE NUMBERS

Why does it matter that businesses have so much information so readily available to them? So Amazon knows what you want and can offer you books you like, instead of trying to make you buy books you don't like. So *what's the problem?*

Is it scary if I'm walking down the street and someone offers to sell me something? Probably not. It's not very scary that people are trying to sell me things. It's not even scary if they're trying to sell me things all the time, which they already apparently are, or if they're not very tasteful in the way they go about it. Sales aren't scary unless you're a salesperson.

Is it scary if I walk down the street and my face is scanned by a camera belonging to a salesperson? It might be offensive; it's probably legal. Is it scary? Maybe not. What does the salesperson know about the person behind the face?

Is it scary if I walk down the street and my face is scanned by a camera belonging to a salesperson, and the scan can be compared automatically to a scan of my face that's on file with a bank or a credit card company? Now, the salesperson may know a good deal more about me: my name, where I bank, where I live.

Is it scary if the camera *doesn't belong to a salesperson?*

In an increasingly consolidated, global, networked economy, information moves everywhere. Sooner or later, it moves to a place where the owner—or anyone in current possession—can do whatever he or she likes with it. That party might be ethical—*might.*

If we've learned one thing from terrorists, not to mention action movies, it's that a tool is also a weapon. Globally accepted credit cards and the databases that support them are tools for taking the friction out of commerce. That's another way of saying that they're tools for extracting money from people with minimum effort on everyone's part.

So it's not a problem if they're trying to sell me stuff. And it's not a problem if it's Amazon. But it might be a problem if it's neither.

I haven't mentioned *identity theft* yet, but surely that's what this is leading to. Identity theft is unauthorized use of the information that identifies me, in order to perpetrate fraud. The more widely my information is known, the greater the number of places where it may be found, and the more likely that more theft will occur. The more information is correlated to a single identifier, the more damage an instance of identity theft may cause.

Identity theft is much feared in our society, though no one has ever died from it or been ruined by it. There are worse things than identity theft, and a universal identifier may lead to those worse things as well.

Wherever universal identification leads, we don't yet know how to manage a world in which *everything can be linked to me, wherever I am.* We don't yet know how to balance the undoubted convenience of this world with the peril—vague, but apparently near—that we sense in the presence of all that information combined and consolidated, if only *logically.*

WHERE DID THE SECRETS GO?

The boundaries are down. Ubiquitous monitoring is technologically feasible and will soon be economically feasible. Any limits that exist will be limits set by agreement and reinforced by constant oversight. Those limits must ultimately be international.

Computers constantly and geometrically increase in power—the power to know and to communicate what is known—while their physical size shrinks. The rate at which they do both is described by Moore's Law, one of the best-known formulas of the second half of the twentieth century. Moore's Law stipulates that the computing power of a transistor of a given size doubles every 18 months. The trend is so well established that we take it for granted that it will continue, or even accelerate, into the indefinite future.

The result isn't just that we're increasingly surrounded by computers of all kinds, including computers that are skin-close—closer than a cell phone in a pocket. We're surrounded by buildings most of the time too, and that's not a big deal. This is more like being surrounded from the *inside out.*

A *system* now consists of nothing more than all the machines that are plugged in and talking to each other. A system can change on a momentary basis. We're not just within the boundaries of a system. We *are* the boundary. *It* moves when *we* do.

Security is about *control within a boundary*. If the boundary is constantly shifting and is impossible to define or predict, what does that imply about security?

Is that why we feel so insecure in the midst of so many powerful machines designed to do our bidding? Or is it that we're not sure whose bidding the machines are really doing at any given moment?

CHAPTER TWO

Streets Without Secrets

On July 2, 2001, Rich Mogull, my colleague at Gartner, posted an e-mail message to the Security Research Community. The message was titled "Here We Go . . . Tampa uses cameras to scan for wanted faces."

Inside was a copy of this Associated Press story, circulated that morning:

July 2, 2001 Posted: 10:22 AM EDT (1422 GMT)

TAMPA, Florida (AP)—Tampa is using high-tech security cameras to scan the city's streets for people wanted for crimes, a law enforcement tactic that some liken to Big Brother.

A computer software program linked to 36 cameras began scanning crowds Friday in Tampa's nightlife district, Ybor City, matching results against a database of mug shots of people with outstanding arrest warrants.

European cities and U.S. government offices, casinos and banks are already using the so-called face-printing system, but Tampa is the first American city to install a permanent system along public streets, *The Tampa Tribune* reported Sunday.

A similar system was used at Super Bowl XXXV, which was held in Tampa last January.

"Tampa is really leading the pack here," said Frances Zelazny, a spokeswoman for Visionics Corp., which produces the "FaceIt" software.

The software has raised concerns over privacy, ethics and government intrusion.

"This is Big Brother actually implemented," said Jack Walters of the Tampa chapter of the American Civil Liberties Union. "I think this just opens the door to it being everywhere."

But Tampa Detective Bill Todd says FaceIt is no different than having a police officer standing on a street holding a mug shot.

At the Super Bowl, a Visionics competitor, Graphco Technologies, wired cameras around Raymond James Stadium and in Ybor City.

The computer spotted 19 people at the crowded stadium with outstanding warrants, all for minor offenses. But no arrests were made.

"During the Super Bowl, we got overwhelmed," Todd said. "That's the other thing: When you get a match, how quickly can you get to these people?"

Business owners have mixed emotions about the new technology.

"I don't know if I like it," said Vicki Doble, who owns The Brew Pub. "It may be a bit too much."

Don Barco, owner of King Corona Cigars Bar & Café, approves of the cameras but says they may not be as effective as the city hopes.

"Sometimes these high-tech toys, they tend to give a little too much credence to what they do," he said.[1]

My colleagues and I debated the implications of this story for days. My first question was: How could this be possible, technically speaking? Only five weeks earlier, another colleague, Andrew Phillips, had circulated his latest research on biometric authentication technologies—stuff that relies on some part of your body, such as your face, fingerprints, or voice to make an identification. In it, he said flatly that *searches of more than one thousand templates* ("template" in this case meaning a biometric database record) *typically compromise performance.*[2] This means that such searches are too inefficient to be practical in applications where immediate response is demanded. "The number of people attending the ball game is irrelevant," he said to me in a subsequent conversation. "What counts is the number of faces of bad guys in the database, not the number of people going through the gate." Yet the Tampa police were apparently using a database with tens of thousands of faces, searching for matches in something close to real time.

It's like Alvin Toffler said: The future arrives too soon and in the wrong order. The people of Tampa don't seem to be ready. Jack Walters of the American Civil Liberties Union (ACLU) invokes Orwell. Vicki Doble doesn't know whether she likes it. Don Barco thinks the *high-tech toys* don't really work. Doble and Barco both use the phrase *too much* to describe their feelings about the technology. Walters doesn't say it's *too much,* but when he talks about its *being everywhere,* there's a definite whiff of *too much* in the air.

None of them understands clearly what's happening, even if they all think it's *too much.* But that's all pretty normal for the future, whenever it arrives.

HOW THE FUTURE WORKED IN THE PAST

Historically, there have been three basic ways to authenticate someone—that is, prove that a person is someone in particular or is the person he or she *claims* to be. Confirm something the person *knows,* something the person *has,* or something the person *is.* In the age of Global Positioning System (GPS) technology, we can now add a fourth technique: some*where* the person is. A password is an example of something you *know.* A token, like a smart card or a secret decoder ring, is an example of something you *have.* (Some people still have secret decoder rings.) A fingerprint or face scan is an example of something you *are.* An office where you're supposed to close on a deal is an example of some*where* you are.

Good authentication is both *singular* and *secure. Passwords* are very widely used, especially on the Internet, not to mention at automatic teller machines (ATMs) everywhere, but they're not a good authentication because they're not very *secure,* and once they're known to more than one person, they're no longer *singular.* Anyone who is watching or listening at the right time might see or overhear a password; anyone who knows something about you might guess it more or less easily. (Is your password based on your birthday?)

A token is not much better. It might be *singular,* but because it's a physical object that generally is portable, it can be stolen, so it's not very *secure.*

Your *location* is both singular and secure—it's pretty tough to fake latitude and longitude—but lots of the things people do that require authentication don't happen in a prearranged place at a prearranged time. Also, you've got to have some other means to ensure that the person in a given location is not a decoy. Location is important, but the applications are limited.

That leaves *who you are.* In general, *who you are*—as literally embodied by your physical person, your *biometrics*—is singular (provided there are ways to effectively distinguish you from anyone else) and is pretty *secure.* It's much harder for someone to fake the characteristics of your voice or your face or your fingerprints than to fake your signature or steal your password or credit card.

A problem with biometric authentication is that it takes lots of work to establish the preconditions or *infrastructure* required to use it. Everyone in the world has fingerprints, but not everyone has been fingerprinted. It takes time to do that, even if everybody involved wants to help. (*I* sure don't.)

A second problem is that, in practice, biometric authentication takes time and some kind of special equipment to process. The more complex the stuff is that's being compared, the longer it takes and the more specialized the equipment must be. (For example, it's currently too demanding to process DNA for biometric authentication anywhere but in the lab. That's only currently, though.) Even if everyone's fingerprints were recorded and filed, you would need some way to take fingerprints in the field and compare them—quickly; ideally, instantly—to fingerprints on file. If you already know who someone is supposed to be, of course, the process is faster. You just compare the prints you took in the field to the prints on file for that person. But you still need lots of fingerprints on file, and you still need to get to them in a hurry. Gathering fingerprints at a crowd site is no picnic when people are standing in line, or even just sitting in their seats at the Super Bowl.

Technology that works faster can speed things up. Even when the technology is driven by Moore's Law, you need more to really get things moving. You need to focus on the things you can compare from a distance, the things you don't need to touch. Fingerprints don't qualify. Now we're talking about something you can hear, like a voice, or something you can see, like a facial scan. We're more likely talking about things you can see, because voice only works when someone's talking and you're close enough to hear, and that's pretty difficult in a crowd.

In the first week of July 2001, most people reading this would have wondered why anybody would want or need to authenticate every person sitting in the stands at the Super Bowl. Every one of them must've had a ticket; what *more* do you need to know? By now, everyone's aware that there's at least one reason why you want to know who is sitting in the stands.

But you don't really need to know who *everybody* in the stands is. Like lots of other things in the World Without Secrets, the only things you really want to look at are the *exceptions*. The point of the authentication isn't necessarily to include everybody. The goal could be to screen out everybody who doesn't matter so you can focus on the few who *might*.

AUTHENTICATION AND THE EXCEPTION ECONOMY

A lot of law enforcement is about exceptions. Criminals are exceptions. If they weren't, cities would need an army, not a police force, to keep things under control. If having an army is not acceptable, the law can be changed to reduce the number of lawbreakers, which is what was done in the United States in the early 1930s, when lawmakers admitted that Prohibition had turned much of the adult population of America into witting criminals and customers for organized crime. (We apparently haven't figured that out where other currently illegal drugs are concerned. We have tried using the military to police the drug trade.)

Among criminals in general, an exceptional few are always responsible for the vast majority of all crimes. (Some studies have concluded that 10 percent of a typical prison population is responsible for 90 percent of the crimes committed by all the inmates.) Police on patrol look for exceptions: people who seem out of place in their surroundings, people who are behaving inappropriately in the context of their environment, people who don't fit in. *Profiling* is about exceptions, about people who exhibit characteristics that make them different. (If everybody matches the profile, you don't need a profiler. Call in the troops instead.)

Biometric identification in law enforcement is historically about exceptions, too. In the United States, we fingerprint people only when they're arrested for a crime, or join the military services, or are accepted for a few other relatively special assignments. We've operated historically on the assumption that the government isn't supposed to know anything it doesn't need to know in order to carry out its lawful duties, which specifically do *not* include keeping track of what everybody is up to all the time.

Scanning—especially in public places—implies something very different to most people. It implies that we're no longer focused on the exceptions. Instead, everything and everyone is being watched, and no secrets are withheld from people about whom we know nothing. This perception is not entirely wrong, even if it's not entirely right, and the vagueness is part of the resulting anxiety.

Detective Bill Todd of the Tampa Police Department (PD) is the Project Coordinator for *FaceIt,* the program described in the Associated Press article (p. 13). He understands that reaction to the program very well. "What most people are afraid of is the unknown," he told me in an interview in September 2001. "When the ACLU says your face is being captured and cataloged and indexed, people get nervous."[3]

Well, sure. If someone thinks you're asking around about him, he gets nervous, especially if he's not exactly sure who's doing the asking around, or why. I talked to Todd about John Woodward's Rand Corporation report, *Super Bowl Surveillance: Facing Up to Biometrics,* which examined the constitutional privacy issues involved in the Tampa PD's use of facial scanning technology at Super Bowl XXXV. In that report, Woodward said:

> The interlinking and interoperability of massive databases could lead to several problems. The most serious of these potential problems is that much more private information is collected and revealed to the government entity than is necessary to achieve the purpose of the surveillance. And as a consequence, the damage caused by inadvertent disclosure or unauthorized access to the database is much greater.[4]

In this statement, Woodward is very close to the real issue. It's not simply all that data piling up in the government's hands (or anyone else's); that's just a necessary precondition. It's the *power* all that information implies, which derives from the potential for misuse of the information for personal, financial, or political advantage. Our fear is that the power can barely be held in check under the best of circumstances, that *inadvertent disclosure or unauthorized access* is all too easily done and far more difficult to undo. The more information is combined, the greater the implied power and incentives for misuse. Woodward leaves open the question of who might misuse the information and to what ends. "Where do you think the limits are?" I asked Todd. "What is permissible in terms of gathering and combining information?"

"My first thought is that it's not technologically feasible," Todd said. "Tampa couldn't afford the hardware to put all that stuff together." His voice was calm and precise. Todd seemed to me to be a practical guy, and he gave a practical answer: You don't need to worry; it's *not feasible.* That's probably true, for reasons including and beyond the one Todd cites. Even if Tampa could afford the hardware, combining lots and lots of databases takes an enormous amount of programming time and skill. It *is* expensive.

But in a world driven by Moore's Law, what's expensive today is cheap tomorrow. The hardware certainly is. The other problems involved in combining multiple databases are solvable, given enough time and money, and the resources available to deal with the problem probably aren't limited ultimately to the information systems budget for the Tampa PD. So this is a temporary obstacle, and the question remains: What's *permissible?*

"I'm not eager to be tracked any more than anyone else," Todd told me.

I believe him. Simply to say so is to acknowledge that the potential to track a whole lot of things, if not everything, is vaguely visible if not yet present. It's unclear whether Jack Walters of the ACLU is reacting to that potential or to what's being done already. "This is Big Brother actually implemented," he says, meaning it's Orwell *now*. But Walters also says, "I think this just opens the door to it being everywhere," meaning it's really Orwell *later*, presumably *soon*.

It's not unusual for people looking at this kind of stuff to confuse what's real now with what could be real later. The subject is complex, and it's hard to get the details straight and even harder to work out what it really means.

As C. S. Lewis said, *"The great mass of people never get it exactly right, but they never get it exactly wrong."*[5] If they don't understand the technology, they understand the implications very well. *The boundaries are down.* Technology doesn't set the boundaries anymore. Policy sets the boundaries. You can't roll back what technology has made possible, but you can roll back policy whenever you feel like it.

Todd's a practical guy, and he's focused on what *is* being done, not what could be done. The policies he has put in place seem to recognize the boundaries in the right kinds of ways. In particular, they're focused on the *exceptions*.

It's worth looking at the details, even if they could change later—or maybe *especially* because they could change later.

How It Works in Tampa

"In 1997, we realized we had a situation in Ybor City in Tampa," Todd told me. "It's like the French Quarter in New Orleans. On Saturday night, we get upwards of 100,000 people there. We have to close the streets to traffic. It creates unique police opportunities."

I've never been to Tampa, but I visit New Orleans every year. If Ybor City is like the French Quarter, where there are crowds of drunken party animals—or ordinary people trying on party animal skins—crowding the streets all night, almost every night, then it creates unique opportunities, and not just for the police.

"Wherever you put large crowds of people, opportunist criminals will go," Todd said. "They have to commit a crime to generate an income, and their chances are better where there's 100,000 people having a good time, not thinking about the criminal.

"And that's where traditional police tools break down. In your neighborhood, you've got neighborhood policing. In every firehouse in Tampa, there's a firehouse cop. His job is to know everybody in the neighborhood. But he can't know everyone in a zone like Ybor City. It's a transient crowd.

"Patrol officers walking in that crowd have trouble seeing what's going on. So we began mounting video cameras on light poles to give police officers a better view of the street.

"There are now 36 cameras deployed throughout the district, with monitoring stations in several zones. When the cameras were installed, we also installed signs all over Ybor City to tell the crowds that police cameras were in use. The officer in a particular monitoring station can dial in a feed from a particular camera. There are 45 police deployed out on the street."

The software is something new. That's only been in place in Ybor City since June 2001. That's the stuff that Doble and Barco, whose businesses are located in Ybor City, think might be *too much.*

"We've interfaced computers into the fiber-optic cable coming from the video cameras," Todd said. "We've updated the signs now to say 'Alert: Computer Enhanced Video Cameras in Use.' " Fair warning. The idea is that the people who ought to be really nervous about the cameras—the opportunist criminals, the *exceptions*—walk away. Do they? Hold that thought.

"The Visionics software reads the video feed and produces a facial geometry scan," Todd says.

Facial geometry isn't the same as a photograph. It's more precise and much more compact in terms of how much space it takes up in a computer. Frances Zelazny explains: "We use a technology called 'local feature analysis.' We create a 'topographical' map of the face, using landmarks like the distance between the eyes. We've defined about 80 nodal points on the face that make up this facial geometry. We only need 14 to 22 to make a positive ID. Some points count more. We concentrate on the 'Golden Triangle,' from temple to temple and to the center of the top lip. That's the central region of the face.

"The key factors in a good scan are pose and lighting. Our software produces reliable results with poses that deviate up to 35 percent from a frontal view. We also need the right kind of lighting for the contrast that exhibits the nodal points. Sharp glare might be as bad as dim lighting. We only need 20 to 25 pixels across the eyes to get good results.

"The size of a facial scan template is only 84 bytes. The smallest fingerprint template is 125 bytes, and at that size it's not good enough to distinguish one person among millions of others. We can do that with our 84-byte template. The small size means we can search databases with millions of records pretty quickly."

Okay, now I know—at least in theoretical terms—how it was possible to scan tens of thousands of people at the Super Bowl more or less in real time.

"The second thing the template size lets you do is take advantage of small storage capabilities, like a smart card or a magnetic stripe," Zelazny says.[6]

Okay, now I know—at least in theoretical terms—how we can create an electronic national ID card with a facial scan on it.

"The system in Ybor City has a capacity of eight faces simultaneously, 100 faces per minute," Todd told me. "We only grab the feed off one camera at a time. There are 36 cameras deployed throughout the district, and an officer in a particular zone can dial in the feed from a particular camera."

The software produces facial geometry scans from the video images. At this point, *everybody passing in front of the camera has been scanned,* and every face is captured on its own 84-byte facial geometry template.

What's already happened—the preparation of the database that the scans are compared to—determines what happens next.

WHAT THE SOFTWARE KNOWS

"There are three categories of scanned faces on our database," Todd said. "Runaways, sexual predators, and wanted felons. Under Florida law, if you're convicted of certain sex crimes, the court labels you a predator. The label puts different obligations on both the convicted predators and the police. For example, some predators may be under house arrest.

"The software compares a new scanned image to the database. If there's no match on the database, the software discards the image," Todd says.

So if you're not a runaway, a wanted felon, or a sexual predator, or you don't look exactly like someone who is—in terms of the geometry of your face, not your hair style—your scanned image lives exactly as long as it takes for the software to find out that you're not in one of those four categories. That happens almost instantly. The 30,000 records stored in Tampa's database aren't a lot, given this technology's capacity.

"If there's a match, the system sounds an audible alarm, and it parks the image on the computer monitor. When the officer clicks on the image, the software puts the new scan and the matching image from the database on the screen, side by side. If the officer concurs that they're the same person, he clicks on a view button, and that brings up bio info on the person from the database. The officer then relays that information, and the suspect's location, to the officers on the street so they can approach that person."

"So they've got probable cause at that point?" I said.

"No, they *don't* have probable cause for an arrest," Todd said. I reminded myself that American police operate in a very proscribed environment; procedure—and the precise terminology that goes with it—matters. "They've got *reasonable suspicion* of the person's identity, so they can proceed to verify. They can ask that person for some other kind of ID, for example."

Zelazny made a similar point to me. "This isn't *forensics*. This technology hasn't been used in a court of law yet. We get requests all the time, asking us to compare photos to determine whether a given photo is a picture of somebody's brother. I have to tell them that we can't prove things like that."

Okay, it's not forensics, and it's about establishing reasonable suspicion, not probable cause. Is it *legal*? Would it pass a constitutional test?

YES, PROBABLY

There's never been a court case in which anyone contested the right of the police to establish reasonable suspicion based on this kind of technology. The way the Tampa PD has it set up, I bet they'd pass.

"If I were to set a police officer on a street corner with an album of photos and he compared them to people going by, and he found a match, he'd be justified in asking people if they were that person," Todd says. That's true. The next question is: Would the officer be justified in having the photos in the first place?

Well, if the photos are all of runaway minors, wanted felons, or convicted sexual predators who are under various kinds of court restrictions, the answer is *Yes*. The police need photos of such people to do the necessary police work, and they get to keep those photos for as long as they need them. In the case of wanted felons and sexual predators, that's basically forever.

So it's legal for the Tampa police to maintain a database like the one they've got now. Is it constitutionally legal for them to scan citizens and run the match? Rand Corporation's Woodward lays it out clearly. The Supreme Court has ruled that "a person does not have a reasonable expectation of privacy with regard to physical characteristics that are constantly exposed to the public," specifically including one's face. If your face is exposed in public, the police can look it at, just like anyone else, whether or not they're using a video camera and software to do it, and ". . . information privacy concerns would probably not arise so long as no information about individuals were retained, disclosed, or linked to any other database."

The Tampa police look at your face. That's legal. They take a picture. That's legal. They process the picture to produce a facial geometry profile. That's legal. They compare it to their database, which contains only facial geometry profiles for people in whom they have a legitimate interest. The comparison and the database are both legal. They discard the picture as soon as the match process comes up negative. That's legal, not to mention reassuring. If the match is positive, they have the right to ask for confirmation of your identity. That's prudent as well as legal.

It looks to me like everything's legal—in constitutional terms—so far. So why do Doble and Barco think this is *too much*? Is it only because they don't understand what's going on? Is it because we somehow feel that there's something more on the way, and it's hard to pin down what it is? *What most people are afraid of is the unknown,* Todd said.

What's next is, by definition, unknown. There's always the chance that it's *too much*.

DOES IT WORK?

In Newham, in the United Kingdom, when scanning technology from Visionics Corporation was installed, two things happened: (1) the crime rate in Newham dropped 34 percent, and (2) the crime rate in surrounding towns *climbed*. "If you create a barrier to entry for criminal activity in one place and not another, the criminals go where the barriers to entry are lower," Frances Zelazny of Visionics, which also supplied the systems used in Newham, told me. "When we installed the system in Newham, Bob Lack, the head constable, saw that the criminals went to surrounding towns, and he was *glad*. *His* job was to get criminals out of

Newham, and he succeeded." Whether you think that's a good thing or not depends on what your postal code is, I guess.

"What effects did the cameras have?" I asked Todd. "Was there a measurable impact on crime rates in Ybor City?"

"Ybor City, like the rest of the city, has had a drop in crime over the last four years. But you can't trace that to the cameras," Todd said. "It's hard to measure, but there's a qualitative impact. They've allowed us to see crimes being committed. Video from those cameras has been used as evidence in court cases, including a murder case. But so far it doesn't seem like they've had a statistical impact on crime."

The cameras have been up for four years. That's long enough to produce a statistical impact.

"We turned the software system on for the first time on June 29 of this year," Todd said. "We only use it two nights a week. It hasn't produced any arrests as of September, and we haven't located any runaways so far." Did the criminals and the runaways all take off when the technology came in? Did they make a point of staying out of view of the cameras? They had warning.

Terry Danner, the Chair of the Criminology Department at St. Leo University in St. Leo, Florida, has studied crime in Ybor City in some detail. In his article "Violent Times: A Case Study Of The Ybor City Historic District," Danner mentions factors contributing to "victimization risks . . . greater than was average for all Tampa." They include "macro-structural forces," like the presence of "motivated offenders"; "populations drawn to the area's nightlife," in particular, young people, who are more frequently both victims and perpetrators of crime; and "the high density of bars."[7] The impact of the Tampa PD's cameras on that greater-than-average risk was apparently negligible. "Maybe they had the cameras in the wrong places," Danner told me in an interview in October 2001. "Maybe it would have made a difference if they had them in the alleys, instead of on the street. That's where the muggings were."[8]

But the Tampa police are sure that the cameras make them a better police force. "We deploy the cameras and the software"—the stuff supplied by Visionics that scans faces and looks for matches on a database— "to make us more efficient and effective," Todd said to me.

That's the idea, but the stats don't prove it. Maybe there's something fundamentally wrong with the approach, or maybe there's something going on that the normal stats can't measure, or maybe it's like Danner said: the cameras aren't in the right places. There's not enough data to prove any of those explanations. But if you believe that the technology is useful, as the Tampa police do, the next step is obvious.

MORE FACES IN VIEW

In Tampa, the video cameras and software linger only on people who've been included in a special database, the *exceptions*. The most important question is, therefore: Who goes on the database next, and why? Who's *exceptional?*

"I'd like to take videotape from a convenience store robbery, use the software to compare it to mug shots or a jail population, and see what you come up with," Todd says. Would that push at the boundaries of the Constitution? Probably not. Mug shots, by definition, are a permanent record of police business. A jail is mostly full of people who've had mug shots taken somewhere. Because 20 percent of the criminals commit 80 percent of the crimes, and those people tend to have police records, there's good reason to look at those populations first for potential matches.

It's easy to think of additional categories of people who might be prime candidates, even though Tampa's not in a hurry to load up its database—missing persons, for example, or people wanted for questioning, or anyone else with whom the police have legitimate business. Todd dismissed the question in a practical way. "It's a dynamic situation," he told me. "It's not worth it for a $15 parking ticket."

The limits ultimately are about *policy*, not technology, and policy is about what's considered important. A $15 parking ticket is *not worth it.* "We have an administration that believes that technology can enhance the police department's mission," Todd told me. Good for them; the mission is important. But even in Tampa, there are limits. *My first thought is that it's not technologically feasible. Tampa couldn't afford the hardware to put all that stuff together.* The cost of the technology is a hard limit, but only at a given point in time. If it's not affordable now, maybe—probably—it will be later; and if not in Tampa, maybe somewhere else. And of course, what's *affordable* all depends on how important it is. Medicine's not affordable until you're sick. Security technology's not affordable until you're *scared.*

WALK WITH ME

Suppose that Tampa were to set up cameras all over the city, not just in Ybor City. Suppose that the police decided to scan *every* face in the city for a match to the convenience store robber. Would that be legal? The short answer is *Yes.* "In a place where's there's no reasonable expectation of privacy," Victor Kovner, the First Amendment scholar, told me, the police can look at as many faces as they like. "The scope of the geography is unimportant."[9] If it's constitutionally legal for a cop to carry a photo of the convenience store robber and walk around and look at everybody in the city, it's legal to scan everyone too.

Let's go farther. Suppose that cameras are all over the city, scanning constantly, feeding the scanned images to intelligent software. That's certainly within the capabilities of the technology that will be available within the next 5 to 10 years. When *any* infraction against the law is committed, images of the crime and the suspected perpetrator are reviewed by a police officer and potentially captured on a database. All other images picked up by the cameras are immediately discarded. Is that constitutionally legal? Yes, and not only for the police. *Where there's no expectation of privacy*—i.e., whenever you're in a public place—"under existing law, it would certainly be legal for private as well as public parties to record and retain what's going on," Kovner told me. Two new thoughts surface: you don't have to be a police officer to use this technology, and you can hold on to the images you've captured. You don't have to dump them instantly.

Now suppose that every camera is also scanning every citizen in its field of view, whether a crime is under way or not. Suppose that the facial geometries constructed in those scans are instantly compared to all the captured images of all the suspects for every offense recorded in the database. Is that constitutionally legal? Assuming that nonmatches are discarded—maybe even if they're not, as per Kovner—why not? It's no different from walking past a police officer who has *seen everything* and *remembers everything*. That's an impossibility, of course, but the collective memory of the police department is certainly something any individual cop could and should have available. The database is just an *automated* collective memory.

Now suppose that the cameras and the databases are installed in every city, and every city's database is available to every other city. Now *every* citizen on the street can be matched to *any* crime committed *anywhere* in the country. If you've committed any infraction at all, any police officer anywhere is going to know about it as soon as you walk in front of the camera. Is that constitutionally legal? Yes, with some reservations. "It's a difficult question," Kovner said. "All the places are open to the public. What bothers me is that the potential for error and abuse increases with a national database. There are people all over the country who look just like each other. So the likelihood of abuse increases as the population increases." But this isn't *forensics;* it's about *reasonable suspicion*. A police officer in Denver may have no real interest in a speeding ticket you've never paid in Star City, Arkansas. But it would certainly be of legitimate interest to a police officer to know that the man walking toward him may be a man who has a criminal record or an outstanding warrant, even if both were generated outside the police officer's jurisdiction.

Suppose, hypothetically, that the facial scan provided identification as strong as a fingerprint. "This hypothetically is quite a stretch," Kovner said. "But assuming the scans were obtained in public places, then there'd be no legal issue as to their acquisition."

We've just established that a national database of facial scans, coupled with a program of ongoing live scans *everywhere in the country,* could at least theoretically be designed to pass a constitutional test.

Do you feel *better*?

KEEP WALKING

Let's go one more step. It's a big one. We're going to stop assuming that the technology is deployed only by conscientious public servants in pursuit of legitimate and legal ends.

Suppose an unpopular war is going on, like the Vietnam conflict. Suppose the government promoting the war decides that opponents of the war (or of the government's policy for conduct of the war) merit special, hostile attention. (Every war has opponents, but governments generally make a point of harassing the opposition only during unpopular wars.) Members of the opposition will be put under surveillance until the government has enough evidence to charge them with crimes or otherwise attack them. In other words, instead of finding the perpetrators responsible for a crime that has been committed, evidence of crimes will be sought in order to charge targeted people.

Government agents map out the places and times where opposition members meet, and they set up cameras to scan everyone who enters those buildings at those times. Then the facial scans are compared to every database available, such as the databases of facial scans used by credit card companies to validate card-not-present transactions. The credit card companies cooperate because this is a matter of national security in wartime.

All members of the opposition are quickly identified. Once identified, all of their electronic transactions—including most of their business, personal, and otherwise—are collected and analyzed to reveal patterns that indicate potentially fruitful avenues for investigation into the private lives of these individuals. Further, the individuals are followed, and all the people they associate with are scanned, identified, and ana-lyzed. The result is an understanding of who—among the entire commu-nity that comprises the opposition and their friends, family, and colleagues—has drug problems, gambles, is in debt, is having extramari-tal affairs, or has any kind of weakness or secret that can be exploited for leverage.

All of this is thoroughly illegal under current law, never mind what-ever future legislation, federal or otherwise, is enacted to manage the use of identification databases. It's illegal to investigate people who are not suspected of a specific crime. It's illegal to examine personal records in the absence of a court order specifying what records may be searched in regard to which specific alleged crimes. It's illegal, but it has been done before, and, in the absence of very strong safeguards—maybe even *with* them—it can happen again. It's especially hard to prevent when the rot starts at the top of the system, which it can. (Need I name names? How many American Presidents in the past 40 years have *not* attempted to mis-use federal resources for personal or political gain?)

DO THE MATH

Have we reached the point yet where you're beginning to feel uncom-fortable about those cameras? Have we reached—or passed—the point where you've decided that even if it's legal, it may be a little *too much*?

Doble, Walters, and Barco reached that point as soon as the software was deployed in Ybor City. Maybe that was just fear of the unknown, like Todd says, and maybe the unknown was only what had already been in-stalled on the streets of Ybor City, which everyone involved in the FaceIt program is glad to explain. But maybe what was unknown was the endgame. That's still unknown, but you can see that most of the people in the indus-trialized world will be in it.

Deployments, to date, of the Visionics technology are generally con-sidered successful by the authorities responsible, not all of whom are in law enforcement or even in the public sector. In the week after the 9-11-01 attacks, Zelazny had to cancel interviews with me twice because she was fielding so many calls from governments and businesses that suddenly con-sidered the Visionics technology important and urgent.

Within the next 5 to 10 years, something that performs the functions contained in the Visionics technology will be effectively ubiquitous on the streets of many major urban zones worldwide. It's likely to be used widely for many other purposes. In addition to *identification*—matching a photo of an unknown individual to a database of known individuals—the technology can also be used for *authentication*—one-to-one matches—in situations where things like credit card numbers or passwords are used now. Within the next five years, video cameras will be button-sized and enabled for wireless communication, and almost anyone will be able to scan anything, anytime, anywhere, if he or she wants to and can afford the gear, which won't be expensive. Converting those images into database records is relatively simple. "We work with existing cameras," Zelazny told me.

Let's start counting all the faces that are likely to be scanned over the next 5 to 10 years. The police—in Tampa, Florida, and in Birmingham and Newham in the United Kingdom, and undoubtedly in lots of other cities, soon—have some wanted felons, runaway minors, and sexual predators on their databases. At the airport in Reykjavik, Iceland, they've got a database containing the faces of 10,000 known terrorists and false asylum seekers. Maybe those can be expanded to include everyone with an arrest record, or anyone who is a suspect in an active investigation. To that database, we can add anyone who's working in a facility where the employees are authorized for various job functions, and probably for entry to the facility itself, via facial or other biometric scans. That could include most people who work for a medium-to-large size company.

Zelazny offers a lengthier list of applications. "Security is convenient and passive when your face is the token," she said, "and people recognize each other by their faces anyway," meaning your face is always available to a system that can *see*. "You could use this to secure your home and your car. You could use it in a smart car to tell the car to sound an alarm when the driver falls asleep, because our scan can tell when the subject's eyes are closed."

So we can add car owners and homeowners. Those databases might be very personal, though. They might live only in the car or in the house, for example. Maybe we can drop those very personal databases from the list. Scratch homeowners and car owners.

"The states of West Virginia and Colorado are using our technology to eliminate duplicate drivers' licenses. They found a guy in one state with 27 different drivers' licenses."

Well, we got all the car owners back. Since we're talking about everybody with a driver's license, we can include all the car *operators* as well as the people who actually own a car.

"In banking, the technology's used to verify an individual's identity at the time of a transaction. Innoventry is a joint venture of Wells Fargo and Bank of America, based in San Francisco. They've got a network of 2,000 ATM machines that use our technology. They've eliminated debit cards from those terminals." *What you have* is replaced by *who you are*. "You just enter a PIN number and show your face. They maintain a watch list of people who've defrauded them, and the terminal won't let you conduct a transaction if you're one of those people. The overall fraud rate in check cashing is 15 percent. This system gets it below one-half percent."

So we can add anyone who's got a bank account. That means we got the homeowners back, too, since they've got mortgage accounts with their banks.

"There's another thing nobody's talking about now," Zelazny said, "but they will when the market picks back up. It has to do with mobile commerce and convenience. PDAs are coming out with built-in cameras that enable video conferencing. That same infrastructure could be used for facial recognition.

"You'll have an account with Visa or some other credit card company, and your scanned image will be on their database. Instead of typing in your credit card number when you do a transaction, you'll show your face, and they'll compare the live image to the database. The same thing will happen at an airline gate."

"When Erickson and Nokia are coming out with one model after another that has a camera in it, it seems like a real possibility," Zelazny said.

The "possibility" includes all the credit card owners and everyone who has a cell phone. Cell phones are cheap and getting cheaper. Even elementary school children carry them now.

"Mexico used Visionics in its latest election, to eliminate duplicate voter registration. They started the project with a random sample of a couple of million registered voters and found that half of 1 percent were duplicates. They decided the results were compelling enough to create a permanent system covering all 64 million registered voters. Every time you register to vote, they check you against the system."

That's *every voter in Mexico*. They're the first in line, not likely the last. Governments at every level are talking now about how (not whether) to implement Internet voting. A real-time facial scan (or some other biometric test) is just the thing to ensure that any person voting remotely (1) is entitled to vote and (2) hasn't already voted in a given election. So let's add at least a healthy plurality of all registered voters in all active democracies worldwide.

When you add it all up, just about everybody over the age of 11, in every industrialized nation, has multiple facial scans on file, and dozens or hundreds of public and private institutions are managing the databases.

DRAW THE LINES

In July 2001, not long after deployment of FaceIt in Ybor City, Dr. Joseph J. Atick, the chairman and CEO of Visionics, called for "federal legislation in the United States to help transform . . . responsible use guidelines into responsible public policy." Atick proposed: guidelines for alerting the public about areas where scanning is underway; rules for managing the reference databases used for comparison to newly scanned images; rules for discarding images and audit trails when comparison to the reference database produces no match; rules for authorizing access to the system and the reference databases; and procedures for enforcing the guidelines—for example, via external oversight and review.[10]

Atick gets *very* specific. It's not enough for scanning technology to be deployed unannounced when national security is involved. He talks about restricting unannounced scanning to specific locations, like airports and borders. Technical measures should be in place to ensure control over a database's size and maintenance. "Technical and physical safeguards" over access should be installed. That may be a complex issue. Access could vary widely by locality. "Florida has one of the most liberal public records laws in the country," Todd told me. "The database I'm using with this software is obtainable with a public record demand." If that's the case, then "authorized access only" isn't a very tough constraint. If police databases were shared by municipalities across the country, someone who wanted access to those databases could simply go to the state that has the least restrictive access laws.

Visionics' call for federal legislation seems intended precisely to address the wide range of policies found in state law. The demand for "oversight procedures and penalties for violation of the above principles" implies that the deployment of the technology isn't complete without an accompanying infrastructure of people, procedures, and tools designed specifically to ensure that it won't be misused.

That's a basic principle for all information systems' security. I note elsewhere in this book that a big majority of serious computer system intrusions are committed by insiders. Financial services companies learned a long time ago that if you don't want to make it easy for programmers to steal from the company, you set up operations so that the people who make changes to programs are not the people who authorize and execute the move of those changes to production status. But implementing that principle requires additional staff, which means additional cost. If you think of security as a cost of doing business, then the cost of doing business is going to go up. That's not a calamity, but it is a fact.

It's realistic and distressing to note that many information systems organizations, including many within governmental agencies, have, to date, poor records for implementing security on their databases, including those that contain sensitive information. In his June 2000 testimony before the House of Representatives Subcommittee on Government Management, Information, and Technology, General Accounting Office (GAO) Assistant Comptroller General Jeffrey Steinhoff noted that the most important reason that 19 out of 20 federal agencies surveyed by the GAO failed a security audit was their inability to control access to sensitive data.[11] Will governments be able to make the case to their citizens that the cost of managing these databases securely is justified?

It's a bad sign when scare stories about cyberwarfare list, among effective defenses, the very basic stuff that ought to be taken for granted, like installing firewalls to protect against unauthorized network intrusions. An article in the October 15, 2001, issue of *Fortune,* titled "Business Goes to War" (and subtitled "Fear Along the Firewall"), noted the following:

> What should corporations be doing now to protect themselves? "The same thing they should have been doing all along," says Howard Schmidt, Microsoft's top information-security executive and an Army Reserve special agent who has been called to Washington to assist in the war on terrorism. Schmidt suggests that computer users strengthen their passwords, stop taping them under keyboards, and keep up with antivirus software.[12]

You mean everybody isn't doing that *already?* This is the cyber-equivalent of *flossing.*

If it takes the threat of a cyber-war to get everybody to *floss,* what's going to happen when things settle back more or less to normal, and there's even more, much *much* more, critically important information to safeguard?

So?

If a facial scan provides the bona fides that makes my credit card, my passport, my airline ticket, and my person valid, then, for good reasons, my facial geometry could be captured and stored in a database located anywhere in the world. Will every database owner everywhere be as careful with that information as the most careful business or government agency anywhere? To ask the question is to answer it.

Visionics' guidelines for responsible use are clearly aimed at government, and many of the databases described above are owned and maintained by businesses and individuals, who are, in general, less constrained than governments when it comes to collecting and trading information, though some restrictions do exist, in the United States and elsewhere, on how personal information may be used by a business. The Gramm-Leach-Bliley Act of November 1999 applies restrictions to the ways in which personal information can be used by financial services companies.[13] For example, consumers must be offered an opportunity to opt out of sharing information with nonaffiliated third parties. However, Gramm-Leach-Bliley doesn't extend to companies that are not "significantly engaged" in financial activities, and databases are used everywhere by everybody. There's no uniform international law on the subject—laws in the European Union are more restrictive; laws elsewhere are less so—and certainly no uniform international enforcement mechanism. The Federal Trade Commission's Web site notes, as of October 2001: "The FTC has encouraged web sites to post privacy notices and honor the promises in them. Many web sites—indeed almost all the top 100 sites—now post their privacy policies."[14] Encouragement is not law, of course, and clearly not even all of the top 100 feel bound to comply. Privacy policies covering information not gathered through the Web aren't mentioned.

Even if stringent laws governing the behavior of business-to-business transfers were in place, there's the matter of business-to-government. When *must* a business provide information about customers to governmental agencies that want to see it? In the current wartime environment, the probable answer is *"On demand,"* if national security is involved in any way. In some countries, it could be *on demand* whether a war is on or not.

We don't really know what *responsible use* means when we're talking about identifiers that can be used to correlate information in databases anywhere in the world. The Gramm-Leach-Bliley Act is an attempt to define responsible use from the perspective of financial institutions, but it's neither international nor comprehensive. The Visionics approach is a start, but it's focused on information gathered by governments about people who are known *threats*. Commercial databases in general don't record people who are threats; they record people who are *targets*.

Information is international. The laws are not. Something's got to change. It won't be the information.

ETERNALLY VIGILANT?

Liberty means responsibility. That is why most men dread it.

—George Bernard Shaw

Within 5 to 10 years, almost everyone will be scanned multiple times daily: at the front door of the office and at one's desk; at the door to one's home and behind the wheel of one's car; on the street and on the telephone. In a world where one's next customer, partner, or enemy may be located anywhere on the planet, some universal means of identifying almost everyone uniquely is required. Biometric identification of one sort or another is the likeliest means. It won't be used sparingly. The tools are too useful—even to the people who think it's *too much*—to imagine that it will be otherwise. People who now oppose using the technology for street scans will accept it as a means to voting, buying, flying, and driving, even though all these uses boil down to *placing your identity in someone else's hands,* if only for a moment.

Is it *too much?* It's a lot. It's pretty clear that, as a society, we don't know how to handle it yet. We don't know how to maintain the boundaries between self and others when one's face is a gateway to almost everything one owns and does. "You have zero privacy," Scott McNealy, CEO of Sun Microsystems, says with his customary brusqueness. "Get over it."[15] *Why?* Privacy is connected to liberty, not tangentially but directly. Why give up something that generations of people fought and died for? Why *get over it?*

We live in a dangerous world, and these tools reduce some of the danger. The Tampa police department knows what it's doing and who it's pursuing, and it has taken pains to get it right. Our police need powerful tools to do their work. *"You have to raise the barriers to entry* for criminals," Zelazny said. *"You have to make it difficult."* But as the barriers to entry for criminals go up, the boundaries that separate the rest of us, and our lives, from everyone else go down. *"It's about convenience,"* Zelazny said. The convenience of being known everywhere is the burden of being known everywhere.

Visionics is on the right track when it insists that policy must be decided now, but it doesn't go quite far enough. This is a global issue, not a federal issue. At most, federal laws are useful preludes to an international agreement, a chance to develop some of the principles that will work, worldwide, for commercial entities as well as governments.

Data is a manmade environment that has to be controlled to preserve an acceptable quality of life, just as industrial activities have to be controlled to preserve a breathable atmosphere and water that's fit for drinking. If we can deal with issues of industrial pollution on a worldwide basis, perhaps we can deal with information issues in the same way.

Can it be done? Certainly not perfectly. Nothing people do is done perfectly. Every system has *noise*. Protection of our physical environment isn't perfect, either.

It remains to be seen whether a society—a world—full of *distracted consumers* can maintain the necessary vigilance and will pay the necessary cost. We're addicted to the convenience—the uninterrupted flow of commerce—that goes with being instantly known everywhere. Every addiction carries a price, including the addiction to frictionless lives.

CHAPTER THREE

Homes Without Secrets

Monitoring in the home implies the same issues as any other setting in a World Without Secrets. It's feasible and inexpensive. It's here now and will be here, in force, within a few years. It changes the dynamics of the family; someone monitors, someone is monitored. The former has power over the latter. Technology won't set the boundaries. Families must set and enforce them, or suffer the consequences in terms of damaged relationships. Businesses must keep the same facts in mind.

It's mid-morning on October 4, 2001. I'm connected, via my computer, to a live streaming demonstration of a Smart Kitchen, courtesy of IBM. After the usual setup work—lots of details involving uniform resource locators (URLs), configuring my monitor, typing in passwords, and so on—an IBM systems engineer named Bill Bodin appears on-screen, moving in the slightly jerky, out-of-focus way that images move in streaming video and audio, even with a 512-kb/second cable connection. So far as I can tell, he's of medium height and build, has short, dark brown hair, and is wearing a dark brown sweater and glasses with dark frames. He seems relaxed. He's in his element, and the stuff he's about to show me works, at least in the environment of an IBM showcase room.

The screen shifts past Bodin and zooms in on a refrigerator to his right. At what seems to be roughly chest level for an adult, a video monitor is built right into the big flat vertical face of the fridge. On the green screen of the monitor is a menu with the following selections:

Browse Fridge	Calendar
Life Networking	Recipes
What's Inside	Dining Out
Shopping List	Safeway

On the bottom edge of the monitor is another set of choices:

Menu/Messages/Family/Web Connections/Information/Help

"I expected to see *Setup* somewhere on the menu," I tell Bodin. We're talking via a regular telephone connection. There's a lot of connecting underway among me, him, our computers, and the stuff in the kitchen.

"That application lives on a network available to a Personal Digital Assistant (PDA)," Bodin says. The PDA communicates wirelessly via the 802.11.B protocol, and Bodin explains that they're working on enabling communications via Bluetooth, another short-range communications protocol. Essentially, the refrigerator is just a device communicating wirelessly with every other device on the network. The network doesn't live in the refrigerator; it lives in the house.

It's supposed to be simple, at least for the people using it. Making it simple seems a little complicated, at least for the engineers configuring the system. "You might start a transaction," Bodin says, "like setting up a calendar, on one device"—like your refrigerator, which can display both a calendar and a "virtual keyboard" for typing in information—"and finish it on another," like a PDA, for example. "The network has to know how to present the information on any given device, in terms of the bandwidth the device can handle, the display characteristics, and so on. WAP"—Wireless Application Protocol, yet another standard—"for example, has limits on what it can display. We're working with IBM human factors people and manufacturers on the engineering aspects."

Bodin touches a couple of virtual buttons on the refrigerator's screen, and a graphic rendering of the kitchen layout—a long view, with the refrigerator to the left—appears. Bodin touches a picture of the kitchen light on the graphic, and the *real* lights in the kitchen dim. Sensors on every light in the house communicate with the fridge, or rather with the network that the fridge communicates with.

"The network has a picture of every room, assembled from the CAD [computer-aided design] drawings used by the builder," Bodin explains.

"Suppose I move stuff around in a room. How would the network know?" I ask.

"You'd have access to applets provided by the builder"—computer programs in a language like Java, running on the house network—"that would allow you to update the drawings."

That sounds like work. The system doesn't know when I make a change. I have to tell it. That doesn't do the whole job, either.

"Suppose I want to see what's actually *in* the living room, like the furniture, for example." The builder's CAD drawings show only the *structure of the building*. There's a lot of my stuff inside that structure. I interact with the furniture more often than I interact with the wall. I definitely *move* it more often.

"You'd need cameras in the rooms," Bodin says. "The network handles those functions. Once the cameras are on the network, you could look at it on your PDA, or on the refrigerator, or any other display device that's talking to the network."

So there are cameras in various rooms in the house. "That kind of erases boundaries, doesn't it?" I ask. "I can see what's going on everywhere in the house. It seems like the family dynamics might have to be readjusted."

"Families will have to decide those issues," Bodin says.

Indeed.

Bodin brings up a family calendar with everyone's schedule on it. "This is great for family information." He brings up the virtual keyboard and changes a few entries. "The interfaces need not be visual," he says. "You could have audio and speech interfaces also." That's very useful for sight-impaired people.

The products stored in the refrigerator are labeled with two or three mil-thick Radio Frequency (RF) tags, "like wireless bar codes," Bodin explains. They communicate with the refrigerator, so it knows what's inside. It can even contribute to the shopping list that's on the main menu screen.

There's more, but you get the idea. Everything in the house has a little brain that's wirelessly connected to a big network. Everything talks to everything else. What's known in one place is known throughout the network.

It's a bit different from a smart car, though some of the basic technologies are the same. But, like everything in the World Without Secrets, it all comes down to comfort and control—and, of course, whose.

I WANT THIS WHY?

There doesn't seem to be an overwhelming demand for smart houses in the traditional sense, or what Neil Scott, Leader and Chief Engineer of the Archimedes Project at Stanford University's Center for the Study of Language and Information, dismissively calls "show homes." "They try to put all the functionality into the structure of the house, which requires design and installation at the time of construction," he told me.[1]

Dr. Egil Juliussen of the Telematics Research Group was trying to make a business of smart houses years ago, long before he got involved with automotive telematics. "Fifteen years ago, my wife and I built an automated home in the Dallas area," he told me in September 2001. "We basically learned that we were 15 years ahead of our time. We got an incredible amount of press worldwide, but it was a financial disaster. We spent our own money, and weren't able to turn it into a viable business." He did learn something important. "Focus groups showed that safety and security were the big issues."[2]

Those are the big issues for automotive telematics, too. But there's a big difference between the value propositions supplied by intelligent devices in the two applications, even though safety and security are the impetus for both. Drivers don't have a lot of ways to get certain kinds of safety and security in the cars without telematics. Anyone in a house has loads of options for achieving safety and security. Many of those options are easier and less expensive than making the house smart. There are telephones, beepers, smoke detectors, and alarm systems, none of which has to be built into the house at design time.

"It probably adds less than 1 percent to the cost for a high-end house," Nicos Peonides, an Information Technologies/Controls engineer and associate at Arup in New York City, told me in September 2001. But that's a lot, especially if your house isn't high-end. And a lot of the houses out there weren't designed or built with this stuff in mind. "Development isn't as fast as we thought it would be. The economic drivers aren't clear," Peonides said.[3]

"Five years from now, how many houses will incorporate this kind of technology?" I asked.

"Within the next five years, less than 1 percent," Peonides said, "if we're talking about houses built with embedded smart materials and integrated smart technologies."

So what's the *real* value proposition for the smart house?

KISS

"The reality for most people is: you go to Radio Shack and buy an X10 module"—a relatively simple device that communicates via the electrical wires in your house—"for the device that you want to control," Scott told me. "You go to the house and set a room code and a unit code, and you've just installed another smart device in your house. That's what most people can handle."

Apparently, they can. The *X10 Zone* (http://www.x10.com) lists dozens of products that support what it calls "wireless living." A variety of wireless camera models is available, along with motion sensors and other security gear. There are more wireless cameras. There are entertainment devices that will transmit from a DVD or CD player to a device like a TV in a different room. And there are more wireless cameras.

These devices don't seem to be smart for the most part; they communicate, but they're not particularly self-aware. They see, but they don't understand what they're seeing. But they're *all* about secrets. They make the people using them smarter, or at least more aware. Did I tell you that the site has *wireless cameras?*

We'll return to X10.com and all those wireless cameras later. In the meantime, Neil Scott has more to say about what makes smart houses work.

"Keep the VCR in mind. A design must be clever on the inside, very *very* simple on the outside. As one of my mentors said, "My job is to make things simple, which doesn't mean making them dumb." As an example, a lock on a door should know when you're allowed to go through or not. So you can send a code from your Palm Pilot, and the door reads that code and knows whether you're allowed entry. It works simply, but it's very sophisticated."

I'm beginning to get the idea. The smart house, for Scott, is just a place where someone is carrying a smart device that talks to a bunch of *other* smart devices in the house. It's something like the evolution of the food astronauts take with them on space flights. In the early days of space flight, NASA tried to engineer foods so they would stand up to an earth-orbit environment. Tang® is just *orange juice redesigned for outer space.* After a while, NASA figured out that you didn't have to engineer the food for outer space; you could engineer the package that contained the food for outer space, and let the astronauts eat *normal* food. In the same way, you don't have to engineer a house to be smart. Just bring some smart stuff into it. You can even use the same devices to make your car smart.

"One of the drivers to adoption of this technology that I'm working on is the aging population," Scott said. "It's very expensive for a person to be put into a facility for a condition that might be manageable in a smart house. Every day you keep them out of hospital, you're saving the insurance companies big dollars. The changes for aged people are incremental. It ends up being like you were hit by a Mack truck, but it takes a while to get there. Along the way, a smart house can have a big impact on quality of life and costs.

"Fifty percent of the population will be over 50 by 2020," Scott said. "We can't wait until then to say 'We've got a big problem.' I'm hoping that the insurance industry and welfare support will provide the funding to implement this technology."

That helps answer one question: Who's going to pay to make the house smart? But we're really not talking about smart houses anymore. You don't need to make the *house smart*. Just plug the stuff in and let it talk to anything that will listen.

Scott is looking for a "killer app," the application that supplies a must-buy reason for a new technology. But one such killer app is already here. Remember those wireless cameras? It's not really about a smart house per se. It's about eliminating secrets.

ABOUT THOSE CAMERAS

A wireless camera is a means to monitoring someone or something. Monitoring always implies control; the one who monitors controls the one who is monitored. The implication is that, in a house with wireless cameras installed, a certain amount of control is going on, more or less all the time.

X10.com's Web site seems to recognize that its clientele is very much interested in being in control. The benefits cited for the technologies the site sells emphasize control applications ranging from trivial to nearly voyeuristic. On the trivial side, various appliance modules remotely control the corresponding appliances, like lights and entertainment equipment. X10 Motion Sensors "supercharge any home and lifestyle. . . . You can now make things happen as soon as you walk in a room!"[4] Moving quickly to more intrusive control-oriented applications, The "Ninja Pan 'n' Tilt Camera Mount" allows the owner to "Quickly check on your entire home or office!" and offers "LIVE Monitoring from ANY Location" via the PanTilt Web site.[5] The "Ultimate Starter Kit," with three wireless cameras, is "The Ultimate for Home Surveillance!" and allows its owner to view "the walkway," "the backyard," "the kids' playroom," "the *kids' bedroom*." "Know what's going on in your 'entire' house as you relax in the bedroom! With this Three-Camera SuperDeal you'll be able to view ALL the action!"[6]

There's a lot of excitement here. Just look at all those exclamation points. (They're in the original copy, in case there's any doubt.) It's almost *prurient.* What's *ALL the action* we're supposed to be viewing in the back-yard, the kids' playroom, the *kids' bedroom* (as *you* relax in *your* bedroom)? Someone is getting off. What are they getting off *on?* It can only be that sense of *control.*

Part of X10.com's site is devoted to stories about the people who buy their products. One such story, titled "A Cynic's Demise," tells how a father and his 11-year-old twin sons turned the tables on their mother, who "adamantly" claimed Halloween "is just for children." The father and children are described in the introduction as "idealists," in direct counter-point to the "cynic," Mom.[7]

According to the story, the mother "always worked late." (One won-ders whether those late hours were any cause for resentment among the more idealistic members of the family.) On Halloween night, the father and his sons made preparations to instill some idealism in Mom. They set up wireless motion sensors outside the house and in the living room, and they set up a wireless camera to allow the twins to monitor the front porch from their upstairs bedroom.

Mom came home. The twins used the motion sensors to detect her ap-proach and the camera monitor to time their attack. At the right moment, they dropped a blanket covered with plastic spiders and a plastic snake onto Mom's head and shoulders. Did I mention that, according to the story, Mom is quite frightened of spiders? Mom screamed and stepped back, at which point her idealistic husband, hiding beneath the porch, grabbed her ankles and growled "as loud as he could." Mom screamed even more loudly. "She surprised even us," says her husband with appar-ent satisfaction.

"Their 'X10 Assault' certainly was funny," the article says. Or so Dad and the twins thought. X10.com's reporter didn't get Mom's reaction. But we don't need to, do we? Mom's the one without the technology. The ide-alists are the ones who have it. *They showed her.* If I were Mom, I'd stop coming home late. Maybe I'd stop coming home, period. Either way, the relationship would be different.

Right now, Dad's running the show—setting up the motion sensors and the camera. The camera is about the size of a golf ball. In five years, the camera will be the size of a button. Many kids will be able to afford one, and it won't be hard to seed a house with them. Dad won't be the only one taking pictures.

Technology no longer sets the limits on what can be done. *Families will have to decide those issues.* Not to mention everybody else. The boundaries are *down. Families will have to decide.*

DATA AT REST

Both Scott and Peonides think that smart devices in the home, embedded or otherwise, will generate plenty of data. Peonides thinks at least some of that data belong outside the house. "For controls and monitoring systems related to environmental comfort, video-conferencing, utility metering, and so on, the trend is to store it on the Internet," he said. "I wouldn't have a closed circuit TV system installed in my house, let alone put the images on the Internet," he added.

I wonder how much of a trend it can be if less than 1 percent of the homes in the country will be smart within five years. "Then outsiders could potentially access it," I said. Stored on the Internet means stored someplace *not* under one's direct control.

"Yes," Peonides agreed, "but you do that now, don't you? Doesn't ADT or somebody already monitor your home when you're away?"

True. But what data are they monitoring, really? Nothing much. The doors are closed. Nobody's walking around. It's not like they have cameras going. And if they did, what's there to see when I'm not around?

"People are getting wired," Peonides said. "They're on the Internet. They'll need firewalls to protect their houses, potentially more than that. You can stop radio frequencies from escaping a space by using an RF screen, building a metal or mesh cage around the building. Special glass is available on the market with embedded wire mesh designed to do exactly that."

Yes, but if your house doesn't have that stuff installed already, it's a major renovation to put it in, and the materials aren't cheap. We're back to the classic, engineered-from-the-ground-up smart house.

"People should and eventually will learn to use these new technologies with caution," said Peonides.

Hard to argue. Certainly people with an Internet-connected computer need a firewall *now*, whether their house is smart or not.

Scott's vision is a little different. "The convenient thing is wireless, but that can be hacked. But now we can carry enormous amounts of memory on us, so we could store data on ourselves and transmit it later via some secure method," if, for example, you wanted one of the devices in your house to tell your doctor about something it noticed.

Scott spun it out for me. "You record the data, then encrypt it for transmission. But how do you know the company doing the transmission is ethical? They may initially promise to maintain your privacy. Then they may be bought out, and there goes your data.

"So, the data is safe enough when it's recorded on my device. It can be made relatively safe during transmission. But once it's at rest in a database I don't control, someone else might get at it.

"The more you can do yourself," he concluded, "the less has to be divulged to the rest of the world."

Regardless of how the house gets smart, lots of devices are talking to lots of other devices, wirelessly. *Wireless* is just a stream of bits in the open air. Bits can be hacked.

The distances over which these wireless devices transmit aren't very large. The Bluetooth protocol, one of the leading standards for unlicensed (meaning you don't need to ask the FCC for permission to turn it on) wireless communications between intelligent devices, currently has a range of about 10 feet. X10 has a range of up to 100 feet—certainly enough to be picked up from the street in many places. *Any* wireless protocol, even an encrypted message, can be cracked once received, if given enough resources, skill, and time.

The same issue—the *hackability* of the bit stream—arises with every wireless device and every wireless communication, but it seems particularly acute in this case. What goes on in one's house is the most private of all private information. It's also acute because it's easier for someone who wants to know about you to find you at your house, compared to following you in your car or on the street.

We'll ignore for the moment the question of why someone might wish to crack the wireless transmissions coming from your home. We'll assume that you're somehow exceptional enough—rich, irritating, or otherwise interesting—to justify the attention. We can assume, for the moment, that anyone who wants to hack your house is either a criminal or a government agent. Criminals don't play by the rules, so if you're being hacked by a criminal, you can expect bad things to happen. As an example of the bad things, consider the potential for identity theft in an environment in which much of the information needed to establish identity is transmitted wirelessly.

Government agents have to play by the rules, at least most of the time, but the rules can change, just as the technology does.

THE RULES

In a legal sense, houses aren't like cars or streets. What goes on in our homes is more private, at least for now—depending, of course, on where you live. The Supreme Court ruled, in *Katz v. United States,*[8] that we have a reasonable expectation of privacy in our houses and, for that matter, where our persons are concerned: what a citizen ". . . seeks to preserve as private, even in an area accessible to the public, may be constitutionally protected." So it's not legal, for example, for government agents to do an infrared scan on your house from the street outside and use the results of the scan to get a search warrant to look for a marijuana farm inside the house. Nor is it legal for government agents to somehow produce a scan of your face while you're inside your house and have your window shades drawn. On the street, you have no reasonable expectation of privacy for things like your face; it can be observed or scanned in a public place at any time.

But it's a little trickier than that. It's not just about what you *seek to preserve as private;* it's about a *reasonable expectation* of privacy. The Pennsylvania Supreme Court took that distinction to the recent limit in August 2001, with its decision in *Commonwealth v. Rekasie.* Justice Ralph Cappy wrote for the majority: "A telephone call received by or placed to another is readily subject to numerous means of intrusion at the other end of the call, all without the knowledge of the individual on the call. Extension telephones and speakerphones render it impossible for one to objectively and *reasonably expect* [my emphasis] that he or she will be free from intrusion."[9]

So, in Pennsylvania, for the moment, no phone call can be considered private. The available technology makes it easy to listen in, so you've got no *reasonable expectation* that anyone won't be listening, and therefore any government agent who wants to *can.* Justice Zappala said it clearly in his dissenting opinion: "Today the majority holds that the Pennsylvania Constitution affords no protection against the government listening to, recording and reporting the details of our private telephone conversations."

The boundaries are down. What *can* be done *will* be done, at least in Pennsylvania, at least for the moment. It all depends on what's *reasonable,* and what's reasonable changes, maybe quickly, because it's about what people *think.* It's reasonable, for example, to assume that anyone can wiretap any wireless communication at any time. *Bits can be hacked, and wireless is just a stream of bits in the open air.* Using the logic of the Pennsylvania Supreme Court, it's therefore *reasonable* to assume that any government agent could wiretap any wireless communication, at any time, without a court order.

Perhaps if a wireless communication were encrypted, one could argue that a reasonable expectation of privacy did in fact exist. Maybe not. Multiple government agencies worldwide have sought official authority to manage the coded "keys" used to encrypt messages. If they had such authority, there would effectively be no such thing as an encrypted message where those agencies were concerned. And if they had no such authority, would everyone desiring to send or receive a private message be required to demonstrate that encryption was used (or intended) to demonstrate that a reasonable expectation of privacy had existed? Would it be necessary to prove that the form of encryption used was technically difficult to break to demonstrate such a reasonable expectation, or would reliance on relatively weak encryption mean that the message was fair game?

In an odd way, the Pennsylvania Supreme Court is thoroughly in tune with its times. Napster was based on the premise that the ability to make and distribute digital copies without compensation to the copyright owners was equivalent to the right to do so. *What can be done will be done.* You don't necessarily expect to see it coming from the state. Maybe that's the expectation that's *unreasonable*.

WE ARE THE BOUNDARY

Scott's advice—*"The more you can do yourself, the less has to be divulged to the rest of the world"*—is good. But it also tells something about how complex this is getting. I record data on a smart device. I keep the data in my house. I transmit them to somebody else. Someone may be listening during the transmission. The people who receive the data may or may not guard them adequately.

Meanwhile, the most personal data possible—stuff that describes my body, my activities in private, and my relationships—are piling up. It's as if the stuff is radioactive. I can't just dump it somewhere, because it's dangerous for at least the next thousand years, especially if it gets into the wrong hands, which is hard to anticipate. How can I possibly know whether the company that does good things for me today is going to be bought out by a bad company tomorrow?

Meanwhile, I'm monitoring my family. They're monitoring me. We know things about each other that we shouldn't know and don't really want to know. But we know.

Welcome to the World Without Secrets.

Families will have to decide, notwithstanding the novelty of the decision. We can add that businesses will have to decide the same kinds of questions, because they also will be privy to much information that they never encountered before, and the relationships are just as delicate.

CHAPTER FOUR

Cars Without Secrets

Make a list of every emotion you can think of—exhilaration, joy, pride, happiness, sadness, fear, anger, regret—and you can probably remember a moment in your life when a car provoked it. Our relationships with cars are deep and complex, and they can probably be summed up simply: We *love* our cars.

Americans change when they're in their cars; or perhaps, as Anne Rice said about aging, they just become more like themselves. Often, they don't change for the better. The American Automobile Association (AAA) estimates that reported incidents of road rage—in which a driver uses his or her car purposely as a means to intimidate or harm another driver— have increased at a rate of about 7 percent per year since 1990 (meaning that they've more than doubled by now), and lots of road rage episodes aren't even reported. Men driving sports cars are more aggressive than men in sedans. Women driving SUVs are more aggressive than men driving SUVs. Over 40,000 Americans die in cars every year, and many times more are seriously injured. The death toll worldwide is over one million. It's unknown how many of those deaths are suicides.

Cars reflect the American struggle between *personal* prerogatives and the *system*. We think of ourselves as rugged individualists—pioneers and frontier fighters—and, to some extent, that image is true. But we also like to build businesses and armies that are as top-down as any in the world, and we like to take our cars onto highways when everyone else who lives or works in the nearest major city is doing the same thing.

Cars are rapidly growing more intelligent. The average car rolling off an assembly line in 2001 has at least 18 to 20 microprocessors in it. A luxury car has twice that many. At this point, the devices mostly communicate with each other, or, more rarely, with the driver. Some cars can communicate with external third parties. The systems used in cars for that purpose are called *telematics*. Within 10 years, at least a quarter of all cars on the road will have such systems installed.

Cars are rolling toward the World Without Secrets, and we're rolling with them.

THE TECHNICAL STUFF: TELEMATICS

David Reid is Motorola's Director of Strategic Marketing for the Automotive Communications and Electronics Systems (ACES) Group. Motorola is one of the largest players moving to establish a position in the nascent telematics market, which the Telematics Research Group (TRG) estimates will generate over $7.3 billion in revenues for products and services by 2006. (The TRG's name is itself a sign of a nascent market poised on the edge of dramatic growth. Somebody's buying their research.)

"From Motorola's perspective," Reid told me in September 2001, "Telematics is integrated wireless communications and location-based services tailored for the vehicle. It could be as simple as an integrated cell phone system where the driver can place calls via voice command, and there's some level of location-based service. More advanced features include embedded diagnostics and communications."[1]

That's mostly consistent with the TRG's definition in the executive summary of its September 2001 report, *Telematics: Technologies, Trends, and Markets*. "Automotive telematics is the wireless exchange or delivery of communication, information and other content between the auto and/or occupants and external sources."[2] The difference is that the TRG's definition is technical; Reid's emphasizes the important applications. You see the overlap when the TRG lists telematics benefits for drivers and other vehicle occupants: enhanced safety and security, improved accident response time, improved health care for crash victims, and improved traffic flow. All these benefits are based on a car's being able to communicate its precise location to a third party, especially when the driver can't (for example, immediately following an accident). (*Precise* in this case means within 100 yards, which is within the capabilities of the state of the art, and close enough for an ambulance or tow truck to find the vehicle.)

WHO HEARS WHAT

"In an overarching sense, telematics services defined today and in the future for the vast majority are event-driven from the vehicle," I was told by Steve Millstein, the CEO of ATX, one of the leading telematics service providers. "We don't cause anything to happen until the vehicle does. It could be a tire blowing out, or an airbag going off, or a nervous driver hitting a button. We can use whatever information is available to the car. For example, the federal government has mandated that certain dashboard notices be given to the driver when there are tire conditions. ATX can use that information."[3]

An accident occurs. The service provider for the telematics system, such as Onstar or ATX, is immediately, automatically, wirelessly informed of the location of the car and the fact that an airbag was deployed. The service provider's operators or response specialists then execute standard procedures for wirelessly contacting the driver of the car, learning about the condition of the vehicle and its passengers, and coordinating help. "We always give people the option of a live operator," Millstein says. "If somebody is hit, it's automatically upgraded to a live operator." An accident is too complex for a machine to handle. Handling the people involved in an accident is *way* too complex for the machines.

This is very simple, compared to what's already on the drawing board. Even so, you can already see control shifting from the *driver* to the *car,* and from the car to the *system.* As usual, the ones giving up the control hope to get *comfort* and *convenience* in return.

THE MORE YOU GIVE, THE MORE YOU GET

A state-of-the-art commercial telematics system doesn't have sensors that would tell it what most of the systems in the car were doing before or after the crash, or where the car was hit and with what force. If a car knew those things, it could notify third parties (such as a service provider like Onstar or ATX, or police, or a hospital) of the nature and severity of a crash, in addition to its location. Dr. Egil Juliussen of the TRG thinks that's revolutionary.

"The first hour after the crash—the 'golden hour'—is what's most important," Juliussen told me. "If they know what kind of impact it was, and the severity, medical personnel can dramatically improve the kind of service they provide. They'll know whether they should send a helicopter, or whether they can afford to take 15 minutes to get to the scene.

"There's going to be a 'black box' in General Motors cars starting in 2005. It'll keep a rolling record of the status of systems in the car for the last 15 seconds. When there's a crash, it'll automatically transmit that data, plus the status of the systems in the 15 seconds immediately after the crash, to a service provider. It's aimed at gathering as much statistics about the vehicle and its behavior as possible. It's a massive data collection, and it'll terrifically improve what we know about accidents and how we allocate medical resources.

"Insurance companies have a lot to gain, too," Juliussen says. "It'll be much easier to settle lawsuits. We'll know who was at fault, or whether it was a mechanical cause."[4]

All that involuntary data transfer from the car means that the people involved in an accident are no longer the authorities on what happened. You give up that control in return for the comfort of knowing that help will be dispatched instantly, whether you can call for it yourself or not.

"Generally speaking, capabilities for diagnosing the condition of the vehicle exceed what's being done today," Millstein says. "We can already connect to the system busses in the car, and get any information available to that bus. We're just developing some of the applications. It's not only knowing that something's wrong, it's doing something with the data. For example, the driver doesn't know what to do when the engine warning light goes on. We can enhance the engine warning light so the customers know they're going to get a call if it's something they need to do something about."

The statement is interesting for at least two reasons. First, if the driver doesn't know what to do when the engine warning light goes on, what's the point of having an engine warning light? Why not just build a message display into the dashboard and tell the driver what's happening and what to do, as opposed to making him or her call out for that information? The second thing that's interesting is that we can easily accept the idea that the car is too complex to be understood by the typical driver. The car has to understand and explain itself, or call on someone to do so on its behalf. The driver, in other words, needs a Mentat (as described in Chapter Seven) on the road. Driving is too complex to go it alone, or the driver's not smart enough, or both. (We'll return to the smartness of the driver later.)

Dr. Juliussen elaborates. "I'm on the road. My car breaks down. I'd certainly be willing to pay fifteen dollars for a remote diagnosis, so I know that I'm not being taken for a ride by the repair shop. Auto manufacturers will gain more information and revenues from ongoing remote diagnostics than from anything else," Juliussen adds. "It's like running Six Sigma after you've sent the stuff out."

Six Sigma is the quality program used to such great effect by Motorola and General Electric. It's aimed at making processes—and, by extension, the products produced by the processes—as close to error-free as is humanly possible. ("Six Sigma" literally means that errors occur at a rate equal to six standard deviations from the norm, or about one error per every 3 million executions of a process.) Six Sigma is very data-intensive, and the only place manufacturers have historically been able to get all those data is inside the factory walls. Juliussen is pointing out that, with telematics, the car can keep talking to the factory long after the customer has driven it away.

The factory personnel, of course, are in a much better position to manage service for you, if you choose to let them. Give them a little control; get some comfort. They're your Mentat too. As such, they're looking forward to a closer relationship with the owners of the cars they build. Such relationships are an aspect of the in-car presence of telematics, which is of great interest to multiple service providers. All *you* have to do is let them in.

WHO'S DRIVING?

We've already got systems—like antilock brakes (ABS)—that augment the driver. With ABS, the only thing the driver does to work the brakes is push on the brake pedal. From then on, the ABS is working the brakes, not the driver. The ABS doesn't make a decision that it's time to hit the brakes. The driver does that, at least for now. That could change.

"If you're in a turn and accelerating too quickly, and the vehicle detects that you're starting to roll too much, the vehicle itself could dynamically lower the throttle to reduce the roll condition," Reid said. There's the car taking charge, deciding that you're putting the car into a roll and it's going to stop the roll if you can't or won't. "It's an advanced version of stability control." Very.

"Some of this technology is on the road today. Mercedes Benz has branded advanced stability control built into the car now. It's not like the futuristic version we're talking about, i.e. taking away control of the vehicle, but it is enhancing the performance of the vehicle," Reid said.

"For lane-following situations, you'd need some means of sensing outside the vehicle, like a camera. You could use the camera for a coarse sense of tracking on a road. Couple that with more specific performance information from the rate or angular sensors. That could help with lane departure or entry. Couple it with distance measurements or radar to help you maintain distances between vehicles."

"In some new systems that've been demonstrated, when adaptive information, like speed, is sent to the car, the car provides tactile feedback, such as increased back pressure on the gas pedal," Juliussen says. "The car adapts to the situation presented. The driver is still in charge, but the car will tell you when something's going on."

A good driver—meaning *a careful and considerate person*—could use that kind of information to adjust the distance to the next car for an extra margin of safety. An aggressive driver—who might be just as *careful*, but is a lot less *considerate*—could use that kind of information to get hairbreadth precision on the distance from another driver's bumper. Better feedback from the car makes the car a more sensitive instrument. How drivers use it is up to them.

WHAT THE OWNER WANTS

Control always involves multiple viewpoints and players. Someone is *in* control. Someone *is* controlled. Even *self*-control implies that the person is split between *someone in control* and *someone being controlled*. Relatively few people seem to have strong self-control while they're driving, so external controls of some sort are always necessary. That's why we have highway patrols.

It's clear that telematics systems open up new possibilities for external control. They communicate to someone who's watching, even if the watcher is not a cop per se. These systems won't necessarily make anyone a better driver, but it can make someone a more *controlled* driver.

"Systems will emerge, over the next 10 years, that are capable of both augmenting the driver and taking over in emergency situations," Juliussen said. "They might be applied to known dangerous drivers, or to people who would like a failsafe if they're old or sick or have other dangerous conditions."

Or they might be applied to cars that are owned by one party and driven by another. They would allow the party that owns the car to maintain control. There's already a class of car owners whose cars are routinely used by other people: rental car companies. Many of those owners are installing fairly advanced control systems. The people who are controlled—the people who *use* the cars—are occasionally reacting with surprise—maybe because the way the controls are applied is sometimes clumsy.

CARS WITHOUT SECRETS, NOW

In June 2001, CNN reported a story straight out of the World Without Secrets:

> An ordinary trip turned into an Orwellian ordeal for one Connecticut driver, forced to pay multiple fines after a car rental company tracked his every move via satellite.
>
> James Turner of New Haven took Acme car rental company to court, calling the technology too intrusive. Acme countered that Turner knew the risks. . . .
>
> When Turner needed a van to drive from New Haven to Virginia some months ago for business, he turned to a merchant near his home that he had relied on many times in the past. But the theater box office manager overlooked a clause in the contract stating that its vehicles were equipped with a Global Positioning Satellite (GPS) system and that going over the speed limit would cost $150 per infraction.
>
> When he returned home and tried to use his ATM card, he discovered that the rental company had taken out $450 from his account. Acme Rent-A-Car had determined that he had gone over the speed limit three times and dipped into his account for each one.
>
> "They took the money out before I returned the car," Turner told CNN this week. "I was very, very surprised. I was not aware of what GPS could do. I thought it was an onboard navigation system, to use when you get lost."

This story confirms a number of important things about a World Without Secrets. First, look at *what was observed and recorded.* The systems in the car and external to it didn't take Mr. Turner's picture or record his voice. They tracked and recorded a few simple labels and numbers: the vehicle identification number (VIN) of the rented van, Mr. Turner's name and credit card account, and the speed and location of the van. *What matters most is what people do, and what they do can often be summed up with labels and numbers.*

Acme had asked its telematics service provider, AirIQ, to set up Acme's system so that their vehicles would report when a speed of over 80 miles per hour was sustained for more than two minutes. (I tend to agree that if you're going that fast for that long you're speeding, assuming that you're not driving on the Autobahn or in Nevada.) Human monitoring and intervention weren't required. The system could do the job. *Data mean something when they are monitored, but not until then.*

We can also see how unaware people are of the presence of intelligent devices like the GPS system in the van. When Mr. Turner signed the rental contract, did he think Acme really had any way to know if he went over the speed limit, short of his getting a speeding ticket? *"I was not aware of what GPS could do,"* he said (or, we presume, of what the merchant was willing to do with the information GPS provided). Acme claimed that pains had indeed been taken to inform Mr. Turner that his speed would be monitored, and he would be subject to penalties for speeding. But even if Turner knew, he might have forgotten, once under way. *Who pays attention to anything that's silent and invisible?*

We can see also that Mr. Turner didn't like being monitored, or being fined. The Connecticut Department of Consumer Protection didn't like it either, and decided, about a month after this incident was reported, to overturn the fines levied on Mr. Turner (and a number of other customers) by Acme, on the grounds that Acme didn't have the authority to levy such fines. The state didn't attempt to rule on the privacy issues. CNN quoted Max Brunswick, Acme's attorney:

> The monitoring system allows Acme to find cars that are not returned, a persistent problem that can drive small car rental companies out of business. Moreover, drivers, knowing their speed is being checked, tend to drive slower, leading to less liability for the company and fewer accidents for the drivers, according to Brunswick.

So it's for the benefit of the *driver,* too. *Everyone* benefits when we all drive slower. It's probably true.

And, of course, *good drivers have nothing to fear.* That is, drivers who have some *self*-control.

WHAT THE CAR KNOWS

The system installed in the Acme car rented by Mr. Turner was provided by a Canadian company called AirIQ, whose business is aimed at commercial fleets, including rental vehicles and trucking companies. AirIQ's Web site describes the company as follows:

> As a wireless application service provider, AirIQ is dedicated to providing the knowledge to protect and manage vehicles, simply and cost-effectively. With AirIQ, clients can access and receive information about their vehicles without ever having to leave the office.

AirIQ OnBoard™ is installed into each vehicle and keeps track of **where the vehicle is, what direction it is going, what speed it is traveling, and records and reports additional vital information** [emphasis mine]. By preselecting parameters, clients choose the circumstances under which a vehicle will report.

This information is forwarded to AirIQ OnLine™ (central computing intelligence), where it is routed to a location selected by the client. Clients can view and access their own fleet information on digitized maps by using AirIQ's Fleet Operator™ service available over the Internet.

In addition, the client's staff can carry out certain control functions directly. For example, a vehicle can be disabled or enabled and the doors can be unlocked with the point and click of a mouse. AirIQ places the power of these capabilities and many more at your fingertips.

You can imagine lots of situations in which people would like to install that kind of technology in other people's cars, compared to relatively few in which people would want it for themselves. Parents might want it for their teenage children. Adult children might want it for their aged parents. Police might want it for drivers who have been convicted of multiple moving violations. And so on. People who want control could like this stuff.

I spoke to Don Simmonds, the CEO of AirIQ, on October 5, 2001.

"We don't comment much on speeding tickets, because that's between the rental car owner and the courts," Simmonds said. "In the Turner case, it's fascinating to us that invasion of privacy was the first issue people picked up on. Over time, the response was that the owner of the property had the right to enforce the rules. It's more common for a renter who exhibits risky driving behavior to be refused the right to rent again," as opposed to being fined by the car owner.[5]

AirIQ doesn't want to be *between the rental car owner, the courts, and so on.* I don't blame them. They want to focus on the real problems they solve for their clients. "Moving assets are the largest single investment of most of our clients," Simmonds said. "The assets were at risk before AirIQ, because they were in the hands of someone else."

This is one of the important things about monitoring technology. The people who want to use it always have legitimate needs and reasons to be *in control.* Law enforcement needs to watch people and situations that are potentially dangerous. Rental car owners need to track their assets. Parents need to know what their children are up to. Did that last item cross the line? It depends on your definition of *legitimate.* It's not a simple question. It's certainly legal for parents to keep tabs on their children. But what's *legal* isn't necessarily *legitimate,* at least not in everybody's eyes. (Are you the one *in control,* or the one *being controlled?*)

Recent events add urgency to the need. "The Oklahoma City bombing (of the Murrah Federal Building, in 1995) was done with a rental truck," Simmonds said. "We've had conversations with law enforcement about it. People are getting a little fed up with the use of rental vehicles for purposes like that. The Turner ruling was a tangent. The deeper issue is that there's a benign asset that's being used for dangerous purposes."

Rental car companies need to track their assets, and, in many ways, the tracking is for the public good as well as the company's. That's legitimate. Was Acme's use of AirIQ's technology legitimate?

"It's not up to a single company like AirIQ to solve these philosophical questions," Simmonds said. "If a customer owns the information and does something with it, that's not a problem we can solve. We always have something to say about our recommended use of the information. We're concerned if our customers don't inform their drivers and customers that the technology exists. But we have no right to say, 'You can only use the information this way or that way.' If you sell a car to a 16-year-old, you can't tell him or her where to drive. You don't have control of the outcome, but you have a social responsibility to raise certain issues. We can tell Acme: 'If you're going to put this technology in your cars, there's some things you ought to keep in mind.' "

Neither Acme nor any other client, nor even the consumers who use their services, has to listen, of course. *We're concerned if our customers don't inform their drivers and customers that the technology exists.* Mr. Turner was informed; he signed a contract that informed him. But he supposedly didn't *understand: I was not aware of what GPS could do.*

Powerful tools get used in all sorts of ways. The people who make them don't always anticipate all the uses. AirIQ gave Acme the tools. Acme decided to do something about renters who speed. Turner thought he was in control. After all, he was driving. But he wasn't *aware of what GPS could do.*

SUPPOSE

Suppose that Acme had set its system up in such a way that when another threshold—say, a speed of 100 miles per hour—was exceeded, a call for assistance, from the van, was automatically generated to the nearest police station. Would a transaction like that be an unconstitutional invasion of privacy? It hasn't been tested in any court, but the answer's probably *No.* U.S. courts have generally ruled that any behavior or fact that's publicly observable is fair game for observation by law enforcement. If a car could be observed by the naked eye (or by a radar gun by the side of a highway) to be traveling at 100 miles per hour, there's probably no constitutional reason why a device on board the car couldn't be used to tell a police officer the same thing.

If a rental company can't charge fines—the State of Connecticut said Acme can't—can the company refuse to allow a customer to operate one of its vehicles in a manner not to its liking? It could certainly refuse to rent to the same customer again. Could it go beyond that? AirIQ's system gives an owner the ability to disable the vehicle. Could an owner demand the immediate return of the car if the driver is operating it recklessly, as defined by sustained speeds well in excess of the speed limit, and disable it otherwise?

Suppose that in the post-9-11-01 environment of vastly enhanced security against terrorism, *every* car is *required* to have technology like AirIQ's installed, on the chance that police might need to track *any* car's whereabouts. Americans are already largely willing to have their e-mail and phone conversations monitored; why not the location of their cars? Not that the police *would* track the location of every car continuously; that's a lot of work for a lot of meaningless information. But perhaps they'd like the option to track anyone who was *exceptional* in some important way.

"Post-September 11, public opinion has swung," Simmonds told me. "More than ever in years to come, society and history will see that event as a marker point for new directions in public conduct." Meaning, I guess, that there's going to be more control.

The most important limit on all these scenarios is the broken and distrustful relationships they imply. Parents monitor children, car rental companies monitor customers, governments monitor *everybody*. The children, the customers, and the citizens are certain to be unhappy with the arrangement. We can guess that Mr. Turner is unlikely to pick Acme the next time he needs a van.

Drivers are still in control, at least for now.

But they may have to behave themselves to stay there.

PRIVATE BY INTENTION

A service provider has to do a lot to avoid the appearance of external control. "Customers are very sensitive to privacy," Millstein explained to me. "A customer might have an accident or a blowout in a part of town where they're not supposed to be. They don't want that information to be public. So we asked from the start: What information do we really need to keep? We were sensitive from day one."

That's a pretty good working definition of sensitivity to privacy: you don't even want to know anything you don't have to know.

"We currently don't permanently store the audio recordings we get from emergency situations involving cars out on the road," Millstein added. "We keep them for two days, mostly for quality assurance. We store the signal information for a year: a printed record of the call, the location, what kind of incident was involved, a few details. We have to pay the wireless company for that call. We have the capability, if an original equipment manufacturer (OEM) or customer ever desired, to pull a lot more: tire pressure, oil pressure, vehicle mileage, what triggered the engine light to go on. Today, despite the capability, we actually don't monitor much of the data we can pull."

The data aren't stored permanently, but before they are discarded they are used to set up follow-on data-mining operations. "We can tell the car companies that a certain tire on a certain car model is having one blowout per million, and a different tire company's tire is having half a blowout per million on the same car," Millstein told me. Like Juliussen said: That's Six Sigma after the car leaves the factory. "The VIN is like the DNA of the vehicle," Millstein said. "It's basically a code for identifying the vehicle's configuration. We can use it to look up corresponding data about the car, supplied by the manufacturer. We don't have to use the VIN to identify the driver."

You could. But you don't have to. The thing that stops you is your customers' sensitivity to privacy. The technology would let you go as far as you wanted to. For that matter, so would the law, in many places. This isn't financial services; Gramm-Leach-Bliley doesn't apply. What a company like ATX has to do is set the boundaries and stick to them. Both activities are at least slightly problematic.

WHAT CAN POLICY DO?

ATX's privacy policies are clear; they're documented, and they're intended to provide strong protection for customers' privacy. I'm going to review the policy in some detail (1) because it's a good example of a good privacy policy, and (2) because it's a good example of what a good privacy policy doesn't do.[6]

The first paragraph of the policy starts with "ATX Technologies, Inc. (ATX), takes your privacy very seriously." The last sentence of the paragraph reads: "Please note that this Policy may be changed from time to time, and that any changes will supersede this Policy."

"Policy may be changed." ATX might change its mind, as Amazon did in September 2000. If ATX does so, the current policy will be superseded. When Amazon changed its policy, customers were informed that Amazon would do whatever it liked with data that customers had previously been told would not be shared with anyone besides Amazon. ATX has no intention of changing its mind, and it understands how important this is to its customers. However, *a policy's not bulletproof, no matter how strongly it's worded.*

Paragraph 2 of the policy states plainly: "We do not sell, trade or rent your information to others." Good. Of course, this is policy, and *policy may be changed.* Amazon's policy was changed *retroactively;* that's one of the most important differences between a corporate policy and the law.

Paragraph 3 adds: "When required, we may release information to comply with the law or to enforce or apply the terms of our Agreements. For example, we may be legally compelled to provide location data and other information to law enforcement agencies." No surprise there. But even strong privacy policies have exceptions.

Paragraph 5 states: "We have security measures in place to protect the loss, misuse, and alteration of the information under our control. . . . Although we take your privacy very seriously and we use industry standard practices to protect the privacy of your information, we cannot guarantee that your information will always remain private." This is a straightforward admission of a simple truth: The security of electronically stored information can't be guaranteed. Is that a problem? No more or less than it is for any other database that contains your personal information. There are many of those for most people, to the point that very few people could count them all with any reasonable degree of certainty.

Perhaps more important from a security, as opposed to a privacy, standpoint is this statement in Paragraph 6, *Security on the Cellular Telephone Network:* "In providing the Services to you, voice and data are transmitted between the response center and your vehicle over the cellular telephone network. This network is complex and not necessarily secure. Therefore, the privacy and security of conversations or data transmitted to and from the vehicle cannot be guaranteed."

Wireless communications, by definition, can be hacked. *Any* communication traveling through the air can be intercepted and interpreted. "I think there'll be telematics wiretaps applied all the time," Juliussen told me. "But as the number of telematics users grows, you can't monitor everybody. You'd have to know that there's someone worth following."

There's an interesting insight. The technological limit on wiretapping in the days of hard-wired lines was that it was hard to do. In a wireless world, it's easy to do, and *that's* the new limit. It's so easy that you can't *afford* to monitor everybody all the time. A wiretapper just gets swamped. But that's really not much of a limit. It's just like our tracking scenario. You have to restrict yourself to eavesdropping on people you already know are interesting.

"I'm more worried that there'll be illegal use of that information," Juliussen told me, "like a snooping private eye wiretapping somebody in a divorce case."

Indeed.

When you add it all up, it's a good policy. It's better than what's provided by many, if not most, companies. It's just not a guarantee of anything but good intentions and best efforts.

CALL ME ANY TIME

In some scenarios developed by the telematics industry, consumers choose to make it easier to find them in their cars. ATX's Web site contains this description of a user who has decided to open the doors to her car wide:

> . . . as telematics becomes more ubiquitous and its use more prolific, tomorrow's telematics services will go a step beyond, telling the environment about the user. What does it mean to tell the environment about the user? The question is most easily answered with a couple of examples: A driver approaches a Starbucks on her way home from work. Information about the restaurant's location, special promotions, and so forth, is automatically offered to the driver, who has indicated her passion for gourmet coffee in the pre-filed profile she completed online with her telematics service provider. In essence, she has given permission for Starbucks to advertise to her, wherever she is.[7]

The boundaries are clearly down. This driver wants contact. She wants it so much that she's willing to *tell the environment* about herself. Who's in that environment, and what does she know about *them?*

Even if the service provider is managing all those contacts, in effect keeping them at arm's length, it's still a little uncomfortable. Doesn't this driver already know how to find a Starbucks that she passes every day on her way home from work? There's some added comfort here, of course. It's nice to get those specials from Starbucks. North Americans really like caffeine. But the driver has to give something up to get it. Somebody out there—maybe lots of people—now knows her *passions*.

We could argue that they know anyway. If the driver buys most of what she buys using a credit card, then anybody with a decent data-mining program can already figure out what she likes. As I said earlier, the stuff that matters is simple labels and numbers, and the more of them there are, the better I know the person who generated them.

But it still seems a little odd for them to call her in the car. It really drives home—no pun intended—the point. As I said, the boundaries are *down*.

SPEAKING OF ENHANCING PERFORMANCE

"The social impact of telematics hasn't been much discussed," Juliussen told me. "It's very important stuff. For example, take health care. It's staggering how many people are killed in transportation accidents: forty thousand every year in the United States, over a million worldwide. It's a major public health problem. Telematics can have a big impact everywhere. It might help the international market more than the United States.

"Simply knowing how to allocate resources makes a big difference," Juliussen continued. "Medical personnel can improve their performance and efficiency and the number of lives they save dramatically." The medical personnel had control at this point all along; this merely makes them more effective. "Telematics won't necessarily reduce the number of accidents immediately, but it may do so over time."

Reducing the number of accidents—as opposed to reducing the impact of accidents—means that the cars, the roads, or the drivers, or all three, get better as a result of telematics. It's taking the long way around to bet that drivers will improve as a result of telematics. It's also not a sure thing.

Take our previous example of a car's providing feedback to the driver about the distance to the car ahead. What if the driver won't listen? What if the driver *wants* to tailgate? What if the driver keeps pushing that gas pedal *down*, no matter how much back pressure he encounters? Don't most people who tailgate *want to*?

We've all got the right to tailgate—sorry, I mean the *ability* to do so, of course—as long as it's our car and a cop's not watching. Part of the freedom of the road is the freedom to drive recklessly, stupidly, *badly*. We all love that freedom. Who *hasn't* driven recklessly and *loved* it?

Does a *smart car* want you to have the freedom to be *stupid?* Will it *dynamically lower the throttle* if you don't *control yourself?* Will you *let it?*

We love our cars. We won't love them so much if they're smarter than we are, and we *really* won't love them if they get in the habit of taking over. A car that won't let you tailgate is a tough sell.

I doubt that most manufacturers will try to sell it. My guess is that we're going to let drivers keep on tailgating, at least for now. We can still use the telematics to call the paramedics.

MAKING THE DRIVERS SMART

"Telematics isn't a substitute for education and training," Reid told me.

It's a good point. It begs two other points: (1) there's no other substitute, either, and (2) very few drivers get any real education or training in driving.

Education starts with assumptions about what the result of the education is supposed to be. We make certain assumptions about drivers from the start, almost everywhere in the world. The first assumption is that *almost everybody's going to drive*. They're going to start young and keep going until they die of old age. Implicitly, we assume that they're going to have to screw up really badly, usually repeatedly, before they're told they can't drive anymore. We think of driving as a right, even if we say it's a privilege.

With or without telematics, there isn't a whole lot of education and training for drivers going on. The typical American state requires fewer than 40 hours of training before a novice driver is handed an unrestricted license. That's all the training most drivers get, ever. Only people who demonstrate incompetence repeatedly, via moving violations or actual accidents, are likely ever to be required to get additional training (or lose their licenses), and a lifetime of driving may last upward of 80 years.

Less than 40 hours of training doesn't seem like much for people who are operating heavy machinery on narrow roads, at high speeds, at all hours of the day and night, in all sorts of weather, traffic, and personal conditions. We certainly ask a lot more of most pilots. SAS's Web site tells prospective applicants for a commercial pilot's job that they need one and a half to two years of formal training, plus 700 to 1,500 hours of flight experience after training is completed, before they can fly an SAS plane.[8] *That's* training.

Does that seem like overkill for drivers? Having 40,000 dead in the United States and over a million killed worldwide seems like literal *overkill* to me. Forty thousand commercial pilots *did not* crash their planes last year in the United States. Our attitudes toward driver training aren't based on the relative likelihood of car crashes versus plane crashes. The planes most frequently involved in accidents are single-engine craft, and a pilot can get a license for one of those without much more training than is needed to drive a car. If we trained airline pilots the way we trained drivers, jumbo jets would be crashing every day.

It's all about *what we want to do*. And what we obviously want to do is make it easy for people to drive. We'd rather concentrate our resources on technical systems that make it easier to pick up the mess, than on human systems that teach people how not to make messes. That's not a value judgment, by the way. It's an attempt to accurately describe the operating model.

SMART CARS, YES

When you take that approach, you end up needing really smart cars, because lots of the drivers aren't very smart or capable. Over time, the cars do more and more of the driving. The cars watch the road and make decisions about when to step on the gas and when to step on the brakes, because the drivers just *screw it up*.

The interesting thing is that this is kind of how we're running the Internet, too. Ten years ago, the Internet was for scientists and academics. Everybody knew the rules of the road, and everybody knew how to drive. Now the Internet is full of people who just bought powerful vehicles— their personal computers. They haven't been trained, but they've got 1,000 free hours from AOL, so they've got a license to drive. They don't know the rules, they don't know how to drive, they don't know how to protect themselves from highway robbers, and they're getting killed (via viruses and identity thefts) in record numbers. And when we talk about protecting them, a lot of the discussion is about making the cars smarter.

If I've devoted too many words to this issue, it's not because I think I'll persuade anyone to change the way we run driver education (or Internet education) in the United States or anywhere else. I'm sure I won't. *Americans love their cars*. We'll keep driving them the way we want to drive them, no matter what, even if eventually we're not really driving anymore.

We'd rather concentrate our resources on technical systems than on human systems. We'd rather *make the cars smart* than *train the drivers*. If you

WHEN DOES TELEMATICS ARRIVE IN FORCE?

The Telematics Research Group (TRG) has estimated that by 2010, over 80 percent of all cars and light trucks sold in North America, and something like a quarter of all cars and light trucks on the road— about 60 million units total—will have telematics systems installed.

David Reid thinks that's a little optimistic. "It may be as low as 50 to 70 percent of manufactured cars by 2010. The TRG figures assume that systems must be embedded in the vehicle by the manufacturer. It's possible that some systems with limited functionality would just offer an interface for a personal digital assistant (PDA) or some other device, which would allow retrofits." Yes, but if you wanted the really great stuff, like roadside diagnostics, sensors and supporting communications would still have to be embedded in the vehicle.

Steve Millstein is pretty close to the TRG's numbers. "We think there'll be 24 million units on the road in 2008, with annual uptake by then of about 16 million units." That adds up to 56 million units on the road by 2010, a little short of TRG's estimates, but not much.

Because these systems are subject to Moore's Law, prices will drop steeply over a 10-year period. Already, the added cost is pretty insignificant for luxury cars; within five years, it will be insignificant for an economy sedan. Potential inhibitors include competing system standards for things like operator interfaces—you certainly don't want to have to retrain every time you get into a different car—and for basic technical architectures. Another potential inhibitor is the interest of state regulatory authorities in ensuring that the operator interfaces for the systems don't distract drivers to the point that they make the cars *less* safe.

Millstein doesn't see these as major issues: "It's a marketing play, not a technology play. It all gets back to the safety of the driver. It always gets back to the need. The lack of universal coverage was supposed to be an inhibitor for wireless, but wireless took off anyway. The privacy issues can be worked around. There's a compelling story with regard to driver safety, and very compelling economic arguments for car companies in terms of better safety." I agree 100 percent with 90 percent of that argument. I'm sure we'll still be working around the privacy issues in 2010. It's a moving target. But by then, 25 percent of the cars on the road will have telematics systems installed.

take the idea that the car—or some third party with access to the car via wireless—can make decisions about what the car's going to do next to its logical extreme, you wind up with a car where the driver is something like a passenger on a very small, trackless train.

I trust that everyone knows I'm not talking about cars.

IT'S SIMPLE, NOT

One can't impose unity out of the blue on a nation that has 265 different kinds of cheese.

—Charles de Gaulle

It's easy to say that telematics is great stuff, because it really is. A lot of people will live longer, safer, happier lives when those systems are installed in their cars. A lot of manufacturers will get the information they need to make their products better. The value propositions are clear, and the market growth will be predictably rapid.

If knowledge is power, then these systems are, to some extent, a mechanism for transferring, or at least sharing, voluntarily or otherwise, the power we currently feel in our cars. Whether the feeling is illusory is beside the point. You don't get the comfort without giving up some control. As the cars get smarter, and the links between the cars and third parties become more fully developed, the cars know more about who we are and what we do. Anybody listening does too, and the nature of the communications medium makes it impossible to know for sure who'll be listening to who.

The World Without Secrets is *just like this, all the time.* The boundaries between my space and everyone else's space are established by policy, not by the laws of the physical world. You have to trust that people are going to adhere to the policy, and you have to wonder what happens when they don't. You give something up for everything you get, some measure of *control* for every *convenience*.

It's not always clear what's being given up, because information—the thing that moves everywhere in the World Without Secrets—means different things to different people, and its value isn't always apparent to the person who possesses it *right now.*

It's not the business of the people who make the systems that make the cars smart to train the drivers. It won't be anybody's business until societal attitudes change significantly. The drivers may not get smart until the cars are doing the driving.

HUNTER'S FIRST LAW

The network is an amplifier.

Formula: The power of a network in a given context equals the square of the number of people on the network, times the intrinsic power of those people in that context.

First Corollary: The instability of a Network Army is directly proportional to the number of Communities in the Army.

Second Corollary: Relationships matter.

Metcalfe's Law is one of the most frequently referenced laws in the brief history of computer technology. It says that *the usefulness or utility of a network equals the square of the number of users on the network.*

That statement alone says that any network is a powerful amplifier, but I think we need to go farther to understand the power of a network. People are not equal in their power, and a network that includes only a few people might be very powerful. The network of *people who applied the economic theories of John Maynard Keynes in 1935* probably numbered in the low hundreds, but it included influential academics, heads of state, and ministers of finance who could change the lives of millions of people by implementing their policies and ideas.

Also, a network has power *in a particular context,* and it may have a very different kind or amount of power in other contexts.

So here's Hunter's First Law, with thanks to Metcalfe: *The power of a network in a given context equals the square of the number of people on the network, times the intrinsic power of those people in that context.*

Whether you're citing Metcalfe's Law or Hunter's First Law, the power of a network increases at a geometric rate. It's easy to be surprised by that power, even when there are no secrets at all, and the networks are combining and forming in plain view.

CHAPTER FIVE

The N Party System: The Era of the Network Army

The assault on the World Trade Organization (WTO) meetings in Seattle in 1999 was planned and carried out by a motley collection of dozens of small organizations: French farmers, environmentalists, animal rights activists, and others far too diverse in their goals to list here. These organizations disagreed on many important issues, but all of them agreed that global trade as defined by the WTO was a very bad idea. The alliance that resulted had little formal leadership or infrastructure and no long-range strategy even for its own viability, much less for resolving the significant policy differences among its members. It nevertheless succeeded in turning the WTO meeting in Seattle into a political and public relations debacle that continued through the 2001 G8 meetings in Genoa, and shows no sign of abating. It was a textbook example of the power of a *Network Army*.

In a World Without Secrets, where so much is shared so openly over great distances, a Network Army forms quickly and becomes an archetypal political and social structure. Its communications are overwhelmingly public, and its formation, via a combination of individuals and small communities, is open to all to see. In fulfillment of Hunter's Second Law—*When everything is known, no one knows everything*—the sudden surge of a Network Army's power is often shocking, as it was to the Seattle police, the representatives of the WTO, and lots of ordinary citizens worldwide who, before the riots, hadn't paid much attention to either the WTO or its opposition.

Network Armies form rapidly and internationally. We've seen Network Armies in politics before, but never so many, growing so quickly and widely, expressing so much power. What's new also is the adoption of the Network Army model in so many spheres of human activity. Individuals, governments, businesses, and institutions of all kinds, legitimate and criminal, will join Network Armies and fight them.

In this chapter, I'll use a technique borrowed from the Global Business Network, *scenario building,* to briefly describe some of the other dominant social structures in the World Without Secrets.[1] Then I'll examine the implications of the Network Army in more detail.

HOW SCENARIOS WORK

Scenario building begins by selecting a pair of continua in which each element is bounded by the extremes along a range of possibilities (for example, "Political power is widely shared" versus "Power is heavily concentrated"). The intersections of the continua produce four *quadrants,* each of which describes a potential future state that is a combination of two extremes, one from each continuum.

The quadrants aren't necessarily mutually exclusive, and the future might shift from one quadrant to another, depending on events that are unpredictable. But the purpose isn't to make a prediction about which quadrant is going to be the right one. The goal is to define a range of possibilities and identify the circumstances that push us from one possible future to another. Ultimately, we're in the best position to deal with the future if we're prepared to deal with any and all of the possible scenarios.

THE SCENARIOS FOR SOCIAL STRUCTURES

The scenarios for social structures in the World Without Secrets begin with two axes: (1) the extent to which value systems are widely shared within society, and (2) the extent to which communities are activist.

When value systems are shared, basic definitions of what matters, why it matters, and how it matters are widely shared throughout the society. To put it another way: When value systems are shared, people are committed to working "within the system," whatever the system is. Such shared value systems are characteristic of the traditional politics of nation-states, which

THE VIETNAM WAR OPPOSITION
AS A NETWORK ARMY

An early example of a Network Army is the movement that coalesced around opposition to the Vietnam War in the late 1960s and early 1970s. The new communication technologies that enabled a Network Army in that era were television and the photocopy machine. (Daniel Ellsberg copied the Pentagon Papers with a Xerox machine, not a computer and a modem connection.)

The antiwar movement was composed of multiple communities with wildly divergent value systems (Dr. Spock and the Black Panthers, for example) that overlapped only in opposition to the war. The Network Army that united against the war was international in scope, and it was supported by a wide range of independent media organizations that operated outside the traditional establishment value system of traditional media (including independent newspapers and leaflets, FM radio, rock music, alternative comic books, and so on). The independent media were thoroughly, often scatologically, opposed to what they saw as the phony neutrality of mainstream media, which reported official government communications with at least token respect.

None of the communities involved in the antiwar Network Army was powerful enough to be a credible opposition by itself. Together, their power was enough to challenge the Cold War value system of the institutions that promoted and managed the war. The Network Army even mounted credible mainstream political challenges via both third parties and traditional party candidates. When the war ended, the antiwar movement disintegrated, and the players pursued their diverging values to take on other challenges (e.g., the Women's Movement, environmental issues).

We can draw two lessons from this example: (1) *Established leaders hasten the Network Army when their actions show that Establishment value systems are phony and corrupt;* and (2) *Network armies are only as permanent as their common agenda.*

WHY SHARED VALUES AND ACTIVIST COMMUNITIES?

A Gartner team that included researchers French Caldwell, Bill Kirwin, Susan Anderson, Michelle Henderson, and myself chose, in June 2001, to look at the future of social structures using these two axes because they're so characteristic of a World Without Secrets.

Value systems in a World Without Secrets are in constant, sometimes rapid flux. Everyone is exposed to everyone else's values, and what's exposed includes more extreme values over time. Any society that's not utterly chaotic must have *some* widely shared values, so the extent to which values are shared is an important factor in the stability and direction of social structures. In a World Without Secrets, like-minded people find each other more easily, and they tend to create communities. The extent to which these *communities are activist* is an important variable for their ultimate impact on the larger society.

include established "legitimate" political parties, clear lines of authority, and clear rules for participation in social structures, usually based on territory, ethnicity, or citizenship.

When value systems are varied, politics and associated lifestyles vary dramatically within a given society. All the rules are open to question, including the rules about who has a say in running the society. (If the issues are global, anyone in the world might claim the right to participate.)

When there is *increased communal activism*, communities that share a common value system seek to influence other communities, and the course of events, via externally focused involvement and activity. When there is *reduced communal activism*, individuals may seek to influence others but they don't channel their efforts through a community, either because they don't want to or because they can't.

THE QUADRANTS

The quadrants for social structures in the World Without Secrets are: *The Engineered Society, The Lost and Lonely, The Conscientious Objectors,* and *The Network Army* (see Figure 5.1). Keep in mind that the quadrants aren't mutually exclusive. Especially in the countries within the postindustrial

FIGURE 5.1   SOCIAL STRUCTURE IN THE WORLD
WITHOUT SECRETS

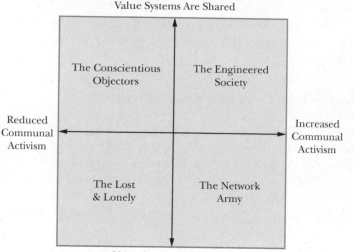

Value Systems Are Shared

The Conscientious
Objectors

The Engineered
Society

Reduced
Communal
Activism

Increased
Communal
Activism

The Lost
& Lonely

The Network
Army

Value Systems Are Varied

world, all of these quadrants are under way now, though the same scenario isn't always dominant.

Movement along the vertical continuum is clearly trending downward, worldwide, toward less unity in value systems, especially in postindustrial nations. It's not coincidental that this movement is occurring at the dawn of a World Without Secrets. Huge masses of information and widespread communications networks make everyone, everywhere, more aware of choices, even if most choices are ultimately rejected (as they must be; nobody can be or do everything).

In the next few pages, I'll probe these quadrants, starting with the world we all used to live in just about all the time: The Engineered Society.

THE ENGINEERED SOCIETY

In Afghanistan, under the Taliban regime, non-Muslims had to wear identifying armbands, and a woman could be stoned to death in the streets for leaving her home without a veil over her face. In such an extreme Engineered Society, there is no tolerance for competing value systems, and most people focus all their energies and activities through the dominant community. (The others spend their time either fighting it or trying to escape.)

Every nation that has an established government is, to some extent, an Engineered Society. Engineered Societies have rules and authorities. They're nationalistic and territorial. It's always clear who's in charge, and change is slow at best. In a corrupt Engineered Society scenario, even legitimate channels for change are blocked or manipulated by the establishment.

The Power of the Dominant Value System

The power of the dominant value system in an Engineered Society is very strong because it's widely shared by people who have a lot of power themselves (like the established leaders). According to Hunter's First Law, that makes the official value system network very powerful indeed.

Anything outside the dominant value system in an Engineered Society is basically invisible, whether or not the mass media are limited to officially sanctioned "news."

It's Where We're Coming From, Not Where We're Going

Right now, in the United States, political conservatives are promoting laws that, among other things, would require schoolchildren to say the Pledge of Allegiance every day. Whether you think it's a good idea or not, no such law would be necessary if the shared values of the Engineered Society hadn't faded since the 1950s. If you had told a typical American citizen in 1955 that schoolchildren in 2001 wouldn't routinely say the Pledge of Allegiance every morning, your listener probably would have imagined a takeover by Communists (the dominant opposing Engineered Society at that time), not a whittling away by a horde of competing value systems.

Vested interests of all kinds yearn for an Engineered Society; it's certainly easier for the people in charge when they can set the rules and everybody else has to stick to them. Most people who've lived in a strong Engineered Society yearn for the sense of shared purpose and camaraderie they felt when they were part of it (or opposed to it, which amounts to the same thing).

The Engineered Society is about concentrated power, and power corrupts. Scandal is a recurrent threat to the legitimacy and power of the Engineered Society, especially in the World Without Secrets, where the private lives of leaders are no longer off limits for discussion. Revulsion at the behavior of leaders can easily be the spark that ignites and unites a Network Army. The rise of the neo-fascist Front Nationale in France in the 1990s, for example, was fueled in large part by public outrage at the fiscal corruption of the dominant Socialist Party.

The Engineered Society is strongest when people don't have viable alternatives or when information moves very, very slowly. In a World Without Secrets, there's lots of information about alternatives, and it moves faster all the time, even in repressive Engineered Societies. *The Engineered Society is constantly on the defensive in the World Without Secrets.*

THE LOST AND LONELY

> *You can hear the fabric ripping.*
>
> —Robert F. Kennedy

The two teenage boys who attacked Columbine High School with machine guns and bombs, killing and wounding teachers and schoolmates before they killed themselves, were immersed in an alienated value system. They acted *against* their community, not *through* a community, and their only agenda was destruction of their perceived enemies. Their alienation and anger were stoked by Internet access to ugly ravings about Nazism and extreme violence. They were Lost and Lonely in every way.

Communal action is about connecting, and The Lost and Lonely can't connect, which is what distinguishes them from a Network Army. As a group, they're apolitical or antipolitical to the point of nihilism. They may express cynicism and contempt for political parties and politicians of all kinds, but they're unwilling or unable to take action either inside or outside the system. Network Army players might not bother to vote because they have other ways to make things happen. The Lost and Lonely don't vote because they don't *care*.

Extreme Lost and Lonely value systems are self-referential and alienated to the point of self-victimization. They include immersion in vices that include drugs, alcohol, pornography, gambling, television, online chatrooms, video games, and other well-known favorites. (What's yours?) These are all readily available in a World Without Secrets, and many of them are legal.

The Lost and Lonely in an Engineered Society

In the United States, we've tried punishing drug addicts, educating them, and hospitalizing them. What we haven't tried lately, and aren't likely to try soon, is leaving them alone. What self-respecting Engineered Society would do that? (Well, sure, the Netherlands, but who *else?*)

SO-CALLED VICES

A very large number of people are involved in one or more of the activities I call "vices" above. For example, over 700 million pornographic videos were rented in the United States in 2000.[2] The number is big enough to imply that there's an audience of millions of people out there who look at some kind of material that could be called "pornographic" at least occasionally. (That doesn't include the audience for the explicit sexual content that's now common in "mainstream" films and TV.)

The National Drug Intelligence Center said in December 2001 that 76 million Americans had used marijuana.[3] It's difficult now to find a candidate for the Presidency or the Supreme Court who hasn't used the stuff. The current President of the United States, a conservative Republican, has admitted (sort of) that he abused both alcohol and cocaine before he straightened out some years ago. Need I ask an American audience whether they've ever gambled or watched TV?

In short, I'm not trying to assess the intrinsic morality of these activities. I'm certainly not saying that everyone who's done any of these things is a pervert, an addict, or Lost and Lonely. I'm noting that the stuff is inherently self-referential and potentially alienating, and *immersion* in any of these things is a symptom and cause of withdrawal from communal activity.

The Lost and Lonely scenario is always coupled with an Engineered Society. (Somebody has to make the trains run on time, and you can bet it's not the Lost and Lonely.) The Engineered Society despises and pities the Lost and Lonely, and veers between hostile and ostensibly helpful controls on them. The Lost and Lonely response is usually to pull deeper into the shadows, where it's even harder to take political or social action to protect themselves. In a World Without Secrets, it's also futile more often than not.

Sometimes the Lost and Lonely response is the opposite: a violent, self-immolating outburst. The apparent increase, worldwide, in alienated, desperate acts of destruction like the Columbine High School massacre is a sign that the Lost and Lonely scenario is unfolding, not only in the United States but in all postindustrial societies.

The Power of a Lost and Lonely Value System

The value systems used by the Lost and Lonely have power, but it's the power to entrap. It belongs to whoever supplies the addictive stuff that's used by the Lost and Lonely. That's what Karl Marx saw in the gin-soaked proletariat of nineteenth-century London, and what "liberty gin," engineered mass hysteria, and two-way television did for Big Brother in George Orwell's totalitarian fantasy, *1984*. It's the power in the opium that the English used to subjugate China in the early 1900s, and it's the dark secret of the extraterrestrial immigrants in the science fiction classic *Alien Nation*.

Even this short list shows that the theme is recurrent in art and life. It's a theme with deep roots in reality, and Engineered Societies fight Lost and Lonely value systems for this reason more than any other: *The Lost and Lonely are controlled by whoever controls their addictions.*

THE LOST AND LONELY SUPPLIER AS SURROGATE ENGINEERED SOCIETY

A criminal cartel that supplies addictive material to the Lost and Lonely acts much like a government. It's heavily armed; it demands and enforces loyalty; it has its own "laws" and (usually severe) penalties for violations; it collects "taxes" from those in its thrall (in the form of fees for access to the addictive material); and it makes war on opposing nations and cartels.

This interpretation is made explicit in Tom Clancy's *Clear and Present Danger*, in which the United States wages war on a Latin American drug cartel as if it was a nation-state. In this sense, opposition by legal authorities to a criminal cartel is a fight between two Engineered Societies for control of the Lost and Lonely.

If I Ever Get Out of Here

Thirty years ago, homosexuality in the United States was widely considered either a tragic mental disease or a horrifying sin, depending on whether a doctor or a preacher was talking about it. Since then, homosexuals have transformed their political and social scenario from Lost and Lonely to Network Army.

IS SILICON VALLEY
LOST AND LONELY?

On July 11, 1999, the *New York Times Sunday Magazine* ran an article ("Instant Company") on an Internet startup called Epinions.com.[4] A fascinating passage described how the small team that founded the company asked potential hires about their "drag coefficient," which equated to anything outside the workplace that might displace a 24–7 commitment to the company: wives, children, even a one-hour commute. "Then they recognized," says the article, "that such talk, even in jest, could be taken as discriminatory." Hey, no *kidding*. Especially if, like Sigmund Freud, you believe that there's no such thing as a joke.

The executive team of Epinions, as shown in a photo accompanying the article, essentially consisted, at startup, of fewer than a dozen work-obsessed young males ("grinding out 15-hour days, seven days a week") intoxicated both by the thrill of a startup and the potential for fabulous riches. If that's not Lost and Lonely, what is? Perhaps categorizing your spouse as a *drag coefficient*? (I grant that a commute is mostly a drag.)

What happens when all the twenty-somethings in Silicon Valley, working 90 hours per week, figure out that the CEO is the only one in the building who's going to get rich, if anyone (besides the VCs [Venture Capitalists]) does, and all they've got for their countless hours of service is lives not lived? Here's a prediction: Their Lost and Lonely scenario turns into an angry Network Army, and goes from there to an Engineered Society institution like a union. Silicon Valley workers certainly know how to put a Network Army together when they need one. What is any Internet startup about, besides creating a community and getting it to act?

Now, an Emmy-winning network-TV series, *Will and Grace*, depicts homosexuals weekly as slightly-funnier-than-ordinary people with jobs, friends, and more or less normally conflicted relationships that happen to be homosexual.

A Lost and Lonely value system transforms into a Network Army scenario when the Lost and Lonely recognize that they have greater mass than they knew. They then stop hiding and begin to take communal action to change their lives for the better. Heavy information flows in the World Without Secrets feed these transformations by connecting the Lost and Lonely—first, to more sources related to their value systems, and then to each other. Social movement—*I am not alone*—becomes political movement when attitudes throughout the society change enough to let the Lost and Lonely emerge from secrecy to make their case. Because of the amplification power of a network, the first surge may be surprisingly powerful even to the newly transformed Lost and Lonely, as the Stonewall Riots were to the New York homosexual community in 1969.

In the United States, a current example of this transformation is *overeating*. Forty percent of the adult population is overweight, and obesity is increasingly common. Before the American population was largely composed of overweight people, overeating was an anxious, private act (like any other addiction) that brought visible consequences. As more of the population self-consciously shared the problem, overeating became a communally supported "disease" attended by doctors and other weight-loss gurus. Now it's a political movement that lobbies to make airplane seats wider. The politics involved are minority politics, but *all* Network Armies are about minority bodies politic that combine, at least temporarily, to form an amplified power base.

Get Ready for More Lost and Lonely

Worldwide drug use is trending upward and is followed closely by incarceration for the people who use the stuff. Gambling is epidemic in the United States and is growing in many other nations. Pornography is a $10 *billion* business in the United States—a bigger draw than professional football and baseball combined, and still growing rapidly. (Wait until the arrival of holographic sex on demand, via *any* technology at all, networked or otherwise. I can't *imagine* how much revenue from the flower, fancy candy, restaurant, and theater industries will permanently transfer to the pornography industry on that day.) Americans watch an average of 3.5 hours of television per day; in the average household, the TV is on seven hours per day. The staggeringly murderous outbursts against strangers that occur frequently in the United States (where even children can be perpetrators) are now, apparently, worldwide phenomena. (When a Japanese man attacks a crowd of Japanese schoolchildren with a knife, something has changed.) The World Without Secrets offers all sorts of value systems to individuals who can't fit into the established mold, whatever it is, and who just want to lose themselves in *something*.

Because the trend in the World Without Secrets is toward increasingly diverse value systems, and away from the restricted choices and confining structure of the Engineered Society, the Lost and Lonely is an important scenario. Because it's ultimately about people being controlled, it's the dark side of politics and society in a World Without Secrets.

The Lost and Lonely aren't the only ones who can't or won't take communal action. They share that condition with Conscientious Objectors, who may be lonely but are never lost.

THE CONSCIENTIOUS OBJECTORS

Timothy McVeigh, whose bombing (solo or otherwise) of the Murrah Federal Building in Oklahoma City was, until September 11, 2001, the single worst act of mass murder in U.S. history, was a Conscientious Objector. So was Alexandr Solzhenitzen, whose three-volume masterpiece, *The Gulag Archipelago,* destroyed the moral foundation of the Soviet Union almost upon publication of the first volume in 1973.

Like the Lost and Lonely, the Conscientious Objectors are always paired with a nemesis Engineered Society. Unlike the Lost and Lonely, the Conscientious Objectors basically agree with the Engineered Society about what matters, but believe that the Engineered Society has lost its moral compass. To put it another way, the Conscientious Objectors want their society to live up to its principles, or to the higher principles it ought to aspire to. The Lost and Lonely want to be left alone; the Conscientious Objectors want to change the world. Like the Lost and Lonely, the Conscientious Objectors will not, or cannot, act through a community.

Conscientious Objectors and Community

McVeigh thought he had a community behind him, but he found out otherwise, too late for his victims. Solzhenitzen was isolated from his national community via imprisonment, as was Nelson Mandela. Larry Flynt's very sexually explicit value system was just too raunchy to gain the support of the respectable community that ordinarily stood up for the First Amendment. Like the Lost and Lonely, and for similar reasons (i.e., official repression and/or private disgust), the Conscientious Objectors can't or won't take action through a community.

For people like Solzhenitzen and Mandela, the community outside the Conscientious Objector's Engineered Society may be as important as, or more important than, any community *in* it. Conscientious Objectors can influence the wider community through example (even if only to talk dirty and buy pornography, in Flynt's case). The World Without Secrets helps them become widely known, making it harder for their Engineered

SOLZHENITZEN AND COMMUNITY

Ironically, when the Soviet Union banished Solzhenitzen, he found his community in the democracies of the West. *The Gulag Archipelago* made Western intellectuals who'd supported the Soviet Union realize that the Soviet system was the moral equivalent of Nazi Germany. In effect, banishment introduced Solzhenitzen to a nascent Network Army and gave him the leverage he needed to destroy the moral rationale behind the Soviet regime.

Societies to (literally or figuratively) bury them. It also sets the stage for the emergence of the Conscientious Objectors at the head of a Network Army, as when Mandela emerged from prison and the Ayatollah Khomeni returned from exile.

THE NETWORK ARMY

> *Things fall apart*
> *The centre cannot hold*
>
> —W. B. Yeats, *The Second Coming*

When Gay Irish men demand to march in the local Saint Patrick's Day parade, a Network Army is ramping up. When a coalition of sympathetic organizations, some flown in from hundreds or thousands of miles away, disrupts the Saint Patrick's Day Parade in New York City in front of dozens of television cameras, the Network Army is in full stride.

In the Network Army scenario, a wide variety of value systems is expressed via communal activism. Absent a dominant value system, the social and political landscape is made up of rapidly shifting alliances of activist communities. These communities are nonterritorial; *it's their value system that matters, not their nationality.*

Network Army communities can be very small (even if internationally based). Their value systems may overlap only at the edges with those of other Network Armies. The communities may not be powerful by themselves, but put them together and—watch out! As always in the World Without Secrets, *the network is an amplifier.* As per Hunter's First Law, when either the number of people in a network or the intrinsic power of the network's members suddenly increases, the power of the network explodes.

Negotiating with a Hydra

If you had wanted to stop the protests at the 1999 WTO meetings in Seattle or the 2001 G8 meeting in Genoa via negotiation, with whom would you have negotiated? An Engineered Society has institutions and leaders—easily identifiable focus points. A Network Army might have no leader, or everyone in it might be a leader who has his or her own agenda. Network Army "negotiation" takes place in public via rhetorical and physical confrontation. Negotiations are concluded when one side or the other announces publicly that it has given up. Until then, the Network Army remains at war. Because *the network is an amplifier,* even a few dissatisfied Network Army elements have the potential to cause lots of trouble for as long as their dissatisfaction lasts. If you think that bodes ill for conventional democratic politics, which is about achieving consensus and moving on, you're right.

A Network Army may make Engineered Society leaders yearn for the good old days when they had only a couple of really *big* enemies to deal with. No one, so far as I know, has seriously suggested that the continuing series of assaults on the WTO has been planned and executed behind the scenes by a shadowy Engineered Society, but the WTO might be on track now if it was.

Communications in the Network Army

One of the most astonishing aspects of Network Army communications is the incredible extent to which they flatten the Network Army's organization. The Open Source movement (as described in Chapter Six), has a "management" structure that consists of four important "influencers," six to eight distributors, about 200 project leaders, and *750,000* developers and other direct contributors. The ratio between leaders and followers is astronomically high by the standards of any business and is *increasing* rapidly. A key enabling factor is the use of Internet-based communications, which allows "influencers" and other key members of the movement to transmit their messages accurately, with zero distortion, to a potentially infinite number of followers. The system works equally well in reverse; movement leaders never have to wonder whether their followers understand what's going on and agree with it.

Communication and coordination between Network Army players in general are handled publicly via mechanisms that include independent media such as http://www.indymedia.org, e-mail, electronic bulletin

MASS MEDIA AND THE NETWORK ARMY

The Network Army is tough on mass media, because the Network Army isn't a stable *mass*. The percentage of the overall audience represented by traditional Engineered Society mass media, like network television and newspapers, has been declining steadily for years, with the end not in sight. Meanwhile, magazines and media aimed at highly specific audiences are growing in numbers and overall circulation. Further, a growing percentage of the population takes time away from traditional media like TV and newspapers to spend it online, where they get tailored information, often from other members of their own Network Armies.

boards, and Internet mailing lists. Because of Hunter's First Law, even such public communications and announcements of intention can be overlooked by opponents of the Network Army until it's too late.

The indie media are explicitly committed to a value system that supports their political or social agenda. (Indymedia.org's home page lists demonstrations and political events, stories about political and economic repression, and contact information—including Internet mailing lists—for various activist organizations.) That puts them in direct opposition to traditional liberal democratic Engineered Society media values of objectivity and neutrality.

Partisan journalism isn't new, of course. What's new is the ease with which anyone, almost anywhere, at any time, can publish to the world, creating a focal point for the development of a new Network Army. What's new also is the ease with which these ideas are communicated internationally. Widespread adoption of English as a de facto international language, as much as the Internet, is the most important accelerator of the Network Army. A technological hyperaccelerator, coming in the next 10 years, is rapid automated language translation.

The Network Army Doesn't Make It Simpler

The Network Army is the quintessential social and political structure in the World Without Secrets. It's the direct result of unrestricted high-velocity information flows, of international visibility for even the most narrowly shared ideas, and of the geometrically expanding power of networks. It's an

WHY THE NETWORK ARMY NOW?

Rapid movement to a Network Army from the Engineered Society is highly dependent on the high-volume information flows of a World Without Secrets. It's also based in the mores of postindustrial, post-materialist societies, whose members generally distrust authority, are not preoccupied with survival issues, and think of self-expression as a moral imperative. For these reasons, a Network Army is a *generational* phenomenon and an *economic* phenomenon.[5]

unstable and unpredictable structure that is difficult to control and difficult to oppose. It will complicate the business of governance and the governance of business.

With so many joining the ranks of the inherently subjugated Lost and Lonely, the rise of the Network Army is the difference between Orwell and Darwin. If it's harder for rulers to rule and leaders to lead in the era of the Network Army, it may also be harder for them to *misrule* and *mislead*.

I REPEAT: THE NETWORK IS AN AMPLIFIER

The power of a network in a given context equals the square of the number of people on the network times the intrinsic power of those people in that context.

In the World Without Secrets, where networks build rapidly, messages are amplified with sudden and increasingly unpredictable force. You never know who will be touched by the network next, and what the intrinsic power of those touched might be. You may not even be able to predict which interests of which communities are peripheral, and what lies at the core.

The next chapter describes a modern Network Army: the Open Source movement.

CHAPTER SIX

Software Without Secrets

Gartner analysts are trained, from the moment of their arrival at the company, to be skeptics. It's our mantra. I was more than usually skeptical when I first heard of the Open Source software movement in 1998. A small but growing percentage of Gartner's clients were using a free (as in zero purchase price) Open Source server operating system called Linux. Linux (the name paid homage to Linus Torvald, the programmer who wrote the operating system kernal) was distributed with its *source code,* and anyone who wanted to copy it, or even change it, could easily do so. Hence the term: *Open Source.*

The clients were pretty happy with the product, so far as we knew, but I was sure that no winning business model in the software industry could be based on giving the entire product line away. As the president of Baan's subsidiary in Brazil said to me, in the summer of 1998, "Software is about volume sales. If you don't know that, you don't know anything." I figured that zero product sales revenue equated, sooner or later, to zero support. People have to do something for a living, and a business model based on volunteer labor had to evaporate. Even if the products were good enough, zero revenue for sales meant zero resources for R&D and support, both of which are critical to long-term product viability and big corporate users. What volunteer was going to show up to fix a broken operating system at 3:00 A.M., anywhere? I also knew that multiple variations of Linux had already appeared, and I wondered why any software vendors would be willing to create versions of their products to run on such an obviously unstable and uncontrollable platform.

My colleagues agreed. At our 1999 Fall Symposium, we predicted that Linux would win less than a 15 percent share in the server operating system market by 2004, mostly in nonmission critical applications where the lack of support wouldn't matter so much.

DISRUPTIVE, QUITE

In retrospect, it's clear to me that I missed the point. Linux is a classic example of what Clayton Christensen, in his book *The Innovator's Dilemma,* calls a *disruptive technology.*[1] It's less functional in many respects than the products it competes with (i.e., Microsoft's operating systems), particularly in ease of use, but it's very functional in certain ways (like ease of modification) that Microsoft isn't. (By law, you can't modify a Microsoft operating system, anymore than you can rewrite someone's novel without permission.) That feature certainly won't appeal to every user but it's very attractive to techies. Linux costs less and the margins for the producers are lower (zero and zero, respectively), so it's not very attractive to the value chain that services and sells the dominant products. It appeals to a different market—in particular, power users for whom ease of use isn't a big deal—than buyers of Microsoft's products.

Once a disruptive technology establishes its beachhead in a new market, its growth rate is exponential. Open Source software fits that profile too. Gartner's latest estimates, done less than two years after the 1999 predictions, are that, by 2003, Linux or other Open Source software will be in use in over *80 percent* of all businesses. Those estimates may still be far too conservative. Members of the Open Source movement argue that Linux will dominate the server *and desktop* operating system markets (the fortified strongholds of Microsoft) within the next few years.

I don't know whether I believe it—like Yogi Berra said, "it's tough to make predictions, especially about the future"—but, by now, I've at least learned not to underestimate the ability of Open Source to grab market share. Christensen notes that, over time, a disruptive technology adds features and functions that drive it deeply into established leader's markets. As I write this, Linux is being extended further into the desktop operating system space, and ease-of-use features are being added to make it more palatable to nontechies. In June 2001, Microsoft admitted to running Open Source Software on some of the servers that support its Passport operations, which includes its Web site, Hotmail service, and other mission-critical applications.

Open Source is clearly good enough, which I guess is to be expected from products whose designers say that their first and foremost goal is to build software that *doesn't suck.*

BUSINESS WITHOUT SECRETS

There's something going on here, and it's not just software. What's happening is a business model for the World Without Secrets, a model designed for the era of the Network Army, a model that leverages the exceptional in every way. In a World Without Secrets, this is a Business Without Secrets, one that has rapidly grown big enough to threaten the biggest Engineered Society in the software business: Microsoft.

The lessons in Open Source are applicable to other intellectual-property industries as well, loathe as the leaders of the movement are to discuss it. As Eric Raymond, one the most influential players in the Open Source culture, said to me, when I interviewed him in September 2001, "Software is unique in many respects. The natural economics of software is that *most of its value is in the requirement for service in its lifetime* (emphasis mine). Artists, including programmers, have a right to control the distribution of their creative work, including proprietary licenses, if they so choose. I think it's self-defeating for software."[2]

If it's self-defeating for software, why not for other intellectual property? Music is a service when it's performed, and such service may be the most viable path to a thriving career for musicians in a World Without Secrets. And perhaps authors will come to see their work as storytelling (like Homer, whose *Odyssey* was a sung poem, a *lyric,* before it was ever written down), not writing fixed-form novels, in which case their value will reside in the service they deliver over their lifetimes.

Let's talk about it.

Openly.

INTERVIEWING RAYMOND

When I set out to interview Eric Raymond, whose essay "The Cathedral and the Bazaar"[3] is widely considered one of the most influential works in the Open Source canon, I did so with some trepidation. Gartner's early stance on Open Source software didn't endear us to anyone in the Open Source movement. At the Open Source Initiative's Web site, you can find a series of documents about the "Halloween Papers," the first of which is an internal Microsoft memo that describes Microsoft's strategy for eliminating Open Source software as a competitive threat.[4] The sixth document in the series (titled "Halloween Document VI," of course, available at http://www.opensource.org/halloween/halloween6.html) includes a discussion by Raymond himself of what he perceives as apparent collusion between Gartner and Microsoft. This passage says it all:

> Far be it from us to suggest that the Gartner Group has fraudulently colluded with Microsoft, however suggestive the evidence. Could it all have been some horrible mistake? Could Gartner Group have been innocently victimized by a Microsoft partisan in its own ranks? Perhaps one of these scenarios is why the reports quietly disappeared—but not before taking much of the Gartner Group's credibility with them, alas. . . .
>
> Ah well. Whatever occurred, I'm sure the large amounts of money that Gartner admits to having received from Microsoft before and after this incident have done much to soothe their upset at looking like patsies.

When I e-mailed Raymond in early September 2001, I figured I'd better address this issue head-on. That happens to be the cultural norm among researchers at Gartner. I wasn't aware then that head-on is the *only* way people in the Open Source movement address anything.

> Mr. Raymond,
>
> I'm a Director of Research at Gartner, Inc. I'm currently working on a book titled *World Without Secrets,* which is about the implications of ubiquitous computing technologies for society.
>
> The more I research the book, the clearer it is to me that issues related to control—who controls what, and who controls who—are paramount in a ubiquitous computing environment. In that regard, I believe that the Open Source Initiative is an extremely important model for how people might . . . behave in this environment. . . . I believe that you may be the best single source for insight on how the Open Source model operates and how it might translate to other domains (outside software). I'm working through the pieces you've written, and I promise that I will be well-prepared for a discussion. . . .
>
> Mr. Raymond, I've read the Halloween VI document at opensource.org,[5] and I can imagine what might have gone through your mind when you read the first sentence of this message. I think Gartner has plenty of integrity, and I know you think otherwise. I won't attempt a point-by-point refutation of your comments here. I will note that it was part of my job at Gartner, until recently, to ensure that no analyst ever fed from a vendor's trough. When we get it wrong, you can blame us and no one else. I agree with you that we underestimated the sticking power of Linux, and I admit that I was one of the analysts at Gartner that did so, though my opinions on the subject never saw

print. I'll be glad to tell you why when we talk, if you're interested. In the meantime, please note that it's my intention to present the information that you provide me as accurately as possible, that I have no intention of abusing you or the Open Source Initiative, and that I have no hidden agenda where OSI is concerned. . . .

By the way, on a personal note, I was unable to find links to your music at your site. (The Cross the Line link is broken.) You can hear mine at www.hunterharp.com if you're interested. There are a half-dozen full-length MP3 samples of my work there, and they're free, of course.

I wouldn't ordinarily include a reference to my music in a business letter, but Raymond's Web site showed that he didn't compartmentalize his ideas and activities the way most businesspeople do. He wasn't one person on the job and a different person off it; he was all himself, all the time. *Openly.* As Robert Heinlein, one of Raymond's favorite authors, said in *The Moon Is a Harsh Mistress:* "When in Rome, shoot off Roman candles."[6] I figured I might as well light mine.

Raymond called a few hours after I sent this message. His first questions were about the Halloween Document VI incident. I told him what I knew, which wasn't anything like a complete explanation, but I guess it was enough to establish that I was all myself, too. We scheduled a phone call for the next day.

HACKERS AND CRACKERS

Our phone interview lasted, in total, well over three hours. That's a lot for a very busy guy like Raymond to offer any interviewer, and it's evidence of another norm of hacker culture as explained by Raymond: A hacker will keep talking as long as you keep asking interesting questions.

Hacker, by the way, means something entirely different to Raymond than it means to the press and the public at large. To the latter, *hacker* is synonymous with *cyber-criminal.* As Reuters News Service put it in a recent headline, *Beware! Some of Your Co-Workers Could Be Hackers, IBM Says.*[7] Not so, says Raymond; he and his cultural peers call such cyber-criminals *crackers.* Here are Raymond's definitions from his *How to Become a Hacker* (http://tuxedo.org/~esr/faqs/hacker-howto.html):

There is a community, a shared culture, of expert programmers and networking wizards that traces its history back through decades to the first time-sharing minicomputers and the earliest ARPAnet experiments. The members of this culture originated the term "hacker." Hackers built the Internet.

Hackers made the Unix operating system what it is today. Hackers run Usenet. Hackers make the World Wide Web work. If you are part of this culture, if you have contributed to it **and other people in it know who you are and call you a hacker** [emphasis mine], you're a hacker. . . . There is another group of people who loudly call themselves hackers, but aren't. These are people (mainly adolescent males) who get a kick out of breaking into computers and phreaking the phone system. Real hackers call these people "crackers" and want nothing to do with them. Real hackers mostly think crackers are lazy, irresponsible, and not very bright, and object that being able to break security doesn't make you a hacker any more than being able to hotwire cars makes you an automotive engineer. Unfortunately, many journalists and writers have been fooled into using the word "hacker" to describe crackers; this irritates real hackers to no end. The basic difference is this: hackers build things, crackers break them.

The Reuters story describes two of IBM's security specialists as "ethical hackers." In Raymond's terms, the phrase is redundant, just as "ethical cracker" is oxymoronic. Hackers are by nature ethical, and crackers are by definition destructive.

Notice also Raymond's comment to the effect that you're a hacker when other hackers *call you a hacker*. This is a community, a shared culture of peers, not a ragged bunch of outlaws. You don't shoot your way in. You earn it. You *prove* you belong.

In deference to Raymond and his tradition, I'll use *hacker* the way he uses it throughout this chapter. If you're one of the mass of the public who trembles at the word, keep in mind while you're reading this that the hackers are the *good guys*.

FROM COMMUNITIES TO NETWORK ARMY

Residency Ain't Community

When you're part of a community, you don't just live in the neighborhood. You hang out there. You play there. Before Raymond and his friends were hackers, they hung out and played together for reasons that had nothing to do with *hacking* and everything to do with the kind of people who *hack*.

Richard Hunter: How did the leaders in the Open Source movement find each other?

Eric Raymond: It was a historical accident. We found each other through the Internet. There are a couple of other cultures in which core members of hacker culture tend to hang out, including science fiction fandom. We all met at science fiction conventions.

RH: Oh, who are the popular authors? William Gibson?

ER: No, Gibson is way down the list.

My Favorite William Gibson World Without Secrets Moment

There's a scene in *Neuromancer* where the protagonist is in an airport. He passes a pay phone. It rings. He picks it up. It's for him. He talks to someone he doesn't know about something he'd rather not discuss, and he hangs up before the caller does. He walks away. A line of pay phones flanks his path, and each phone rings *once,* in turn, as he passes.

We know who you are, and we know exactly where to find you.

Now back to our story.

I was surprised to hear that. Gibson is generally credited with inventing the term "cyberspace" in his book *Neuromancer,* and I thought he'd rate pretty highly among hackers. I pressed on.

RH: Philip Dick?

ER: No, NO! Not him!

I was even more surprised, but I shouldn't have been. Dick is the author of a number of works that have achieved mass popularity in movie form. *Blade Runner* was based on Dick's *Do Androids Dream of Electric Sheep?* Other Dick stories that were successful with mass film audiences include *Total Recall* and *Johnny Mnemonic.* It figures that sheer mass popularity means nothing to a hacker; these are Critical Thinkers tending to One-Dimensional Expertise (as described in Chapter Seven). Raymond laid it out for me.

ER: We've got the most affinity for "hard" SF authors like Robert Heinlein, John Brunner [whose novel *The Shockwave Rider* introduced much of the terminology now common in cyberculture] and Vernon Vinge. We're also into the Society for Creative Anachronisms. They're a hobby group who recreate medieval events. They're not as international as SF fandom; they're really only important in the U.S. There's also a higher proportion of neo-pagans in the hacker culture than anywhere else, including parody religions and Wicca. I'm a Wiccan myself.

Well, that's a pretty wide range of interests. Raymond anticipated the next question.

Visible

ER: What all these cultures have in common, an important part of the link to hackers, is that they encourage constructive use of the imagination. They don't use imagination for mere daydreaming. They exteriorize the imagination, make it take visible and effective form.

Raymond elaborates on the communities from which hackers come in the section of his piece "How to Become a Hacker" titled *Extra Points for Style:*[8]

> . . . to be a hacker, you have to enter the hacker mindset. There are some things you can do when you're not at a computer that seem to help. They're not substitutes for hacking (nothing is) but many hackers do them, and feel that **they connect in some basic way with the essence of hacking** [emphasis mine].
>
> - Learn to write your native language well. Though it's a common stereotype that programmers can't write, a surprising number of hackers (including all the best ones I know of) are able writers.
> - Read science fiction. Go to science fiction conventions (a good way to meet hackers and protohackers).
> - Study Zen, and/or take up martial arts. (The mental discipline seems similar in important ways.)
> - Develop an analytical ear for music. Learn to appreciate peculiar kinds of music. [Notice the emphasis on *peculiar* kinds of music. As Raymond said to me, *Hackers are iconoclasts.*] Learn to play some musical instrument well, or how to sing.
> - Develop your appreciation of puns and wordplay.

"It's been noted for a number of years—I was the first to write it down—that lots of hackers do martial arts disciplines," Raymond told me. (Linus Torvald's wife was a six-time karate champion of Finland.) "It fosters certain kinds of mental concentration that are closely related to the flow states you need to hack effectively. At one time, hackers admired the culture but didn't do it. Now that it's generally available; a lot of us do it. The connection to neo-paganism is similar. Neo-paganism is like martial arts; it values certain flow states and altered states of consciousness. It's closely related to the states that hackers need to function."

Why these things in particular is not completely clear, Raymond says at his site, *but they're connected with a mix of left- and right-brain skills that seems to be important (hackers need to be able to both reason logically and step outside the apparent logic of a problem at a moment's notice).*

I told Raymond that I knew why music mattered to hackers. I'd been thinking about it since I wrote a piece on the subject for *Information Week* in 1989.

"Training for music is like training for programming," I said. "Musicians learn to work in small teams. They learn to read and write code. ('Sheet music' isn't music; it's really a coded set of instructions to a performer.) They learn to look at the big picture and the little picture, the entire piece and the moment, at the same time . . ."

Raymond broke in excitedly the moment I said that. *"Yes!"* he said. *"That's it!* The big picture and the little picture at the same time. That's the fundamental design skill for *everything*. There are neurological commonalities between the machinery we use to process programming and music. This is widely perceived as true in the hacker culture."

Affinity Ain't Community

Throughout this part of my conversation with Raymond, I was experiencing a weird kind of shock of recognition. I've been involved in all the things he was talking about. I write. (I'm writing now, by the way.) I read science fiction, and I read it obsessively when I was in my teens. I studied karate in my twenties. I've composed and performed music since I was nine. (I wouldn't call my music peculiar—I call it "beautiful"—but compositions for solo harmonica definitely don't qualify as *mainstream*.) In my twenties, I was an avid follower of the writings of Carlos Casteñeda, the anthropologist who documented the teachings of Don Juan, a Yacqui Indian sorcerer. It's not Wicca, but it qualifies as pagan. I don't write code anymore, but I did it for a living for half of the 1980s.

The more of these things you already do, the more likely it is that you are natural hacker material, Raymond says at his site.

I don't know if this applies to me, but I know that one of the reasons Raymond was willing to spend over three hours talking to me is that we were both having fun.

You Only See the Power When the Edges Align

Let's go back to the 1970s. The technical roots of Open Source were planted years earlier, in the late 1960s, in the ARPAnet experiments, the MIT Artificial Intelligence laboratory, and other projects related to the new Internet. Now, hackers are beginning to find each other in lots of places, at work and at play.

Raymond and his friends are hanging out. Their pursuits are interesting, if slightly arcane, but no one watching from the outside would think their role-playing games are going to change the world. These guys are far outside the mainstream. You don't change the world by recreating medieval events and talking up guys you meet at SF conventions. You do that by playing golf with Jack Welch and setting up a lobbying office in Washington.

But look at what's latent in this crowd, the power just waiting for the cause that will align the edges of these communities into a Network Army. These people are killer smart. They're verbal; they communicate clearly and frequently. They exercise their right brains playing music, and their left brains analyzing it. They've spent their formative years with one foot in the past, recreating medieval events, and the other in the multiple futures their favorite writers have created. *They're not compartmentalized.* They see no reason why they can't build any world they can imagine. They build worlds in software every day. They're ready to build any world they want, *as soon as they know what it is.*

Now We Know

In the early 1980s, the Unix operating system is distributed without cost by AT&T, which invented it and owns all rights to the code. Unix is widely used on minicomputers, which means it's widely used in universities everywhere. Lots of hackers make their living at those universities, and they use Unix every day.

In 1984, AT&T decides to begin charging for Unix. That decision is a trigger event. It provokes Richard Stallman, a brilliant, iconoclastic programmer at MIT, to define a formal concept of "free" software as an organized and licensed initiative, to found the Free Software Society, and to initiate the GNU (GNU's Not Unix) project, aimed at creating a new, nonproprietary, *free* operating system. Eric Raymond is one of the earliest contributors to the GNU project.

The cause is beginning to emerge.

But Stallman's idea—that software inherently *wants to be free*—is a little too radical for a lot of the people in the communities that are beginning to align in a Network Army. Not everybody agrees that the people who write software have no property rights. "Stallman has a bunch of political concerns," Raymond told me tactfully. "We differ seriously in some respects."

In 1991, Linus Torvald starts writing the Linux kernal and talking about how to write and maintain Open Source code. Open Source sidesteps all the contentious issues related to property rights. You can charge people to buy the software you make if you want to. (You probably won't make much money that way, but there are other ways to make money in this scenario.) Whether you charge them or not, you've got to give them the *source code,* the keys to the kingdom, with every distribution of the product, and you've got to give them the right to modify that source if they want to.

Torvald's goal isn't to liberate software and make it free (like Stallman's); it's to write great code. Great code, he thinks, happens when anybody who's got the brains and the desire to write code has carte blanche to do so, whether the product being worked on "belongs" to that person or not. The more hackers you attract to a project, the better the chances that the resulting project will not suck.

Not everyone is immediately convinced. As Raymond describes his 1996 conversion to Open Source advocacy in *The Cathedral and the Bazaar:*

> Linus Torvalds's style of development—release early and often, delegate everything you can, be open to the point of promiscuity—came as a surprise. No quiet, reverent cathedral-building here—rather, the Linux community seemed to resemble a great babbling bazaar of differing agendas and approaches (aptly symbolized by the Linux archive sites, who'd take submissions from anyone) out of which a coherent and stable system could seemingly emerge only by a succession of miracles. The fact that this bazaar style seemed to work, and work well, came as a distinct shock. As I learned my way around, I worked hard not just at individual projects, but also at trying to understand why the Linux world not only didn't fly apart in confusion but seemed to go from strength to strength at a speed barely imaginable to cathedral-builders.

Torvald's model for development has a lot of things going for it. Most importantly, it's just a whole lot more fun. The hacker community likes fun. Unlike many people, especially the ones who work in big companies, they're not ashamed to say so. (The people I worked for in the insurance industry certainly didn't think work was supposed to be fun. God help anybody who didn't act like it was all *serious business*.)

It's fun because the hackers get to work on stuff they like—*a hacker will keep talking as long as you keep asking interesting questions*—and because the code that results is something they're proud to put their names on. It's fun because they're hanging out in the bazaar, sampling all the wares, talking loudly to be heard above all the hubbub, flaming and being flamed in return, and the stuff that comes out is as beautiful and intricate as any cathedral, even if nobody has a grand design (or an overseer) when they start. It's fun because it all just keeps getting better—the code, the arguments, the excitement of hanging out and working with all those fiery brains—as it goes along, and more hackers join in, and more code comes out.

The hackers have got their cause, and it's nonideological. *They're going to write software that doesn't suck.* How can you not agree with that?

Ten years later, they've got a Network Army with 750,000 soldiers. Remember Hunter's First Law: A *network is an amplifier*. This network army is getting louder and there's no reason to think it's turned it up all the way yet. It turns out that writing code that doesn't suck can change the world, and Torvald figured out how.

In a World Without Secrets, these guys are already open, exteriorized, and visible. What power can secrets possibly have over them?

OPEN SOURCE IS MORE THAN OPEN SOURCE

Open Source is more than one thing, and the *gestalt* is important to understanding the impact the Open Source movement has had on the software industry.

"It's basically a culture," Raymond told me. "It's not quite the same thing as an official movement. I want to avoid the political connotations of the word 'movement.'" Maybe he means that Open Source doesn't have an established organization with membership cards and dues, offices, directors, and a budget for lobbyists. When you've got 750,000 active participants supporting your efforts, it looks like a movement to me.

"It's also a marketing approach," Raymond adds. "We don't like to talk about marketing a lot, but it's true. It's also a major threat to Microsoft."

Enough to be noticed, anyway. *Software that doesn't suck* is a pretty exceptional message for an Exception Economy, not to mention *Open Source* in an industry where the leaders are all struggling to keep their software as secret as possible.

It's basically a culture, Raymond said. Before we discuss the threat, let's talk about how the culture of Open Source works.

YEAH, IT'S A HIGH-PERFORMANCE TEAM

The key thing to understand about the operations of Open Source is this: it's a Network Army. There are no leaders—or, everyone's a leader. There are no management layers; there is little or no *management.* It's a high-performance team with three quarters of a million team members.

In his book *Organizing Genius,* Warren Bennis describes some of the most important characteristics of what he calls Great Groups, examples of which include the Manhattan Project; the team, led by Steve Jobs, that built the MacIntosh operating system; and the team Walt Disney led to create the first animated feature-length film, *Snow White and the Seven Dwarfs.*[9] Those characteristics include:

- *Extraordinary talent.* The members of these teams are the best in their respective fields. Team membership is considered an honor by the members. What could have been a greater honor for a physicist in 1942 than being asked to join the Manhattan Project?

- *A clear vision of the goal.* The Manhattan Project used the new science of atomic physics to create a weapon that would end World War II. Disney sought to prove the viability of animation as an expressive art form on a level with any other film genre.

- *A deadly enemy.* The Manhattan Project fought Hitler. The Apple team demonized IBM. Disney and his crew fought the sheer impossibility of their task: to bring *human emotions* to *cartoons.*

- *Extraordinary tools, co-located teams in dull buildings.* High-performance teams work together out of quarters that are unexciting at best, but their *tools* are the very best available. Disney put a Movieola machine for editing film on the desk of every animator on his team. In modern terms, that's the equivalent of a $50,000 workstation. It was a nontrivial investment in 1935.

- *Autonomy and responsibility.* Disney didn't tell his animators *how to draw;* he told them when the animations were good enough to put in front of an audience. The animators devised their own solutions to their own problems.

Here's a quick comparison of Bennis's model and the Open Source culture:

- *Extraordinary talent.* As per Raymond in *How to Become a Hacker: If you are part of this culture, if you have contributed to it and other people in it know who you are and call you a hacker, you're a hacker.* "You can't gain status or influence without doing lots of high-quality work that's seen as high quality by others," Raymond told me.

- *A clear vision of the goal.* "Build software that doesn't suck" qualifies as an extraordinary goal. To appreciate how extraordinary it is, the average reader probably needs to know that multiple studies have confirmed that the typical software program contains at least 65 errors for every 1,000 lines of code, many of which can produce significant errors in operations and output. To put it bluntly, *most software sucks,* and the bigger and more complex it is, *the more it sucks.*

- *A deadly enemy.* Bad software was the enemy when the movement began. Since then, Microsoft has managed to become the movement's demon. I'll discuss the consequences for Microsoft and the Open Source movement later.

- *Extraordinary tools, co-located teams in dull buildings.* Hackers have extraordinary tools for building software. Beyond that, the Internet is their tool, and they built it. When they need new tools, they build them and share them with other hackers. I discuss the issue of co-location below.

- *Autonomy and responsibility.* Open Source culture takes personal autonomy and responsibility to new levels. "Authority follows responsibility. We're all mavericks," Raymond told me. "We seek the absolute minimum level of conformance required to function together. All of my legitimacy as an influence leader comes from the perception of 750,000 people that I speak for them. The most I do is anticipate where they're going anyway."

The emphasis on personal autonomy goes right to the project level. No one in the culture takes orders from anyone else. People start projects because the problems are interesting. People work on a project because they want to. "Some projects aren't interesting or useful," Raymond says. "Some are interesting and useful but the people who launch them bungle the communications. These projects die." In other words, project leaders who suck, like code that sucks, just go away. There are over 10,000 Open Source projects registered with the Open Source Initiative; only about 250 of those projects are active. The other 9,750 projects will be active when somebody cares enough.

The culture of Open Source exhibits all of the characteristics of Bennis's model except one: The members of the development teams are spread out all over the Internet, not located in a single building. *The Internet is their office building*.

The fascinating thing about that is the apparent effect it has on the unity of the organization's direction and purpose. It strengthens it.

IS THIS MESSAGE CLEAR?

The "organizational structure" of the movement consists of: four major *influencers*—Torvald, Raymond, Stallman, and Larry Wall; six to eight major *distributors* who package Linux releases for distribution to the world; 10 to 20 major *project leads;* another 200 or so active project leads; and 750,000 *developers* who participate in writing or critiquing code. That's a lot of people in a basically horizontal structure, and no one is managing anyone else. *How do they get everybody moving in the same direction?*

In a typical company of 100,000 people, you have at least eight layers of management from the top to the bottom of the employee roster. Any message from the top travels through all eight layers before it gets to the bottom, and every layer of management adds distortion to the message before passing it on. That's not the way it works in the Open Source Network Army.

"The Internet makes co-location unnecessary," Raymond said. "I've looked at the MIT Media lab and other high-performance organizations, and all these cultures are quite limited in size. Humans can't form social groups of more than 250 without bureaucratizing. But with the Internet, 250 people can exert direct influence over a much larger group. The Internet can move arbitrarily complex communications structures at very low overhead. Social machines that are functionally equivalent to intense teams like Xerox PARC or the MIT Media lab are much bigger and [are] distributed all over the planet."

"I get it," I told him. "Here's how it works. There's no mediation. The communication is one to many, with exactly two levels. There's zero distortion, zero lag. Everyone gets the same message from the same source at the same time. That's something you only get with the Internet."

In a World Without Secrets, this is Management Without Secrets—except, of course, that no one is being managed. Perhaps it would be better to call it *Influence Without Secrets.*

THE MEDIUM AND THE MESSAGE

The Internet is the best possible medium for this kind of message to this kind of audience. It is much better than TV, radio, or any other kind of mass communication medium we know about. The subject is complex and abstract. No matter how smart you are—and these people are very, *very* smart—you have to read it and reread it and think it over to understand what it's all about. A picture—like a diagram of a proposed system architecture—might help, especially if you could print it out and scribble your own ideas and comments all over it, but a video of Torvald talking over a sound track wouldn't help at all.

When the primaries for the 2000 United States presidential election were under way, Gartner analysts wondered what kind of impact the Internet was really having. John McCain seemed to be doing well with fundraising on the Internet, but it didn't appear that the Net was swinging lots of votes to him. Then it hit us: *Internet users, especially the older ones, are readers.* They're Critical Thinkers. They knew plenty about the candidates and their positions before they found the candidates' Web sites. That's why fund-raising worked on the Internet, and swinging votes didn't. Television was the thing to swing votes, because people who watch lots of TV don't tend to think in complex, abstract terms about candidates (or anything else). They're the impressionable ones.

We can bet that Raymond and his friends don't spend lots of time watching TV. Raymond didn't mention it in the list of pursuits he provided to me, and I don't see anything about Favorite Hacker TV shows on his Web site. (I might guess *Star Trek,* but I doubt the science on that show is hard enough for hackers.) This is a Network Army of *Critical Thinkers.* TV is for *Distracted Consumers.*

WHY THEY LISTEN

We could add that everybody in the Open Source Network Army is listening to the influencers because they care what Linus Torvald and Larry Wall and Eric Raymond and Richard Stallman think, not because they might lose their jobs if they don't listen (or if they do). They want to listen. They can leave any time they like.

They don't leave, though. Where else are they going to go? Where else are they going to have that much fun? "Being a hacker is lots of fun," Raymond says, "but it's a kind of fun that takes lots of effort." Yeah, but it's *fun*.

There's coin in this realm, but it's not money, or surrogates like stock options. "Like most cultures without a money economy, hackerdom runs on reputation," Raymond writes in *How to Become a Hacker*. "Hackerdom is what anthropologists call a gift culture. You gain status and reputation in it not by dominating other people, nor by being beautiful, nor by having things other people want, but rather by giving things away."

Well, the bad news is: You don't get money. The good news is that the organization, the *movement*, is much less subject to the fluctuations in work force that reliance on money as a motivator causes. Nobody in the Open Source movement is going to leave because their stock options are under water. They're going to leave when they decide to stop having fun.

Or, perhaps, when it stops being fun.

POWER GRABS, NOT

Exciting movements that begin with a few idealistic, highly committed people get killed by power grabs, lack of mechanisms for handling conflicts that result in ideological wars and splintering of the movement, slow diffusion of the values and ideals of the movement as membership grows, and leader corruption.

It's clear that the Open Source movement isn't highly susceptible to a power grab. I mean, what do you *grab*? "Stalin succeeded by stealing the apparatus of the state," I said to Raymond. "But in Open Source it seems that there's no apparatus, so a Stalin can't succeed."

"That's one of the strongest cultural norms," Raymond said. "We avoid establishment of any kind of state. A core value of the culture is that *you don't do things that deprive people of the option to fork.*" ("Forking" means taking the code in a new direction, with or without the support of anyone else.) "That's why attempts to compromise with the hacker culture, like Sun's community source license—you can look at the source, but you can't fork it—don't work."

The structure of the movement includes basic controls that prevent rogue actions with big impacts. "There are checks and balances built into the system," Raymond elaborated. "Distributors don't decide what's developed. Developers don't decide what's distributed. There are limited exceptions, like when distributors sponsor development work. Distributors are part of the peer review. The influencers—Linus, Stallman, Wall, me—set tone and help define general direction for the culture. For example, Torvald can say 'We need to pay more attention to the desktop.' He says that and projects are under way within months."

IDEOLOGICAL CONFLICT AND CORRUPTION

You can't force a Network Army to follow the leaders; they're volunteers. Network Armies follow their leaders because they share commitment to the same ideals and values. What happens if the leaders are corrupted?

A significant threat to Great Groups is a rift, ideological or otherwise, between leaders. Warren Bennis tells the story, in *Organizing Genius,* of how personal and professional differences between Andrew Rice and Irving Knickerbocker, at Black Mountain College in 1936, split the community, resulting first in the forced departure of Knickerbocker, then the voluntary departure of about a third of the faculty and students. Rice resigned soon after, when an affair with a student was exposed. Lots of conflict, lots of losses. What happens to Open Source if the values of the leaders change or the leaders are corrupted somehow?

"That would be a crisis of the first order," Raymond said. "Some people would say we've already passed through a spiritual crisis and failed, in the rift between us and the Free Software Movement.

"Stallman was responsible for the first major step in transitioning hacker culture from an unconscious implicit culture to an explicit conscious culture. He was the first to propose, in 1993, that hacker culture could and should have an explicit agenda. He was the original hacker revolutionary. He said, 'What we're doing is cool, but what we ought to be doing is saying *software is free.*'

"His belief system never commanded more than minority support, but, for a long time, it was the only ideology available. Hackers are moral creatures. When they hear something like that, they react to it. They're not indifferent. Hackers aligned within the culture either for or against Stallman's ideas. Therefore, by default, he was the apex of the culture. From 1993 to 1995, Stallman was *the* moral arbiter of hacker culture.

"That all started to change when Torvald became an influential figure in 1995–1996. Torvald rejected Stallman's ideology without explicitly saying so, by saying, 'Proprietary software is okay sometimes.' What's more important is that Torvald succeeded at something that Stallman hadn't. He built an operating system kernal that worked. The practical importance was that it unified previous free software work aimed at building a common platform and tool kit. The symbolic importance is that the kernal is the center of the OS."

"So, symbolically," I said, "he'd created a new center to the hacker universe."

"He'd created a challenge to Stallman's moral authority," Raymond said. "Then I came along, and, from Stallman's view, I made things worse. Without realizing it, I proposed a specific ideology in *The Cathedral and the Bazaar,* a new organizing principle for the culture. Instead of a moral standard based on free software, I proposed a standard based on the functional superiority of Open Source. In doing so, I implied that the Free Software Foundation philosophy wasn't necessary.

"If it's enough to justify an operating system on the results, there's no need to go on a crusade against intellectual property. It'll wither away on its own. Or not, which would still be okay. It took me a year to realize that I was in competition with Stallman. Stallman saw what I'd written as hostile. He thought me and Torvald hijacked his revolution."

I remembered Stallman's insisting to me that Open Source was a *model for development.* No moral standard there; it's a way to run a project, period.

But if Stallman chose to handle the challenge to his moral authority by ignoring it, he'd still handled it. The leaders fought their battle. Nobody died, including Open Source. Nobody was forced out, the way Knickerbocker and, later, Rice were forced out of Black Mountain. But in the Open Source movement, you can't really be forced out because nobody's really got a job.

That doesn't answer the question of how this Network Army would deal with first-order corruption—say, evidence that Torvald was taking bribes from IBM, or how the movement would handle the loss of all the top influencers in a plane crash. It's reasonable to say that a Network Army, like a democracy, is relatively immune to the loss of a single leader. Beyond that, moral dependence on the major influencers remains the clearest vulnerability for the Open Source movement.

NEMESIS AND THE NETWORK ARMY

A Network Army is *a set of communities aligned on a cause.* Here's a tip for businesses and governments everywhere: Whatever you do, *don't make your-self the cause that unites an angry Network Army.* You may win or you may not, but you're in a war either way.

Big armies with big guns tend to think that little armies with little guns are easy kills. But *a Network Army is not an easy kill.* It's not even a very solid target. Think France and Algeria; the United States and Somalia.

Think *Microsoft and the Open Source movement.*

CAN I BE YOUR ENEMY?

The Open Source movement's cause was nothing more or less than *soft-ware that doesn't suck* until Microsoft identified the movement as a poten-tial threat to its operating system monopoly, in late 1998. *Software that doesn't suck* is, in itself, a big enough cause to keep a whole Network Army occupied forever. It's not easy to achieve, and it's a moving target.

If Microsoft had left well enough alone, it might've stayed that way in-definitely. But in late 1998, Microsoft did two things that guaranteed a war:

1. It created an internal study—"Open Source Software: A (New?) Development Methodology"[10]—that defined the Open Source move-ment in Microsoft's terms and proposed a variety of strategies for de-feating the movement and eliminating Open Source. For example, the study said: "OSS projects have been able to gain a foothold in many server applications because of the wide utility of highly com-moditized, simple protocols. By extending these protocols and devel-oping new protocols, we can deny OSS projects entry into the market." In other words, new protocols would be developed not because they provided added value for users, but because they were proprietary

solutions that Open Source could not use. Those *highly commoditized, simple protocols,* of course, are the basic fabric of the Internet. What Microsoft proposed here was simply to make the Internet entirely dependent on proprietary Microsoft technology. That's the extent of control necessary to "deny OSS projects entry into the market."

2. It allowed the study to fall into the hands of influential Open Source members shortly after its release internally at Microsoft in August 1998. Eric Raymond published it on his Web site under the name "The Halloween Papers" in October 1998, and Microsoft reluctantly authenticated it. It became a permanent, public testament to Microsoft's animosity for Open Source, an animosity that members of the movement considered unjust and undeserved. There's no doubt that Raymond took it personally; just read the invective he lavishes on Microsoft at his site.

These mistakes were especially grave because of the nature of the Open Source movement. This Network Army is a *Great Group* in Warren Bennis's terms. According to Bennis, ". . . virtually every Great Group defines itself in terms of an enemy. . . . In Great Groups the engagement of the enemy is both deadly serious and a lark." Deadly serious and a lark—what could be more attractive to the iconoclastic, combative, brilliant, *fun-loving* influencers who lead the Open Source movement? These are medieval jousters, martial artists, poet warriors. It's not just a war for them. It's a *quest.*

Until Microsoft stepped up to fill the role, the Open Source movement didn't have a real nemesis—an enemy with a name and an address. From Microsoft's point of view, it was a mistake even to let the movement get one. The arrival of a nemesis could only amplify the already growing energy of the movement. It was a very grave mistake to effectively volunteer to *be* the nemesis. Among other things, it made it easy for other powerful Microsoft enemies—companies like IBM, Sun, and Oracle, none of which makes any real money selling operating systems, and most of which make very big money selling *services*—to line up behind Open Source, further amplifying the movement while risking little themselves.

GENERALS ARE ALWAYS FIGHTING THE LAST WAR

Microsoft has high confidence in its own abilities to create solid products and market them effectively, and especially in its ability to outstrategize its competition. (Microsoft has big guns.) Microsoft may have believed that it would easily overcome these relatively disorganized opponents. (Open Source apparently has few guns and obviously has few generals.) Microsoft didn't seem to realize that many of the weapons it had used effectively against other opponents wouldn't work against the Open Source Network Army.

Open Source players didn't collect revenues from product sales, so Microsoft couldn't undercut their prices or introduce a new product and give it away to destroy their revenue base (as they did with their browser against Netscape). In any case, the primary Open Source product was an operating system, and Microsoft couldn't give *that* away without destroying its own revenue base. There was no such corporate entity as "Open Source, Inc.," so the movement couldn't be bought—or bought out and quietly disassembled. The movement was a Network Army with no executives or managers, so there was no one to negotiate with.

That last fact seems like a problem for the movement, but, to an opponent, it's a deadly problem. If there's no way to negotiate, *the war ends when Open Source is eradicated or Microsoft surrenders.* Open Source isn't a company with assets and customers. It's nothing but the people who create it. They can't be eliminated—it's not a *shooting* war—and won't be diverted, so Microsoft has no easy way out.

And there's no guarantee that Microsoft will win.

The Message and the Medium, and the Audience for Linux

The user base—highly skilled technicians—for Open Source products like Linux is much more knowledgeable than the typical Microsoft buyer. Plenty of Windows desktop users have never been exposed to any operating system not built by Microsoft and wouldn't know how to compare operating systems if they wanted to. They're Distracted Consumers where software is concerned; they just want what everyone else is using. *Microsoft's their Mentat.* If you tell those people Linux doesn't work, they'll believe it.

But the people who might choose Linux for their shops are highly trained pros, *Critical Thinkers and One-Dimensional Experts.* They have all sorts of tools for measuring uptime and unplanned downtime, and output and throughput, and transactions per second, and anything else they might need or want to measure.

Microsoft can tell them that Linux is unreliable, that it won't perform, and that they'll never be able to get anyone to fix it when, not if, it breaks. That'll work with Critical Thinkers and One-Dimensional Experts under one or both of exactly two conditions: (1) if it's true, or (2) if they never try Linux, which increasingly is only a matter of time for many technology pros. When they try Linux and find out it's not true, the Critical Thinkers stop thinking of Microsoft as a Mentat, at least where Linux is concerned. The One-Dimensional Experts get *angry*.

All the while, those direct, undistorted, textually dense messages from Torvald and other Open Source experts are waiting for them on the Internet, at Web sites that professionals like these can easily find. Torvald speaks to them, one-to-many, in a voice that they understand and immediately know to be authoritative. It's the voice of a natural leader. *Their* leader.

They may not be recruited into the Network Army yet. But more and more of them are joining all the time. In the battle with the Open Source Network Army for the hearts and minds of the professional information systems organization, Microsoft is not winning. I'll repeat Gartner's most recent prediction: *By 2003, Linux or other Open Source software will be in use in over 80 percent of all businesses.* Open Source is gaining ground.

IF YOU'RE LOSING THE BATTLES, CHANGE THE BATTLEFIELD

A common practice in sales is to escalate the sales pitch to a higher level of the organization when a manager at a lower level isn't buying. Microsoft understands sales. Its official pronouncements on Open Source are now going over the heads of technical professionals (who are increasingly ignoring Microsoft's message) and being addressed to the general public.

On May 3, 2001, Craig Mundie, Microsoft Senior Vice President, spoke at The New York University Stern School of Business on the subject of "The Commercial Software Model."[11] The real subject was Open Source software and the dangers inherent therein. Here's part of what Mundie had to say:

> During the last year, the U.S. economy has hit what could be regarded as its most substantial speed bump of the past two decades. Illustrated most starkly by the declining valuation of the NASDAQ, we've witnessed a notable

decline in consumer confidence that has people wondering whether we're at a brief respite or whether we've reached the end of an economic era.

Mundie soon made it clear what the cause of this economic crisis really is:

> . . . Companies and investors need to focus on business models that can be sustainable over the long term in the real world economy. A common trait of many of the companies that failed is that they gave away for free or at a loss the very thing they produced that was of greatest value—in the hope that somehow they'd make money selling something else. . . . As we've learned—or really relearned—one can't build a business or our economic future on that type of flimsy foundation. . . .
>
> . . . In this sense, Open Source software based on the GPL mirrors the .com business models that proved the least successful during the past year. They ask software developers to give away for free the very thing they create that is of greatest value in the hope that somehow they'll make money selling something else. In effect, it puts at risk the continued vitality of the independent software sector.

FREE STUFF KILLS COMPETITORS, NOT MARKETS

It's true that certain software companies have failed because free software was available. Netscape, for example, failed when Microsoft erased Netscape's revenue base by bundling Internet Explorer into Windows, which deprived Netscape of a market for its browser software. So far two federal courts have agreed that, in doing so, Microsoft illegally exercised its monopoly power.

". . . As we've learned—or really relearned," Mundie says, "one can't build a business or our economic future on that type of flimsy foundation. . . . "

It's clear that a company that's trying to charge for software that's available elsewhere at no cost can't build a future on it. The company that's giving it away seems to do just fine. Microsoft is still in business. Netscape is no longer a serious contender. Microsoft's new operating system, Windows XP, does the same thing with CD burners, digital audio and video players, and firewalls that it did previously with the Internet browser: it bundles them into the operating system. If someone dies as a result, it'll be Adaptec, Real, or McAfee—not Microsoft.

This is a technology-driven business model that Gartner calls the *market breaker*. A market breaker gives something away for free in order to sell something else. It's certainly tough for the companies that sell whatever's being given away by the market breaker. Since Travelocity went online, thousands of independent travel agents in the United States have gone out of business. That's not very pretty, but free markets go where consumers go.

If consumers don't think the services independent travel agents offer are worth paying for when Travelocity offers what the traveler wants for free, the independent agents are going to disappear. Period. And no one will claim that the economy is failing as a result, no matter how many travel agents have to find a new career.

The Open Source software model is a market breaker model as well. *Software* is given away; *services* are sold. "The natural economics of software is that most of its value is in the requirement for service in its lifetime," Raymond said to me. Mundie doesn't like this model at all:

> The business model for OSS (Open Source Software) may well be attractive for software as an adjunct to hardware—the model of the '60s and '70s —or for service businesses that do not generate the revenue needed for major investments in technology. But as history has shown, while this type of model may have a place, it isn't successful in building a mass market and making powerful, easy-to-use software broadly accessible to consumers.

Mundie's dislike for the model may be influenced by Microsoft's overwhelming dependence on software licenses for revenue. IBM has a multibillion-dollar *services* business and is spending $1 billion worldwide in 2001–2002 to develop Linux support and services offerings. IBM can apparently earn good money in the services business by making powerful, easy-to-use Linux software broadly available to consumers, even if Microsoft can't.

Regardless of whose economics are correct, it's obviously more painful to be on the receiving end of a market breaker's attack than to be the market breaker.

WHY NOT JUST LET THE MARKET DO ITS WORK?

If the Open Software model is indeed deeply flawed—if "one can't build a business or our economic future on that type of flimsy foundation"—

then why not just let Open Source *die?* If the fools in the Open Source movement didn't get the message when all the dot-coms that were giving stuff away died off, why not let them find out for themselves? Isn't that how markets work?

The problem is that Mundie doesn't seem to think that the deeply flawed Open Source Software business model is going to fail. In his scenario, Open Source can only be a threat to the *vitality of the independent software industry* if it *succeeds.* Mundie seems to believe that there is a real possibility that it may do so. Otherwise, why sound the warning?

But if it succeeds, then the business model, by definition, can't be deeply flawed, *even if it puts everybody else out of business.* Isn't that what Microsoft did in the operating system market? And the *browser* market? And the *office applications* market? Ninety percent of the personal computers sold worldwide are equipped at the factory with a Microsoft operating system. Over 95 percent of personal computers sold to businesses are equipped with a Microsoft operating system, a set of Microsoft Office applications, and a Microsoft browser. Was it a problem that Microsoft put so many other software vendors out of business, and may eliminate more soon? Has Microsoft's near-total domination of some of the most critically important software markets threatened *the continued vitality of the independent software sector?*

In a free market, success is its own justification. The winners need not apologize. The losers can try again.

Viability's not a permanent appointment, even for a monopoly.

MAYBE SOMEONE CAN BE CONVINCED

What I see in Mundie's speech is that Microsoft's leaders understand that they're at war with the Open Source movement. They understand that the threat is serious. They understand that they're losing ground among technical users, and they're taking the battle to consumers and business executives, who are more easily persuaded that Open Source is not just a threat to Microsoft, but to the economy as well. They're trying, with those audiences, the same arguments that have apparently failed in the technical community. Here's Mundie:

> The OSS development model leads to a strong possibility of unhealthy "forking" of a code base, resulting in the development of multiple incompatible versions of programs, weakened interoperability, product instability, and

hindering businesses' ability to strategically plan for the future. Furthermore, it has inherent security risks and can force intellectual property into the public domain.

In a World Without Secrets, it's hard to make these accusations stick. (The bit about "inherent security risks," coming from the company whose software was the *only* target for the most widely spread viruses in recent history, Nimda and Code Red, is ludicrous to the point of embarrassment.) Because the experts who serve as Mentats to the business press in matters technical know the charges to be false, the press has been highly skeptical. Here's the *Wall Street Journal Online,* reporting on June 18, 2001:[12]

> Microsoft Corp., even while mounting a new campaign against open-source software, has quietly been using such free computer code in several major products, as well as on key portions of a popular Web site—despite denying last week that it did so.
>
> Software connected with the FreeBSD open-source operating system is used in several places deep inside several versions of Microsoft's Windows software, such as in the "TCP/IP" section that arranges all connections to the Internet. The company also uses FreeBSD on numerous "server" computers that manage major functions at its Hotmail free e-mail service, whose registered users exceed 100 million and make it one of the Web's busiest sites.
>
> Microsoft acknowledged its repeated use of open-source code Friday, in response to questions about the matter. Just two days earlier, it had specifically denied the existence of any such software at Hotmail.
>
> . . . Microsoft's statements Friday suggest the company has itself been taking advantage of the very technology it has insisted would bring dire consequences to others . . . one employee of the Redmond, Wash., company said Microsoft has deliberately kept FreeBSD in parts of Hotmail because of its technical superiority over Windows in important functions and furthermore had decided to actually increase its reliance on FreeBSD. Many of the company's Web sites went down much of a day in January, and this person said FreeBSD was judged to be better than Windows at helping to prevent a recurrence of the problem. . . .
>
> . . . In its campaign against open-source, Microsoft has been unable to come up with examples of companies being harmed by it.

Indeed. Note also how Microsoft's use of Open Source was discovered:

> Much of Microsoft's use of the software at Hotmail was uncovered Thursday evening by Trevor Johnson, a FreeBSD developer in Los Angeles who used standard Internet monitoring tools to check on the computers at

Hotmail. Johnson said he acted because he was skeptical of Microsoft's claim, in a *Wall Street Journal* article Thursday, that there was no FreeBSD left at the service.

Mr. Johnson is a de facto member of the Open Source Network Army. He doesn't have to wait for orders, and he knows whom to call.

A network is an amplifier. The louder the message gets, *the louder it gets.*

HOW DID THINGS GET SO BAD?

How did a smart company like Microsoft let itself encourage a growing Network Army to make Microsoft its chief adversary? How did Microsoft get to the point where a senior vice president has to argue in public that a product that competes with Microsoft is a *threat to the vitality of the software industry,* when other Microsoft competitors, including software companies like IBM, are cheerfully spending a billion dollars to support the same product?

What was Microsoft thinking?

More to the point, what could it have done to avoid what is on track to becoming an even bigger problem?

How does any company handle a Network Army?

A FEW POINTERS FOR ENGINEERED SOCIETY GENERALS

Actions Speak Louder

I've already described the most important rule for dealing with a Network Army: *Don't make yourself the cause that brings an angry Network Army together.* It's a whole lot easier to start a fight with a Network Army than to end one. A Network Army *cares.* Its members are not in it for the money. They've got values, a cause, a *moral goal.* ("Hackers are moral creatures," Raymond said.)

If you screw up Rule Number One, remember this: Negotiations with a Network Army are public and include actions as well as words. No one in a Network Army can negotiate on behalf of everyone. ("We're all mavericks," Raymond said. "We seek the absolute minimum level of conformance required to function together.") Negotiations have to be public and visible. The Network Army is only satisfied when its target does the right thing, publicly. You can't talk your way out of a fight with a network army.

Microsoft's misrepresentations about Open Source, and particularly its own use of Open Source, first damaged Microsoft's credibility with the Open Source movement, and are now damaging Microsoft's credibility with the people who read the *Wall Street Journal* Online. When you're facing a Network Army, don't lie about yourself or them, and don't leave a paper trail or a bit trail to prove that you did. In a World Without Secrets, *bit trails are public documents.*

Simple Precautions

Microsoft could have done, earlier, a few simple things that would have made a difference in the intensity of the assault it is now facing. It might have said some nice things about Open Source and the people who write it. It might have incorporated Open Source into a few more of its products, and accepted the resulting distribution of the Microsoft source code as an acceptable cost of doing business.

It might have accepted the idea that it could coexist with the Open Source movement and neither side would kill the other. Coexistence will probably be easier for a lot of companies facing other Network Armies than it will ever be for Microsoft. Microsoft's strategies have always been based not on being Number One or Number Two in its markets, like Jack Welch at GE, but on *eliminating* competition in its markets.

Along those lines, Microsoft might easily have avoided drawing up a formal set of plans to kill Open Source. In a World Without Secrets, having such plans is tantamount to distributing them on every street corner, which of course is exactly what happened. Microsoft didn't produce a viable strategy for fighting Open Source, but it succeeded in stiffening the spine of every soldier in the Open Source Network Army.

Microsoft might have opened an official channel to the leaders of the Open Source movement, updated them regularly on Microsoft's plans for their operating systems, and asked their opinions. Or, it might have done something real, like committing to support common protocols that were not Microsoft-specific so that Microsoft products would work easily with Open Source products. The giant might have showed a little respect and candor, publicly and privately, instead of relentlessly disparaging the products and the movement.

What *Not* to Do

Microsoft offers a textbook case for everything one shouldn't do with a Network Army. It might have made some interesting and useful (if somewhat caustic and argumentative) friends. Instead, it made the Open Source movement into a nemesis bent on Microsoft's destruction. The movement may or may not kill Microsoft, probably not—but it has already hurt plenty, and it's going to hurt more.

Whatever damage the Open Source movement is capable of causing, Microsoft will have to live with it. There's no way to turn back, and little or no way to strike back.

I've said it twice already, and it's important enough to close with, indeed to write on a sign that hangs on the wall opposite one's desk: *Don't make yourself the cause that brings an angry Network Army together.*

HUNTER'S SECOND LAW

When everything is known, no one knows everything.

A practical consequence of Hunter's Second Law is that much of the world is hiding in plain sight most of the time.

A second consequence is that we need expert help just to get through an average day.

A third consequence is that more and more people qualify as *experts*.

CHAPTER SEVEN

The Rise of the Mentat

You yourself, Baron, could outperform those machines.

> —Mentat assassin Piter de Vries to Baron
> Vladimir Harkonnen in Frank Herbert's *Dune*

In a World Without Secrets, tremendous amounts of information are generated. Anybody can find out anything he or she wants to know, but there's so much to know, and no one's time increases at all. It's inevitable that, over time, what anyone knows becomes a smaller and smaller percentage of *all* that's known. These simple facts are the basis of Hunter's Second Law: *When everything is known, no one knows everything.*

In this information-flooded environment, most people will agree when I say: We don't need more information; we need *less* information and *better* information. Simultaneous provision of *less* and *better* information in a World Without Secrets can't be done effectively by machines. It's the role of the *Mentat,* and it's one of the most powerful roles of the next decade. *Mentats will define what is within our field of vision, and so will shape our world.*

MENTAT DEFINED

The word *Mentat* was invented by novelist Frank Herbert in his science-fiction classic, *Dune.* I'll borrow Herbert's concept for this discussion; it's a close fit to the role that's developing in our world.

In the world of *Dune,* computers are outlawed. As described by Herbert, a Mentat is a substitute, ostensibly a more powerful one: a *human*

DO YOU REALLY NEED THE NUMBERS?

You want me to *prove* that you're inundated with more information than ever? Okay. Count all the periodicals you acquired in the past week, including the ones you haven't read yet (and the ones you're never going to read, like all those *New Yorkers* stacked up next to the couch) and the newspapers you read today. Count all the mail-order catalogs, commercial mail offers, personal letters, and e-mails you got today. If you carry a pager or a Palm Pilot, count the number of messages you got on those. Count the number of Web pages you viewed today. Count the number of phone messages you listened to, and the number of people you actually talked to on the phone. Count the number of CDs or MP3 files you listened to and the movies you saw in a theater or on videotape or DVD. Count the number of books you opened. (Count this one.) Count the number of meetings you went to. Count the number of paper memos you got, if you still get paper memos. Count the number of hours you spent watching TV and listening to a radio.

Now, what was the question?

If you've got a count greater than *one* in all or most of the categories listed above, you didn't need to run this exercise to know that you're being flooded with information. If you're still unconvinced, I envy you the simplicity of your life.

thinking machine, trained to assimilate huge quantities of information and analyze them rapidly.

Herbert's Mentats are brilliant, but no more perfect than any other human. They're powerful thinkers, but not necessarily "good" in moral terms. One of the characters in *Dune* is Piter de Vries, Mentat assassin, a brilliant monster who kills and wipes his bloody blade with a look of "creamy satisfaction." (Well, he's a very bad man, but at least he has a capacity for pleasure.) Character traits aside, Mentats also make mistakes, especially when they're operating on incorrect or incomplete information.

Mentats guide us rapidly to effective decisions, hiding the details. What should I buy? Where should I live? What should I *know*? The Mentat's role in such decisions is either to define the framework for the decision or to provide the information that goes into the decision—or both. Either way, *the Mentat has decided what matters, why it matters, and how it matters before the audience sees it.*

Imperfect human Mentats have great power in the World Without Secrets. Mentats are required in the world of *Dune* because computers are unavailable. Mentats are required in our world because computers are inadequate in so many ways. Hard decisions must be made about what will be included and excluded in the relatively small stream of information that we divert to ourselves from the growing flood of all the information there is.

Let's look at the reasons why computers can't fulfill that role in more detail.

Computers Have No Values

I don't think about global warming every day, but it's probably the most important issue of the past 30 years. (If you're not convinced that global warming is under way, then the critical issue is whether it's really happening, as opposed to what ought to be done about it. Either way, it's critically important.) Should I be paying attention to global warming? Probably. Should I tell the computer that screens news for me to inform me of articles about it? If I don't, I may never see another article on global warming again. The computer doesn't know whether that's a good thing or not. (It's not.) It only knows what I asked for, and it can only assume that I know what I'm doing. If I don't, a computer that simply reflects my values isn't helping me. It's putting me deeper into a hole.

Computers don't have values. Computers don't know what's important, why it's important, or how it's important unless they're explicitly told by a human being. Once told, computers don't know when or why to change unless a human tells them to. Until then, computers rigidly obey whatever rules they were last given for making choices.

Over time, as the sheer volume of what's known increases rapidly and the volume of what *I* know increases at a much slower rate, it's more and more likely that I'm ignoring something critically important. Because computer models for filtering information aren't self-updating or self-controlling, any gaps in my understanding will inevitably be reflected in the automated filters I create. Ultimately, a feedback loop is created in which gaps in my filters exacerbate gaps in my knowledge, which results in bigger gaps in my filters, and so on. *This is a critical issue for everyone—individuals and institutions alike—in the World Without Secrets.* We'll examine it in greater depth later in this chapter.

Computers Don't Rock

Your music is my noise. My computer may know what music I like, but does it know why? No. It never will.

Right now, Lucinda Williams is selling lots of records after a couple of decades in the music business in which she didn't sell many at all. No computer can tell us why "Car Wheels on a Gravel Road" sounds so good to so many people, or why it sounds better to so many more people than Williams's first few records did. Computer analysis can only tell us that lots of people like Williams's new music *after the fact,* by observing that lots of people bought the record.

Even in a technical assessment, when hard data regarding performance are often available, quantitative analysis may not work. Does a CD sound better than a vinyl record? The specifications for signal-to-noise ratios for CDs are certainly superior, but audiophiles almost unanimously prefer the sound of vinyl records.

LIMITS TO COMPREHENSIVENESS

Search engines like Alta Vista and Google are good examples of the limits to *comprehensiveness,* because their whole reason for being is (supposedly, at least) to list *everything.* So it's a little daunting that the ability of current Internet search engines to keep track of what's already available is arguably not very good and is likely to fall further behind.

No search engine—Google.com being the largest (though not the most heavily used) as of this writing—even indexes a majority of the pages available on the Web. Because more is not necessarily better, it can be argued that what's unknown doesn't matter. Danny Sullivan, chief editor of the Internet-based SearchEngineWatch.com, wrote, in August 2000:

> . . . BrightPlanet estimates that the inaccessible part of the web is about 500 times larger than what search engines already provide

LIMITS TO COMPREHENSIVENESS (CONTINUED)

access to. . . . That sounds terrible, but . . . the size of a search engine does not necessarily equate to its relevancy or usefulness. (http://www.searchenginewatch.com/sereport/00/08-deepweb.html)[1]

I agree that not everything known is relevant or useful, but that doesn't mean that what is *not* known is irrelevant or useless (especially if what's unknown is 500 times larger than the known stuff). To say otherwise is to act like the man in the old joke who searches under a streetlamp for a lost contact lens, not because he lost his lens there, but because the light under the streetlamp is better. (Of course, anything connected to the Internet can be accessed, whether or not a search engine can find it, if you already know the URL of whatever you're looking for, but we're not talking about people who already know where to find everything they want. Anyway, people who already know where to find everything they want to know don't want to know very much.)

Using more powerful processors in search engines may eventually help to reduce the difference between what's theoretically *available* and what's *known and cataloged*, but I doubt it. The raw volume of electronically stored information is increasing more rapidly than raw processing power (i.e., at a rate faster than Moore's Law). By some estimates, enough data storage capacity will soon be available on the planet to electronically document, in sounds and images, every moment of every person's life, with plenty left over for mundane tasks like managing businesses. If that's true, then it's more likely that the current gap between what's known and what's catalogued will grow larger.

There are potential wild cards, such as the discovery of a processing technology whose rate of increase in power dramatically exceeds Moore's Law, or the development of far more intelligent and efficient language-analysis software. Such technologies are not currently viable in the laboratory, which means that they will certainly not appear in commercially available products within the next five years.

So every search engine begins with a handicap: it doesn't know where to find everything it needs to be sure that it retrieved the most important stuff. If this is true of search engines, it's likely to be true of any other catalogue for the next five to ten years.

Computers Don't Know What We're Talking About

Machines have made it possible for us to do lots of searching and re-
trieving via our computers, but there are big limits to what they can do,
and the limits will be there for a long time. In particular, computers
can't guarantee *comprehensiveness,* and there are significant limits on
what they can *understand.*

LIMITS TO UNDERSTANDING

It's very, *very* hard for a machine to understand the meaning of complex material, such as narrative text. (Forget about sounds and images, period, unless they're accompanied by text that describes them
in detail, e.g.,"a photo of Winston Churchill at age 60 smoking a cigar
and painting a picture.") *Understand* here means the machine knows
not only what words are used within a source like a document, but
what it's *about.* This will be very difficult for machines during at least
the next five years, probably the next 10, because language is inherently very complex, and it's impossible to understand meaning without understanding language.

To know what something is about, a machine also has to compare
it to the concepts, relationships, and language used in one or more
domains. This is more complex than matching on a word or phrase.
A document might be about "a treatment for diabetes" even when the
word *treatment* doesn't appear anywhere in the document. Really intelligent helpers must know a lot about the subject *before* they start
looking. They need a "map" that describes language and the underlying concepts for the domain they're searching.

Some public and private institutions are already building such
maps in fields like health care, business, and information technology. Such maps—often called *taxonomies* or *ontologies*—can be implemented in technologies like XML, an emerging standard for data
description, to make them both understandable and shareable by
computers.

Once a taxonomy is available, a machine can use techniques for
statistical and semantical analysis to see whether a piece of narrative
text is related to a certain set of concepts. Such a machine could
tell whether a document answers a complex question, like: "What

LIMITS TO UNDERSTANDING (CONTINUED)

treatments for diabetes are most effective?" even if the words *treatment* and *effective* never appear in the document.

Construction of detailed, accurate taxonomies takes tremendous human effort. A taxonomy for a complex domain like health care might take 100 person-years of effort to build, and a big portion of that, annually, to update. No technology within the next five years— or probably within the next 10—will be able to build a detailed, a curate taxonomy of any domain automatically. The state of the art for taxonomy-building in the near future is a team of smart people (like Yahoo! uses to build its directories), not a battery of smart machines.

Highly commercial domains will be the first mapped, followed by those supported by committed communities. Examples of the first group include health care, pornography, gambling, film, and finance; examples of the second include Morris dancing and academic research.

By 2008 to 2010, the computer will be much smarter. Improvements in natural-language processing will allow a machine to understand and respond to conversational statements from a human, as opposed to strictly structured commands. Once a statement is received, the machines will be able to reference conceptual and semantic models of specific knowledge domains, such as health care, to *really* understand what the person is talking about. At that point, the machine can offer a response that's truly meaningful. It can do what's called "content-based retrieval," for example, where it answers my question by supplying material (such as text or photos or sounds) that's really *about* my question, as opposed to merely containing words that I used in my question.

Even if a machine had a taxonomy to work with and knew what a document was about, it would still be unable to tell whether it was *good*, let alone *better* than everything else available. The machine might know whether a certain person said it was good, but that's just another way of saying the machine doesn't know until it asks a human.

A quantitative alternative to qualitative analysis is to quantify what other people are saying or doing about the subject under consideration. That's essentially what Amazon does when it tells you that lots of other people liked a certain set of books. They're not telling you that the other books are *good*. They're advising you of a statistical fact. If lots of people are buying stock in a company, for example, or if lots of Wall Street analysts are recommending the company, it must be a winner, right?

That approach hasn't worked for me, and recent analysis of the track records of investment advisers indicates that it doesn't work generally. Successful investments usually make money precisely because they run contrary to conventional wisdom. Warren Buffett has made an art of capitalizing on the stock market's misunderstanding of the intrinsic value of companies, and that art has made him very wealthy. (Note that if it was a science as opposed to an art, computer-based analysis could duplicate Buffett's success.)

A quantitative analysis of references for a company bringing a new technology to a new market would *always* say it was going to fail, because there wouldn't be any history or body of references to draw on. (Most such companies, but not all, *will* fail, of course, and not because they don't have a history already.) The same issues apply to a new work of art. If no one has seen it, read it, or heard it yet, there's no body of references to draw on, and quantitative analysis à la Amazon won't tell us whether it's worthy of our attention.

How did you pick your spouse? Did you run a quantitative analysis on his or her reviews by previous significant others? Okay, bad example. Given the current divorce rate, about 50 percent of the people reading this probably wish they had. Anyway, a computer wouldn't have helped much. Typical samples are too small, unless your spouse had *lots* of significant others, in which case just seeing the size of the sample probably would have told you what you needed to know, without running the analysis.

WHY MENTATS?

Mentats assimilate vast quantities of information and provide concise advice (as opposed to *more information*) rapidly. They add value when *decisions are complex and the data are not definitive*. Even when definitive data are available, in a World Without Secrets, a Mentat is often needed to identify *which* data, out of the huge mass of *all* data, are both relevant and definitive.

Mentats do what computers can't and won't do for the next 10 years: make decisions and predictions based on qualitative factors like judgment,

beliefs, values, and emotions. Mentats fill a number of increasingly important roles in the World Without Secrets:

- Mentats tell us *what matters, why, and how.* In other words, they provide the frameworks we use to interpret the world (or a certain piece
of it).

- A framework is based on values, so it's one of the things that defines a community. In other words, *a Mentat leads a community.*

- Like other leaders, Mentats *make decisions,* or assist us in doing so.

- Mentats filter *out* as much information as possible, so what remains (at least ostensibly) is the *good* stuff.

- Mentats inform us when *something important has changed* that requires us to reconsider our ideas and frameworks.

- Mentats provide a basis for *personal trust* to resolve the claims of
competing information.

MENTATS HAVE (HIDDEN) POWER

When I rent videos, I check the video boxes for reviews by Roger Ebert.
How many movies does Ebert look at or think about before deciding to review a relative handful? Of all the movies released worldwide in a given
year, what percentage is that? I have no idea. I make my decisions based
on what Ebert says about the movies he reviews, not the ones he doesn't.
How can anyone see what isn't there?

Under normal circumstances, much of a Mentat's power is invisible to the user because *the user never sees what the Mentat has excluded*. This point is so important that it bears repeating: *Under normal circumstances, much of a Mentat's power is invisible to the user*. This is especially important when the Mentat's real agenda is hidden from the user—for example, when the Mentat's purpose is not to *inform* the user but to *mislead or misinform* the user. (For a more detailed case study of the hidden power of Mentats, see Chapter Eight).

MENTATS PROVIDE LESS INFORMATION

No one wants more information. In a World Without Secrets, simply providing information is less than worthless. Information is so common that it's oppressive and annoying. Mentats will increasingly be measured not by their ability to provide more information, but by their ability to *make accurate predictions, give concise advice, and* reduce *the amount of information their clients must handle.* Of course, this increases the hidden power of the Mentat.

Old-school Mentat journals like the *New York Times* and the *Wall Street Journal* aim to provide lots of information ("All the News That's Fit to Print," as the *Times* says; *all* of it?). They can expect that the declines in readership each has experienced during the past decade will accelerate in the next decade unless the model changes.

THE NETWORK MENTAT

Matt Drudge uses the Internet as a low-cost platform for distribution of his muckraking news via the "Drudge Report" Web site.[3] Headlines on August 3, 2001, included: "Ben Affleck in Rehab" and "Clinton Keeps $1 Million in Basic Checking Account." A balanced analysis, critical or otherwise, of Affleck's or Clinton's careers and achievements is unlikely to appear at this Web site, one gathers—but so what?

Drudge's commitment to sensationalism has won him a very large audience; as of August 3, 2001, the site proclaimed over 2,600,000 visitors in the past 24 hours, and over 637 million in the past year. As the audience grows, Drudge's power increases as per Hunter's First Law. His credentials probably wouldn't get him a job at the *New York Times,* but he has appeared alongside Establishment journalists, including *New York Times* reporters, on panels and TV talk shows. His audience apparently considers him an important source of information, and if they do, he is. Drudge is a *network Mentat,* an adviser to what I call a Network Army elsewhere in this book, and an example of an emerging model in the World Without Secrets.

The network Mentat may be an independent media organization (such as http://www.indymedia.org, or Drudge), or a member of such an organization, or a self-appointed expert acting independently. I'm an example of the latter. I appointed myself as Mentat to a Network Army of harmonica players and fans when I created my Web site (http://www.hunterharp.com) in 1997; it now draws about 800 hits a week. My credentials (author of a method for jazz harmonica players; session player for 15 years for film, TV, record, and commercial work; two CDs released under my name as leader, and so on) apparently qualify me for the role, but other harmonica Mentat Web sites are offering advice to players, and some that are attracting as many (or more) visitors as mine are run by novices who've never released a recording or played a note for pay. (I mean, who elected *them?*) In my case, theirs, and Drudge's, the ultimate proof of qualification is the arrival of a fascinated Network Army at our doorsteps.

The Network Mentat Is (Apparently) Committed and (Certainly) Influential

Beyond expertise, a network Mentat offers commitment to a cause. (If you don't think harmonica is a *cause,* you've never had to tell an idiot guitarist—is that two words?—that you know the difference between the keys of C and G.) The Mentat's commitment translates to credibility with an audience. (The commitment may be a cover for a hidden agenda, of course. *Caveat emptor.*)

How much of Drudge's audience wonders whether what they're seeing is really true, or even worth knowing? Some people are sure to listen when you talk through a megaphone, even if you don't say much that's worth hearing. A Web page, coupled with a constant stream of fresh communications to a target audience, may be all that's needed to expand on a Mentat's initial credibility, especially if the audience is unsophisticated or undemanding.

Because *the network is an amplifier,* the network Mentat is influential. Millions of people visited Drudge's Web site daily when the Clinton/ Lewinsky scandal was current. Whether or not his reporting was accurate, balanced, or even newsworthy in the traditional sense, it became part of the history of the event.

THE MENTAT REVIEWER

Morningstar, which rates the performance of mutual fund managers, is an example of a *Mentat reviewer*. As the information flood gathers velocity in the World Without Secrets, the role of Mentats in excluding what's irrelevant and unimportant is more and more critical, and the choice of Mentat becomes more important to the audience. As a result, an increasingly large class of Mentats exists solely to rate the performance of other Mentats.

In a World Without Secrets, the ability of Mentats to predict accurately is often precisely measurable. For example, a recent quantitative analysis of stockbrokers' performance over a five-year period showed that more than 90 percent of these investment Mentats gave advice that resulted in losses for their clients. The continuing rise of discount brokers shows that much of the investing public already thinks it needs little advice from Wall Street. Investors are already more inclined to follow the advice of the Mentat *reviewer* instead of the Mentat.

CHOOSE YOUR MENTAT

In a rational world, such analysis would instantly kill the Mentat industry in question. The world is not rational, and people don't choose Mentats solely on the basis of accuracy (see Figure 7.1).

Like everyone else in the World Without Secrets, no Mentat knows all. Mentats have specific expertise and interests, and they're first discovered or chosen by an audience on that basis. (Type in "harmonica" in the search field on Google.com, and there I am.) Beyond that, the characteristics of the audience are critical to Mentat selection, and no Mentat will satisfy all audiences.

We can characterize Mentat audiences broadly, based on two characteristics:

- *Bandwidth*, the audience's ability to process and retain high volumes of information, and
- *Focus*, the scope or breadth of the audience's interests.

Four Mentat audiences result from the intersection of these characteristics.

1. The *One-Dimensional Expert* has *high bandwidth and narrow focus*, which equates to deep expertise in a narrowly defined subject. The

FIGURE 7.1 MENTAT AUDIENCES

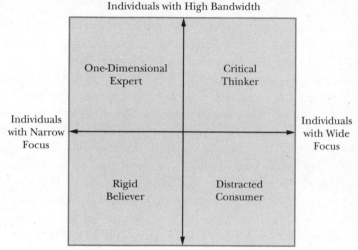

Individuals with High Bandwidth

One-Dimensional Expert

Critical Thinker

Individuals with Narrow Focus

Individuals with Wide Focus

Rigid Believer

Distracted Consumer

Individuals with Low Bandwidth

frameworks used by the One-Dimensional Expert are often his or her own, and the One-Dimensional Expert is often a Mentat for his or her network(s). For better or worse, other Mentats have very little control over the One-Dimensional Expert.

2. The *Rigid Believer* has *low bandwidth and narrow focus.* This equates to a deep commitment to a relatively simple belief system. The Rigid Believer has very little tolerance for information that's either unrelated to or conflicting with that belief system, and in a World Without Secrets there's more of *that* all the time. The Rigid Believer's Mentats are approved by (or the same as) authorities in the belief system. Those Mentats ensure that any content that seriously questions the Rigid Belief system is filtered out (or distorted, if necessary) before it gets to the Rigid Believer.

3. The *Distracted Consumer* has *low bandwidth and wide focus,* which means that he or she lacks deep expertise and is easily persuaded to follow whatever leads are provided. The Distracted Consumer has neither the critical skills to separate reality from lies, nor the belief system that protects the Rigid Believer from the complexity of the World Without Secrets. He or she prefers Mentats who are popular with large numbers of people, and distrusts Mentats who are specialized or use obviously complex frameworks. The Mentats who filter information for the Distracted Consumer are oriented to mass audiences and are often explicitly commercial, like network television. The primary role of those Mentats is to

IS LARRY KING A JOURNALIST?

Larry King was castigated in a memo by his CNN colleague John King (no relation), who said that he felt "shame and horror" when he witnessed Larry King's on-camera embrace of the newly inaugurated President of the United States, George W. Bush, at the latter's Inaugural ceremony on January 18, 2001.[4] John King apparently felt that Larry King was supposed to act like a journalist, that is, according to the demanding rules required of a Mentat serving an audience of Critical Thinkers. Those rules obviously prohibit partisan displays. However, Larry King is apparently a Mentat to an audience of Distracted Consumers, not Critical Thinkers. *That* audience can't be bothered with complex rules about journalistic ethics, and they wouldn't apply those rules to Larry King in any case. All this implies that Larry King is perceived by a substantial part of his audience, if not himself and his colleagues, as an *entertainment* Mentat, not a journalist.

keep things as simple as possible, which gives them a *lot* of control over the Distracted Consumer.

Distracted Consumers tend to be in a hurry, and they're willing to trade the power of real knowledge for the convenience that their Mentats provide. Because of Hunter's Second Law, many (if not most) people are Distracted Consumers at least some of the time. To put it bluntly, most of us simply believe what we're told; we don't ask what we're *not* being told. The consequences for society are serious; see Chapter Eight for an example.

4. The *Critical Thinker* has *high bandwidth and wide focus* and can handle lots of information effectively. He or she understands the strengths and weaknesses of particular Mentats and can easily see through the self-serving stratagems of mass-market commercial Mentats. The Critical Thinker uses a wide range of Mentats for different situations, and may serve as Mentat in one or more networks.

TRUST MATTERS

For all these audiences, *trust* is a key part of Mentat selection, but the *criteria that establish trust* vary dramatically.

If you want to be a Mentat to a One-Dimensional Expert, you'd better be an expert yourself, and you'd better show your respect for the One-Dimensional Expert.

If you want to be a Mentat to a Rigid Believer, show that you believe what the Rigid Believer believes—and then some. (You might not have to *behave* as if you believe it. Some people still trust Jimmy Swaggart. He certainly *talks* a good game.)

If you want to be a Mentat to a Distracted Consumer, talk only about popular subjects, and keep the dialogue simple. In other words, follow the lead of Larry King. In his August 20, 2001, column in *USA Today*, King talks about Drew Carey's recent angioplasty; lavishes praise on a new Michael Douglas thriller and a book by Patrick Walsh, M.D., on prostate cancer; pleads for patience from those who would pan Bill Clinton's memoirs before publication; and offers brief thoughts on abortion, capital punishment, the lack of an NFL team in Los Angeles, Marc Rich, Tim Hudson, and Hideo Nomo—mostly in three sentences or less. That's 10 almost completely unrelated pop subjects in about 700 words. Talk about a *Distracted Consumer.*

If you want to be a Mentat to a Critical Thinker, get ready to prove it over and over. A Critical Thinker's trust is complex and situational, and a given Mentat is trusted to perform only *in a certain context.* Critical Thinkers keep score, too, which can be embarrassing to Mentats who frequently get it wrong.

MENTATS AND THE LAW OF INERTIA

It takes time and energy to select a Mentat, as it does to develop any relationship, and when someone has invested in a relationship, it takes energy to break it up. That's good news for all the stockbrokers out there. It's one reason why intelligence agencies worldwide are still in business, even though the analyses they do can already be developed almost entirely from "open" (public) sources in the World Without Secrets. (During a research visit to a U.S. armed forces base while I was writing this book, an officer nonchalantly told me that he routinely gets important intelligence from CNN days or weeks before he hears it from an intelligence agency. A second officer nodded briefly in agreement, as if to say that the point was obvious enough to require no further discussion.)

On the other hand, Mentats are subject to Hunter's Second Law—*When everything is known, no one knows everything*—as much as anyone else. It's a constant struggle for any Mentat to stay ahead of the network the Mentat serves, and the struggle will only get harder. The automated tools available to Mentats are really no better than the tools available to anyone else. (How could it be otherwise in a World Without Secrets?)

Professional Mentats—especially those serving audiences of Critical Thinkers and One-Dimensional Experts—increasingly will be driven to collaborate with other Mentats in *Mentat networks,* in order to retain their status. The alternative is to fall further and further behind until a Mentat Reviewer arrives to administer the final *coup de grace.*

MENTATS AND I-FILTERS

A Mentat's viewpoint can be embedded in software, at which point it's an automated information filter, or *I-Filter,* that can be applied automatically to large volumes of material. Yahoo!'s information hierarchies are a well-known example of an I-Filter: they organize information and screen out or demote stuff that's supposedly less relevant or important.

I say "supposedly" because there's a difference between Yahoo!'s (and most other search engines') *apparent* agenda and the *covert* agenda. The apparent agenda is to present information that's precisely relevant to the users' interests. The covert agenda is to present relevant information for which advertising fees have been paid. Most search engines now use the services of GoTo.com in ordering search results, and GoTo orders results by how much Web sites have paid to be listed first. (Google.com is the most widely used search engine that orders search results strictly by relevancy alone. It's also the fastest growing search engine in terms of number of users, and the third most widely used overall. My guess is that it's the engine of choice for Critical Thinkers and One-Dimensional Experts.)

I said earlier that, *under normal circumstances, much of a Mentat's power is invisible to the user.* The same goes for any I-Filter. *The user only sees what's there and never sees what the I-Filter doesn't show.*

HUNTER'S SECOND LAW—PERSONAL AND INSTITUTIONAL CONFLICT

In the World Without Secrets, we all struggle, all the time, to filter *out* more and more information. Because of Hunter's Second Law, we are all in danger of being trapped—by our Mentats, I-Filters, and personal limitations—into seeing only information that reflects what we already know or believe.

In the World Without Secrets, viewpoints inevitably become deeper and narrower. People who don't share Mentats and I-Filters are more likely to resolve disputes via confrontation and conflict. They don't negotiate because they understand so little about each other's ideas and assumptions.

Beyond the increased potential for conflict, there are other, more insidious dangers. Clayton Christensen notes, in *The Innovator's Dilemma*, that a successful value chain becomes, over time, increasingly focused on the needs of its established markets. When a disruptive technology appears and begins to serve new markets with a new value proposition, the entire value chain is blindsided to the point of extinction. This tendency is exacerbated in the World Without Secrets. *The effort involved in keeping up with enormous volumes of information in established markets pushes aside ideas and information about new opportunities and markets.* This is true of individuals and institutions alike in the World Without Secrets, and it's a direct result of Hunter's Second Law.

BREAKING THE BUBBLE

In *Heaven Can Wait*, Warren Beatty's deceased-industrial-tycoon-possessed-by-a-mistakenly-deceased-but-magically-revived-football-player invites a delegation of environmental activists into a board meeting, where he discusses their ideas and the affairs of the business openly. The joke in the scene is obvious: no real CEO would do that sort of thing. The real joke in a World Without Secrets is that CEOs are going to have to start doing exactly that kind of thing to avoid being trapped by their own unavoidably limited ideas and knowledge.

If they want to stay in front, individuals and businesses must make extraordinary efforts to evade the limits of their Mentats and I-Filters. The most straightforward way to do so is to constantly challenge one's own value systems and beliefs. Here are a few suggestions:

- Change channels/stations on your television/radio randomly for 15 minutes every day. When you find something of a kind you've never seen before, or something you really dislike, stay tuned to that channel/station for at least another 15 minutes.

- Read a speech by a politician you despise.

- Buy a magazine that features something you find either uninteresting or distasteful, and read the whole issue.

- Invite the leader of a political splinter group that's opposed to your plans and strategy to become a member of your board of directors.

- Do what Robert Oppenheimer did on the Manhattan Project: When two people disagree, *don't allow them to argue for their own positions until each can state the other's position to the other's satisfaction.*

- Hire consultants regularly to "war-game" your strategy and tear it to pieces.

- Create a new business unit and mandate it to put the *old* business unit out of business.

Another way to evade the limits of one's filters is to do what the Open Source movement has done: enable direct communications, without mediation or translation, among leaders, followers, and other interested parties within and outside the organization. There's no question that everyone in the movement is getting regularly dosed with viewpoints that are sometimes abrasively contrary. (For more on the extraordinary flatness and transparency of the Open Source movement, see Chapter Six.)

WOULD BREAKING THE BUBBLE HAVE SAVED CISCO?

In the spring of 2001, Cisco, one of the most successful companies in the history of commerce, took a much-publicized inventory write-down of about $2.5 billion. The company had previously enjoyed years of consistent growth at a phenomenal compound annual rate of 60 percent. The information systems that supported Cisco's business, including its inventory management systems, were legendarily comprehensive and effective. How did this extraordinarily well-managed company miss the signs of such a massive inventory buildup?

It didn't. Cisco's management knew that inventory was increasing but was not alarmed. About six months earlier, the company had lost hundreds of millions of dollars' worth of business when it ran short of inventory. Managers were determined not to let that happen twice. Even when they saw signs that demand might slack—many of the telcos among Cisco's customers were consolidating or going bankrupt—they continued to manufacture equipment, sure that it would soon be sold.

I suspect that Cisco's management was caught inside its own bubble. The managers saw signs of a slowdown but interpreted the information in ways consistent with their beliefs, desires, and values. After years of phenomenal growth, they were unable to imagine a future in which growth had slowed or had become negative.

More information might not have kept Cisco's management from making that mistake. Cisco already had better (and more) information than practically any other corporation in the world. *Exposure to a Mentat with a different viewpoint might have helped.* Such a Mentat could have aggressively attacked Cisco's assumptions and described an alternative future, not the one imagined by management. Such a Mentat could have helped Cisco's management to understand the *meaning* of their information —*what matters, why it matters, and how it matters*—in a different way.

Cisco's management has now achieved exactly that sort of understanding, of course. The company has been strong enough to absorb a $2.5-billion blow and remain solvent. Few others could have done the same.

REALITY ALWAYS WINS (IN THE WORLD WITHOUT SECRETS AND EVERYWHERE ELSE)

In a World Without Secrets, Mentats and I-Filters are both necessary and dangerous. Because of Hunter's Second Law, using them effectively means questioning them constantly. It's the only way to avoid a massive shock when reality finally cuts through. And it will.

ON THE INTERACTIONS OF LAWS

The necessary knowledge is that of what to observe.

—Edgar Allan Poe, *The Murders in the Rue Morgue*

Hunter's Second Law: *When everything is known, no one knows everything.*
Hunter's First Law: *A network is an amplifier.*

Q: What do you get when you put Hunter's Second Law and Hunter's First Law together?

A: You get a whole lot of people who don't know *anything* and believe they know *something for sure.*

CHAPTER EIGHT

Distracted Consumers, Mentats, and Timothy McVeigh

How could there be any secrets left in the story of the bombing of the Alfred P. Murrah Federal Building in Oklahoma City on April 19, 1995? The events, and the people involved in them, are as notorious and well-documented as anything or anyone in the past decade. The story continues to play out in the press months after the convicted perpetrator, Timothy McVeigh, was executed for the crime on June 11, 2001.

Most of us *know* there aren't any secrets in that story. We *know* what we've read and heard. We heard it from the media, who heard it from the FBI, who learned it through dogged investigation. The details of the story have been repeated everywhere, and they're believed by almost everyone. Given Hunter's First Law—*A network is an amplifier*—this is one of the loudest messages in the history of the world: *McVeigh did it, all by himself.*

Does it matter that some well-informed observers—independent Mentats—believe that message is false, or even fraudulent? Well, matter *how*? It's not the first time that Americans have been told by their officials that a big, very public crime was committed by a lone killer. It's hard to remember now that most Americans accepted, with gratitude and relief, the judgment of the Warren Commission that Lee Harvey Oswald acted alone in Dallas on November 22, 1963. For a long time, anyone who said otherwise was widely considered a kook or a fraud. Almost 40 years later, a majority of Americans doubt the Commission's findings, with good reason, but no one has named the co-conspirators, if any. If they exist, they didn't leave a paper trail. (*There's* an important rule for conspirators in a World Without Secrets.)

I think it's worth asking the same kinds of questions about McVeigh, if only to show how Mentats fail, especially when they're in a hurry. When we're in a hurry, we act like Distracted Consumers, and we rely on Mentats for everything. If we stop to think about it, we may know that much of a Mentat's power derives from what the Mentat hides, but when we're in a hurry *we don't stop to think.*

The thing is, in a World Without Secrets, everyone's in a hurry, all the time, and stopping for any reason, even to think, isn't what anyone likes to do.

THE PATH OF LEAST RESISTANCE

The substance of the U.S. government's successful case against McVeigh was that he was a bitter loser who acted essentially alone in retribution for the massacre of 80 Americans at the Branch Davidian compound at Waco, Texas, in April 1993. As *Time* put it, in an August 21, 1995, story titled (somewhat dismissively) "A Two-Bit Conspiracy":

> No wide-ranging conspiracy. No criminal masterminds. Not even any hardened zealots dedicating their life to the disciplined terrorist pursuit of an ideological cause. Just two drifters and misfits with a rented truck and a homemade bomb . . . the alleged conspiracy was a small-time affair in everything except the horror of its results.[1]

Americans, including myself, have generally accepted this explanation, whose source (according to *Time*) is the Federal indictment against McVeigh and his co-conspirator, Terry Nichols. It's simple enough for any Distracted Consumer to understand instantly. *"Just two drifters and misfits with a rented truck and a homemade bomb."* It's plausible, too. We all know what bombs can do, and we all know misfits can and do make them. (Here's the first question a Mentat could have asked—as Distracted Consumers, we don't know enough to ask for ourselves: Was the *specific* bomb in McVeigh's rented Ryder truck powerful enough to take down a reinforced-concrete building? I'll return to that question later.)

The FBI conducted the investigation that led to the indictment; *Time* was just reporting on what the FBI said. The FBI provided all the answers about *who, what, when, where,* and *why* this crime was done; they're the Mentats here. The FBI's got something going for them already: *we want to believe them,* especially when *somebody* is running around blowing up buildings, and the people in them, to smithereens. *We want it to stop right now.* An odd kind of relief oozes from that *Time* story, the tantalizing near-satisfaction of our urgent need to *get it all over with:*

> The government is continuing to look for possible accomplices, but, said Attorney General Janet Reno, "Most of these leads have been pursued and exhausted." Investigators generally think that if any additional plotters do turn up, there will be only a few and they will prove to be mere "facilitators." In particular, some investigators have come to doubt that the far-famed John Doe No. 2 actually exists; others think that even if he does, he is only a minor figure in the plot. All of which makes the horror that much more chilling.

IT'S EASIER IF YOU DON'T ASK

The last sentence above is strikingly, almost unbelievably disingenuous. *More chilling?* Oh, please. Elmore Leonard already told us, in *Glitz,* that losers cause all the trouble in the world. What's chilling is the idea that there might be *more* of those guys running around with *more* bombs. It's *chilling* to think that the bombing was the work of a conspiracy, and we don't know who the rest of the conspirators are. A solitary killer locked up behind bars is no problem for anyone.

What's also chilling is how quickly the government's story is accepted at face value; *Time* moves on, completely surrendering its own Mentat status, which is based entirely on asking questions. (As per Edgar Allan Poe's detective Dupin, *"The necessary knowledge is that of what to observe."*) Ah, the *horror,* the unspeakable *chilling* horror of the misfit drifter with a bomb! So much easier, even for a Mentat, to succumb to the horror than to ask *who, what, when, where, why?*

But why worry? Don't Janet Reno's comments make it perfectly clear that we're all supposed to relax, now that the game is all over except for the paperwork? But even in *Time's* brief description, there are disturbing signs of holes in the government's story, starting with the investigation itself.

Most of the leads in the case, Reno says, have been *pursued and exhausted.* And it seems she's already pretty sure what's going to happen to the remaining leads: not much. Our desire to see this awful thing done with is what keeps us from asking her, at this point, *why* she's so sure that

JOHN DOE NO. 2

When the FBI revealed, a week before Timothy McVeigh's scheduled execution in May 2001, that they'd neglected to turn over 4,000 pages of evidence to McVeigh's attorneys, among the papers was new information about John Doe No. 2. Why don't we let *Time* tell it for us again:

> Among the facts lawyers want Judge Matsch to consider are witness reports that resurrect nagging questions about whether a larger conspiracy led to the April 1995 bombing that took 168 lives. One of the documents, for instance, summarizes a call received by the FBI from Morris John Kuper Jr., who told investigators to check out activities in a parking lot a block away from the Murrah Federal Building about an hour before it was blown apart. Kuper later testified that he had seen a man resembling McVeigh walking with a dark-haired, muscular companion—a description that matches those by other witnesses of a man who came to be known as John Doe 2. Investigators eventually concluded the mystery accomplice didn't exist and tried to disprove some of the reported sightings. Kuper, for instance, was discredited by prosecutors for not having come forward until five months or so after the bombing. But the new document turned over to McVeigh's defense team shows that Kuper had passed along his lead to the FBI just two days after the bombing.[2]
>
> (Playing For a Stay, *Time*, June 11, 2001, p. 31.
> © Time Inc. reprinted by permission.)

These few facts open a whole new set of *Why* questions. *Why* did prosecutors or the FBI, or both, go out of their way to discredit Kuper and other witnesses to a conspiracy? *Why* did they try to *disprove reported sightings*? *Why* was McVeigh prosecuted as a lone perpetrator when possible conspirators remained unidentified and uninvestigated? *Time* again reports on the machinations of the players without *ever* asking *Why*?

the leads she hasn't examined yet are going nowhere. Reno the Mentat is exercising her hidden power. *Time* is going along for the ride. So are we. We are *so* glad to learn that *there is nothing more to learn.* We want out of this horror show, *fast.*

Time's story then shifts from Reno to other nameless government "investigator" Mentats, and they go farther than Reno in telling us to ignore any information that might contradict the indictment and slow things down. The "far-famed" bombing suspect, John Doe No. 2, probably doesn't even exist, they say; and if he does, he's a *mere "facilitator."* (How any participatory role in the violent mass murder of hundreds of people, including infants, could possibly qualify for the adjective *mere* is unexplained.) Nowhere does *Time* note that the reason John Doe No. 2 is "far-famed" (how dismissive, again, that term is!) is that he was seen with McVeigh, before the bombing, by reliable eyewitnesses.

Even more disturbing is the question of how these investigator Mentats know John Doe No. 2's role in the bombing and judge it as *merely* trivial *"facilitation" before they even know who he is!* What other crimes has John Doe No. 2 *facilitated,* and what is he going to *facilitate next?* What is being hidden here—what the investigators *know,* or what they *don't?*

Time neglects to ask. But never mind. John Doe No. 2 must be just a *drifter* or a *misfit* like McVeigh, if he exists at all, which *some investigators have come to doubt.* In either case, he can't be very important, can he? One thing is sure: the FBI isn't going to waste any effort finding him.

Time never asks the obvious question: *Why?* Neither do we. We don't want to focus on the holes. We want to know that *everything's going to be all right.* We want to know it *now.* We're Distracted Consumers, and we want to trust *somebody.*

We're like a crowd milling around on a sidewalk in the aftermath of a seizure, an accident, a mugging; we're straining for a look, asking each other: *What happened? Move along, folks. There's nothing to look at here.*

Sooner or later, that's what we do. After all, we've got things to do.

SO WHY LOOK?

A network is an amplifier. The sheer scale of mass acceptance of the government's story—the size of the network of *people who believe McVeigh acted alone*—gives it tremendous power. *When everything is known, no one knows everything,* and we all have little patience for those who don't share what *we* know to be true. Anyone outside the network of *people who believe McVeigh acted alone* must therefore be a kook or a fraud. Have you already decided that *I'm* a kook or a fraud—after my simple deconstruction of two brief paragraphs—for questioning *Time's* willingness to pass on, without question, highly questionable information from unnamed sources in the FBI?

One of the best-known books about the Warren Commission was titled *Rush to Judgment,* and it's the *rush* that matters here. As I said at the beginning of this chapter, in the World Without Secrets *we're all in a hurry, all the time.* While we're in a hurry, we act like Distracted Consumers, and we count on our Mentats to eliminate information that's unimportant. We take it for granted that they do so on our behalf, and most of the time we don't ask questions. That's what the Mentats are supposed to do for us.

But what if the Mentats don't ask the right questions? The path that *Time's* information traveled, from its source to its readers, is short but not necessarily clear. *Much of a Mentat's power is hidden from the user.* Do you believe the FBI, given that all or most of what you've heard about this case ultimately came directly from that source? Are you willing to accept that the Bureau made the right decisions for you when it decided what not to tell you about how it investigated the case and what it did or didn't find?

DID McVEIGH DO IT?

This isn't about whether McVeigh did it or not. The FBI's story is the one McVeigh confirmed in interviews just prior to his execution. He ought to know. Whether he was telling what he knew is another question. There's plenty of reason to doubt that some of the people involved in this case are telling all they know.

The real question is: *Whom do you believe?* not *What do you know?* Only a handful of people in the world saw firsthand what happened before, during, and after the bombing of the Murrah Federal Building, and one of the most informed, McVeigh, is now dead. Almost everyone else—including professional Mentats like the reporters from *Time*—is relying on what they have heard. Because we rely on Mentats to tell us *what matters, why it matters, and how it matters,* we Distracted Consumers can easily be persuaded to ignore inconvenient facts in favor of a simple explanation, even in a World Without Secrets.

It's not a secret that John Doe No. 2 was seen by eyewitnesses, but it doesn't matter, because either *he doesn't exist* or *he's a mere facilitator.* The

INCONVENIENT FACTS

As I said before, I don't know if McVeigh acted alone. I am concerned that the government's investigation seemed to run like a game of *Jeopardy*, where the answer was: "He's the sole person responsible for the Murrah Building bombing"; the question was: "Who is Timothy McVeigh?"; and any facts that didn't support the answer were ignored or rejected.

Regarding the bomb used in the attack, retired Air Force General Benton Partin, and Samuel Cohen, a physicist and designer of the neutron bomb, have stated publicly that the fertilizer bomb in McVeigh's truck was physically incapable of causing the damage that occurred to the Murrah Federal Building.[3] Both men believe that additional bombs, placed, for example, at the base of reinforced concrete columns in the Murrah Building, must have been used in the attack, to cause the extensive damage that resulted. If so, one possible implication is that additional *bombers* were involved. A certain implication is that the attack did not occur as it was presented in the government's case, i.e., via detonation of a single bomb, whether or not a single bomber was involved. Given his qualifications, Mr. Cohen may be presumed to understand the physics of weapons and explosives pretty thoroughly—certainly better than the average federal prosecutor. Mr. Partin can be presumed to have at least a solid practical knowledge of what makes buildings fall down and go *boom!*

This chapter is about the perils of belief in Mentats, not Timothy McVeigh per se, and there's little point in listing inconvenient facts *ad nauseum*. Mentats who propose theories that don't account for all the known facts are misleading their followers. Period.

FBI said so, and we believe them. We may not distrust the evidence of our own eyes—we may in fact trust it too much—but we're willing to believe that almost any *other* evidence is of no importance when our Mentats tell us so.

This is so important that it bears repeating: *We believe that something matters when our Mentats tell us so.* In the World Without Secrets, everything is recorded and anyone can get any information that is wanted badly enough. Only one camera was running when JFK was assassinated. The

Warren Commission chose to ignore or explain away key evidence in that film when it decided officially that there was only one gunman. There were no cameras running at the Murrah Federal Building on April 19, 1995, but 10 years from now there will be hundreds running in every public space everywhere. That doesn't mean that *truth will out,* or that anyone (much less everyone) will pay attention when it does.

The *truth* is that multiple eyewitnesses saw John Doe No. 2, and the government tried to discredit all of them, for reasons unknown. Did you care then? Do you care now? Do you wonder *why?*

Would you care or wonder more if John Doe No. 2 had been video-recorded, or would he still be only a *mere facilitator?*

THE NECESSARY KNOWLEDGE IS THAT OF WHAT TO OBSERVE

I'm tempted to close this chapter with a quote from *The X-Files:* "No matter how paranoid you are, you're not paranoid enough." But paranoia per se—blanket distrust—isn't a useful operating model. It's too simple. Anyway, you knew before you read this chapter that governments lie, didn't you? (I grew up in the 1960s, and it's hard for me to believe that governments don't lie *all the time.*) If you weren't paranoid before, why start now?

Here's what matters: *Mentats have hidden power.* The way to understand the hidden power of a Mentat is to bring it to the surface. The only way to do that is to constantly ask: *Why? Why* does the Mentat want me to believe this? *Why* do *I* want to believe it?

It takes time to ask *why,* and Distracted Consumers, above all else, don't have time. Because more of us have less and less time in a World Without Secrets, a straight-line extrapolation says that more and more of us will be Distracted Consumers who are led by our Mentats.

I'm comforted by the thought that straight-line extrapolations are always wrong, but I'm still scared. The irony is that, in a World Without Secrets, where all is visible, we can so easily be led, by our own unthinking haste, to believe whatever we are told.

WHAT DO YOU SEE?

Hunter's Second Law:
When everything is known, no one knows everything.

Second Corollary:
People see only what they want to see, and that's usually what lies on the path of least resistance.

Third Corollary:
People mostly see the exceptions.

In the midst of a flood, what do you *see*?
Not the stuff in the *middle*.

CHAPTER NINE

In the Exception Economy, Be Exceptional

The Exception Economy is obvious in any professional sport. A few hundred players at the top of any game are making millions of dollars a year, like the entire roster of the NBA, and a very few are making hundreds of millions, like Michael Jordan. A few thousand more players in colleges and the minor leagues are on their way up or down and are making a lot less. Everyone else—tens of millions of individuals—is a spectator, or an amateur playing for love of the game, making zero. The shelf is abrupt, and the dropoff is sheer. There is no in-between.

Hunter's Second Law says that *When everything is known, no one knows everything.* No one can keep track of everything that's going on, and in a World Without Secrets there's more and more going on all the time. Most people will tend, over time, to pay attention only to what's *exceptional:* the stuff at the very top and the very bottom, or the stuff that's *sui generis*— too weird, beautiful, or gripping to ignore. Those exceptions become the focus of our attention, our gratitude, and our wrath.

That's the *Exception Economy.* It's gathering velocity every day as we strive to reduce what's in view to the minimum necessary to navigate a very cluttered World Without Secrets. It's a great world for superstars, because superstars thrive on attention (at least where their professional lives are concerned). It's a tougher world for everyone else, including the people who used to be more or less safely ensconced in the middle,

FORD AND FIRESTONE

The Ford Explorer/Firestone debacle is a fascinating example of how the normal—high levels of automobile accidents—can become *exceptional,* and how massive amounts of data can help to confuse the issues.

Fatal accidents involving tire failures and rollovers on Ford Explorers fitted with Firestone Wilderness AV tires began occurring in Venezuela and Saudi Arabia at least two years ago. The accidents were no secret, but Americans don't usually pay attention to auto accidents in their own country, let alone accidents in Latin America and the Middle East. When the same kind of accidents killed 80 Americans in a short period of time, not only was the problem visible; it became *exceptional,* even though, statistically speaking, about .001 percent of the Explorers on the road were involved in the accidents.

Ford and Firestone were immediately enmeshed in a scandal revolving around a single question: Whose product was at fault? The *Wall Street Journal* described in detail a meeting between Ford and Firestone engineers at which Ford used Firestone's own data to show that all the failed tires were manufactured in a single Firestone plant. (The meeting and the article are clear evidence in themselves that what used to be closely guarded corporate secrets are public knowledge in a World Without Secrets.)

Firestone countered publicly with reams of data, claiming that tire underinflation caused the problem. Ford's CEO, Jacques Nasser, in turn released data at a public press conference that purportedly proved that Firestone's tires were the sole cause of failure. Both companies are now facing lawsuits. Bridgestone/Firestone Inc.'s Chairman, John Lampe, is testifying in person in a case in Texas, an exceptional event that's clearly aimed at the entire enthralled public as well as the jury.

Both Ford and Firestone may sincerely believe that their defense is truthful. One or both may not, and may have decided that the only chance to avoid disaster is to confuse the public by throwing as much blame as possible, accompanied by masses of technical data, into the discussion. Both have suffered significant damage already; as of this writing, Ford has spent $2.1 billion on tire replacements for Explorers, and Firestone's net worth has dropped from $2.4 billion to $1.3 billion, according to Lampe. Whether or not the technical data support either company's argument, because of Hunter's Second Law— *When everything is known, no one knows everything*—there's a chance that utter disaster can at least be delayed, if not evaded.

because superstars also command a disproportionate and increasing share of rewards.

WHAT DRIVES THE EXCEPTION ECONOMY?

It's the Exceptions, Stupid

In the summer of 2001, two Americans—a man celebrating his anniversary in the Bahamas and a child on a beach in Florida—were attacked and seriously injured by sharks. Were these relatively isolated incidents more important than the more than 10,000 deaths and 50,000 injuries that occurred on American highways in the summer of 2001? They were certainly more *exceptional,* and they generated, on national television, many more hours of discussion that summer than the statistics related to motor vehicle accidents.

About 40,000 people die every year in the United States in automobile crashes, and several times that number are seriously injured. Any American now living is millions of times more likely to die or be seriously injured in a car crash than in a shark attack. A society ruled by numbers alone would be constantly aghast at the carnage happening on our highways, but, unless we happen to know one of the victims, we barely notice the accidents listed almost daily in the local paper. We've all seen *lots* of car crashes, and we're *jaded* with them. As a society, we're generally willing to let drunken 16-year-olds drive their cars, and never mind the predictable consequences. (Consider what's certain to happen in the United States in the next 5 to 10 years as a generation of inexperienced teenage drivers inherits an armada of used SUVs. Those consequences are predictable too, and we're just as unlikely to take steps to stop them.)

It's obvious, but it must be said: The first thing that drives the exception economy is *exceptions,* usually big ones. Anything that occurs frequently, any constant stimulus (no matter how intense), any product that is directly comparable in every way to any other is business as usual and inherently unnoticeable. (Ever wonder why the Rolling Stones don't tour every year?)

Relationships Matter

Multiple studies show that executives who play golf with the boss are more likely to be promoted than those who turn in outstanding performances

ARE LOW PRICES EXCEPTIONAL?

In *The Race to the Bottom* (*The McKinsey Quarterly,* 2001, No. 3),[1] Andreas Florissen, Boris Maurer, Bernhard Schmidt, and Thomas Vahlenkamp of McKinsey & Co. wrote:

> In the deregulating markets we have examined . . . incumbents almost by default worry about the lowest price being offered **rather than the most relevant.** Incumbents, in setting their own prices, should focus on those of **the competitor that is best known in the market** and has the greatest chance of luring away customers." [emphasis mine]

In other words: Watch the exceptional competitor. In a World Without Secrets, brand is more exceptional than low prices. What could be more *normal* in a world driven by Moore's Law than *falling prices?*

Along those lines, we can note that the Linux operating system's success in grabbing increasing market share from Microsoft—one of the most feared and capable competitors in the world—is based on more than the price of the software, which is zero. The story of the Open Source movement, the development model behind Linux, is exceptional. The expertise and evangelistic zeal of the individuals who lead the movement are exceptional. The software itself is high-quality, which matters in terms of holding on to the people whose attention is drawn to the product, but it's not the superiority of the software that's made Linux one of the strongest competitors to Windows NT and Windows 2000. It's the stark, exceptional contrast Linux presents to every commercial software vendor in the world.

and don't socialize. It's a simple demonstration of a simple truth: *Relationships matter.*

Relationships are exceptional. Specific places—Silicon Valley, the Research Triangle, Hollywood, Wall Street—continue to have power and cachet even in the World Without Secrets, where high-bandwidth communications are ubiquitous, and place apparently should mean little or nothing. These places represent relationships between people who are excited by and committed to the same things. There's no substitute for those relationships, no quantity of data transmitted at any speed that engenders the same kind of warmth and trust. The people, places, and things to which I have a personal attachment are, by definition, exceptional to me, just as I'm exceptional to them.

We may not trust what or whom we know, but we definitely don't trust what we don't know. Relationships authenticate us, and they authenticate others—and what they know—to us. They sustain us against both the vast, unfathomable seas of information and the threat of sudden attention in the World Without Secrets, where almost anyone can be the target of a Network Army—an army of strangers—at almost any time, for unforeseeable reasons.

People and businesses that neglect their relationships—as the record industry has neglected its relationships with the people who buy the records ceding that ground entirely to artists—will pay, possibly with their existence. If there's one thing above all that everyone should remember and do in the World Without Secrets, it's this: *Nurture relationships.*

Policy Matters

Policy plays a key role in driving the Exception Economy, because policy defines what matters and therefore what is measured. Standardized data about the effectiveness of teachers and schools will be available, starting in a few years, because the federal government is demanding it. Data about the effectiveness of doctors and hospitals will be available in the next decade because insurers and the large companies that pay for the insurance are demanding them. Information about publicly traded companies' financial results became available to all investors at the same time, instead of a chosen few, because the SEC mandated it. The inevitable result, in all these cases, is increasing rewards for highly-rated players and increasing desperation for poorly-rated ones.

Mentats Matter

Tens of thousands of novels are published every year. It's fair to say that hundreds of these are worthy or better, and dozens are brilliant works that can forever change the way a reader experiences the world. The only ones that are certain to be immediate best-sellers, regardless of their subject

CLIVE DAVIS AS MENTAT

What makes singer/songwriter Alicia Keyes exceptional? Her talent, of course; her looks; the presence of both in a single person. But what *really* makes her exceptional is the enthusiastic public recommendation of Clive Davis, the legendary executive who built Columbia Records and Arista Records into music industry powerhouses during the industry's dramatic period of expansion, from the mid-1960s on. Davis has appeared with Keyes on television to introduce her *personally* to a mass audience. In that capacity, he's acting as a powerful *Mentat,* not just the head of the record company that will profit from Keyes's success. It's Davis's cachet and reputation that tell the audience Keyes is more exceptional than every other talented, beautiful woman who has released a record this year.

Davis's Mentat status has been built via increasing public recognition of his role in pop music's most lucrative era, including a recent TV special devoted entirely to Arista Records' history and featuring many of the stars (like Whitney Houston and Carlos Santana) whose careers he promoted. The music industry executive's role as Mentat is well-established and crucial—*somebody's* got to identify the talent—but it's typically behind-the-scenes. How many people would listen seriously to any personal hype from Tommy Mottola regarding one of Sony's artists, notwithstanding that it's Mottola's job to pick winners and he has done very well at it? Davis's role as a public Mentat in this industry is exceptional.

or brilliance, are the ones Oprah Winfrey selects for her Book Club. Need I say more about the power of a Mentat to make a person, product, or event exceptional? (I will.)

To be singled out by a Mentat as an exception is not always a good thing. In late 2000, *Barron's Weekly* published a short list of Internet start-ups that *Barron's* had calculated to be perilously close to running out of cash. The crash of the Internet economy was still months away, but the stocks of those companies fell straight into big, smoking holes in the ground, within weeks of the article's publication. The Exception Economy cuts both ways.

Fewer Exceptions in More Categories = More Exceptions/Smaller Exceptions

I have a friend who teaches at Salisbury State College in Maryland. This man is very possibly the world's leading expert in biting midges, a small, unloved (biting bugs are kind of unpleasant), and very numerous insect that's found in many variations in geographies worldwide. (He's also an avid amateur harmonica player, which is how we met when I was on a consulting engagement in Salisbury.) Such specialization isn't unique in academia; a search on "academic + degree + proliferation" on www.google .com reveals hundreds of universities that are concerned about controlling increases in the number of degree programs they offer, and many others that entice degree candidates by talking about the massive proliferation of information in a given discipline. In 1999, over 40,000 doctoral degrees were awarded by American universities. Each degree candidate had to produce original research in his or her field. As a result, the fields in question are being sliced finer and finer, to the tune of 40,000 slices per year.

This expansion of knowledge is one reason why we know now when a unique variant of a species, like a snail darter, is threatened with extinction. For the snail darter, that *exception* makes a difference. Of course, the snail darter, like many leaders in relatively minor categories, is still basically a very small fish, but at least it's not extinct. (I should talk. *Harmonica?*)

Consider the explosion in the variety of sporting events at the Olympics. I was *amazed* when synchronized swimming became an official Olympic event. (I mean, *Come on!* If an announcer has to keep reminding you that what you're looking at is *really hard,* as NBC's commentators at the 2000 Summer Olympics in Sydney kept doing in reference to synchronized swimmers, then *why are we watching?* Nobody has to tell you that running 100 meters in less than 11 seconds, or doing a triple Axel, is really hard.) Now synchronized diving has made it to the exhibition stage, along with beach volleyball and lots of other rather specialized entertainments. Each of these newly minted events offers gold, silver, and bronze medalists the opportunity to be exceptional every four years.

There's only room for a few exceptions at the top of any category. (The bottom is infinitely expandable, and the middle tends to the bottom. Who placed fourth in synchronized swimming at the 2000 Summer Olympics? Who placed *second?*) In the World Without Secrets, interests and knowledge are increasingly refined and deepened, *categories multiply exponentially, and more people are offered the chance to be exceptional,* if only to a small network.

But the size of the network can be misleading. As per Hunter's First Law, *the network is an amplifier,* and a slight shift in perspective or context can cause a wider audience to see the subject at the center of the network in the same exceptional terms, even if it seems at first to be just a very small fish (or a little biting insect).

Context Matters

Stephen Ambrose sold 700,000 copies of his 1994 book *D-Day,* a massive total for any nonfiction book. He has followed it with several other books of straight history that have all been massive popular best-sellers. That's exceptional for any historian.

Ambrose jokes that his first book, which was aimed at an academic audience, sold 20 copies out of a total of 500 printed. The numbers of books he has sold lately are definitely exceptional, but he was a very good historian for decades before a big network found him. It was a shift in the context of his work—from events to the experiences of the people involved in those events—that made Ambrose resonate with a larger network. A second context—the timing of *D-Day's* publication, in the year of the fiftieth anniversary of the Normandy invasion—helped as well. Ambrose's book reached print just as popular media worldwide were preparing their own perspectives on the invasion. He became an exceptional spokesperson for NBC and added their audience to his, further amplifying his own network.

The newly popular string quartet *Bond* is composed of four young women who look and dress like pop stars and play popular styles like house, in addition to a classical repertoire. "We dress quite normally for girls our age," says one of the members of the group, like that's not outside the norm for classical musicians. It's as exceptional for a classical audience to see four bitchin' babes in street-babe clothes on stage as it is for pop audiences to hear a group like that jump from house to classical.

There's only room for a few exceptions in any category. The success-ful players, like Ambrose, become something like a brand. Any successful brand almost always has a few successful competitors, even in a minor cat-egory, but in the Exception Economy it's never more than a few.

The Network Matters

In a World Without Secrets, networks matter. *Networks are amplifiers.* Given Hunter's Second Law—*When everything is known, no one knows everything*—the amplification provided by a network is the difference between infor-mation that's effectively invisible and something that everyone knows.

A couple of years ago, a company called Antares introduced *MicMod-eler,* a piece of software that takes a digitally recorded sound and applies the sonic "signature" of any one of a few hundred microphones to it. It's a great tool for any studio that can't afford a closet full of expensive mi-crophones, and it's very useful even for the relatively few that can. ("Ex-pensive" in this class means anywhere from $2,000 to $10,000. Try loading up a cabinet with 10, 20, or 50 of those on a working person's salary.) I don't own any mics as expensive as a Neumann U-47, a Coles 4038, or a Lawson MP-47, but MicModeler makes it sound like I own all of them, and it costs a tenth of the price of one of them.

The company already had a hit product called *Auto-Tune,* which cor-rects out-of-tune notes on a recorded track. (Imagine how singers and en-gineers swoon over *that.* There are very, *very* few hit records nowadays that haven't had the Auto-Tune treatment.) Auto-Tune's success gave Antares a chance to make its case to professional audio engineers, who were nat-urally skeptical of the company's ability to duplicate the sound of their fa-vorite rare, expensive microphones in software.

While MicModeler was in development, Antares began building a net-work among pro owners of rare mics. About 150 such mics were selected by Antares to produce software "models" for the product. Involving the owners of those mics early on ensured that their ears would be enlisted in the testing of the models, and that they'd feel some sense of ownership in the development of the product as well. Antares doesn't give its products away to get testimonials, so building commitment via participation (and eliminating potential sources of opposition in the process) was essential to the development of the network.

The ability of MicModeler to satisfy the ears of prestige mic owners was an important early indicator of success. It also gave Antares an opportunity to educate users to some of the less obvious uses for the software, like taking a recorded track and changing subtle characteristics of the recording (such as the singer's apparent distance from the mic) to make the track sit better in a mix. Those applications were useful even to studios that already owned every rare, expensive mic ever made.

Beyond the exceptional technical nature of MicModeler, Antares tapped into the exceptional mystique of these rare instruments. Antares is a small company, but it spent some of its development money on a good intellectual-property lawyer, who managed to work out a way for Antares to use the actual names of the microphones for their models. "What people are buying here is dreams," Marco Alpert, vice president of marketing for Antares, told me in September 2001.[2] "It's a dream for most engineers to own these mics. The name is a big part of the dream."

When MicModeler was released, Antares flooded musicians' networks—magazines, Web sites, and word of mouth among professionals—with the news. The work already done to bring rare mic owners on board bore fruit immediately. Hunter's First Law says: *The power of a network in a given context equals the square of the number of people on the network, times the intrinsic power of those people in that context.* Antares's initial network of owner-pros had massive intrinsic power in terms of their ability to influence other pros and Mentats in the industry.

Articles in *Keyboard* and *Electronic Musician* described how engineers in major studios were using MicModeler on everything from vocals to string tracks. The engineer on a harmonica session I did for a children's record around then raved about it as he set up a Lawson MP-47 for me. "I know it's just EQ," he said (meaning that the software simply changes *equalization,* or frequency emphasis, in a track), "but it's weird. It seems like it's *more* than just EQ, y'know?" Within weeks, feedback from extremely satisfied customers began showing up at Web sites like Harmony Central (http://www.harmonycentral.com), where musicians report on their experiences with all sorts of instruments. Antares made a fully functional version of the software (with a 10-day expiration date) available at its Web site; I was one of the thousands of people who tried that download, and it had the intended effect on me.

As of this writing, Antares has sold thousands of copies of MicModeler. Software products in this specialized class are generally considered a reasonable success if they sell 50 copies a month. No competing software product has even been introduced, and the only competitive hardware product is made by Antares. MicModeler is an Exception Economy unto itself.

You, Me, and The Second and Third Corollaries to Hunter's Second Law

Hunter's Second Law says: *When everything is known, no one knows everything.* The second corollary states: *People see only what they want to see,* and the third corollary says: *People mostly see the exceptions.*

Lots of people want to know what's going on in the lives of professional athletes and other celebrities (who, by definition, are exceptional), so somebody's always looking where they're concerned, and we all know almost anything we care to know about them. Most of the rest of us are lucky enough not to have that kind of attention focused on us. (As Bill Murray said in an interview, "If you think you want to be rich and famous, why don't you just try rich, and see if that doesn't do it for you?") In a World Without Secrets, more and more of us are likely to catch someone else's interest for any of a thousand personal, professional, or inscrutable reasons. (As I write this, a copy of *People* is on my desk, open to an article about Congressman Gary Condit's formerly very private wife. Being close to any of the people involved in a murder case is enough to turn any private person into an unwilling celebrity.) Once something makes us exceptional, our ability to keep our lives private is less than that of most celebrities, who have better resources and more practice in protecting themselves.

A fascinating and disturbing example of how quickly anyone can become a noteworthy exception in a World Without Secrets can be seen at http://www.fishingcreekfarm.com, where a couple has published a documented history of their prolonged conflict with their neighbors in the Fishing Creek Farm community of Maryland. The site has drawn as many as 12,000 visitors in a single day, and has drawn e-mail comments from around the world. The progression from private dispute to public lawsuit to international *cause célèbre* (or *cause macabre*) isn't common, but it's an archetypical expansion of networks in the World Without Secrets. In a previous era, local squabbles, with rare exceptions, stayed local. Now, anyone, anywhere can choose to take a case to a worldwide court of public opinion. It's no longer necessary to wait for Jerry Springer to call.

A PORTRAIT OF THE ARTIST AS A VERY BIG (OR LITTLE) NUMBER

Film and record producers make a point of telling us how much was spent on their works, as if the fact that the remake of *Planet of the Apes* cost $100 million is important to anyone besides the studio accountants. And it is, isn't it? When you see that number, are you *completely* indifferent to it? It's a big number, man. A hundred million of *anything* gets *my* attention. (If they'd used 100 million *apes* to make that movie, I'd *have* to see it, probably twice, to make sure I didn't miss a *single ape*. To hell with the *people;* I can see 100 million of *those* any time I want.)

THE THREE TENORS

The Three Tenors are clearly exceptions. There's a huge difference in visibility (and income) for The Three Tenors compared to The Other Nine Hundred Ninety-Seven Tenors on the Planet. (Y'know, if all those other tenors got together in a group with that name, I'll bet they could get some great gigs.)

Kornfeld International, The Three Tenors' management team, has certainly created a widespread perception that The Three Tenors are significantly different, starting with the group's name. *Three* tenors are obviously, measurably different from any other (solitary) tenor. The implied significance of the difference is that these are the *three very best* tenors anywhere, so why bother with any other tenor, especially since you never heard of 'em anyway? (They might as well be named *The Only Three Tenors*. Most people can't even name two of the three tenors in The Three Tenors, let alone any other tenor.)

And what about the other 997 world-class tenors on the planet, anyway? Some of them are getting the message; one new trio of singers is called *Three Mo' Tenors*. Of course, they're just three *more* tenors, not *The* Three Tenors.

We can argue about whether that's a good thing for music in general, and in particular for the kind of music represented by The Three Tenors. My guess is that it's not, but so what? In a World Without Secrets, where Hunter's Second Law operates with increasing strength every day, we're all subject to the Exception Economy, like it or not.

In a World Without Secrets, where so many artists compete for decreasing mental bandwidth in an audience that's flooded with information, audiences are increasingly alert to *exceptional* numbers. The price of a painting, the dollars taken in by a movie in its first weekend after release, the money spent to record a new Michael Jackson record versus the number of copies sold, are more and more important in drawing our attention to exceptional works. The more extreme the numbers are—bigger *or* smaller—the better. People are just as impressed by the amazingly tiny budgets of *El Mariachi* and *The Blair Witch Project* as they are by the massive sums spent on *Pearl Harbor* or any other summer blockbuster movie. The friend who told me about Lucinda Williams's *Car Wheels on a Gravel Road* made sure I knew that it took Williams six years to make that record, and I was just as impressed as when I found out that Nirvana recorded *Nevermind* in 10 days.

BUSINESS WITHOUT SECRETS

It's *performance,* not *money,* that makes a person or a business a *player,* though money may be the most important metric to Americans. We live in a money culture, and money is one metric that's comparable in precisely the same terms everywhere.

But money isn't the first metric in any way. As in sport, money happens after an exceptional performance. It's a lagging indicator, not a leading indicator. We all know a lot already about lagging indicators that describe the flow of money through businesses worldwide. In the World Without Secrets, we'll know much, much more, and it'll be all about *performance* and *relationships*—leading indicators that are followed by money.

For a picture of what's coming in every business, look at any professional sport. Professional athletes live in an intense World Without Secrets for most of their lives. Beginning in grade school, their performance statistics are collected under carefully controlled, universally standardized conditions. At any point in an athlete's career, his or her performance can be precisely compared to that of anyone else who has ever played the same sport. From a very early age, the exceptional players get exceptional attention from everyone: coaches, parents, other players, fans, and media. Unexceptional players become exceptional, or move on to purely local amateur leagues by their early twenties, or drop the sport entirely.

The greatest players know it's not enough to master their games; they seek a role on a championship team. In the World Without Secrets, just as in sport, the arrival or departure of key performers and the relationships of leaders and followers are visible leading indicators of the presence or absence of a virtuous cycle of high performance in the business. Over time, great teams and great players find each other and create a virtuous cycle that reinforces their mutual powers. That's the essence of a dynasty like the Montreal Canadiens in hockey, or of a multigenerational business leader like General Electric.

In the World Without Secrets, as in sport, the unexceptional players and teams—those in the middle as well as those at the bottom—are increasingly forced down and out. Like athletes, *businesses, professions, and professionals are closely observed and measured.* More businesses are more like the business of sport. Exceptional performance—performance above a defined "minimum" that's set high to start and keeps going up—is the price of entry and continued participation.

The information that's available about businesses in the World Without Secrets is far more predictive, not just more but *different.* The trend that began with the arrival of the Internet—a shift in power from suppliers to customers, based on widespread availability of information—will intensify at all levels of the value chain.

THE BUSINESS IS A NETWORK

Businesses historically had lots of secrets, even from their suppliers and partners. That worked in an era when everybody, including suppliers and partners, was an adversary in one way or another. (In 1988, I attended an old-school seminar in negotiation. It was very clear, in that class, that suppliers were adversaries when it came to negotiating terms.) That approach doesn't work in the World Without Secrets. *Modern businesses are networks,* and there's very little room for secrets in a high-performance network. Everyone depends too much on everyone else.

Successful businesses focus relentlessly on their "core competencies," the relatively few things that they do better than anyone else. Anything else is outsourced to a business that makes it its core competency. The result is a value chain—essentially, a network—of businesses that have complementary core competencies and have organized their processes around a customer's value proposition. Everyone in such a network depends on everyone else, because nothing is achieved until value is delivered to the customer.

Participants in these hubs must know each other's capacities, capabilities, skills, strengths, and weaknesses. There's no other way to maintain responsiveness in such a network. Increasingly, they know about each other in concrete numeric terms that are directly comparable across all members of the network.

The End of Business-to-Business Secrets

As an example of the kinds of measurement and exchanges this implies, consider Gartner's Business Performance Measurement Framework, which is used to measure performance in what they call the "connected economy." This framework offers a measurement model for real-time exchanges of performance information between businesses. The sidebar titled *Gartner Business Performance Measurements* describes in some detail the metrics involved in measuring supply chain operational performance. (The full detail, which I'll spare the reader, makes it even more obvious how much information networked enterprises are willing to share. A given set of monitors—such as the ones for measuring supplier performance—might summarize several thousand data points to derive a handful of metrics for presentation.)

By way of full disclosure, I served previously as Vice President for Consulting in Gartner eMetrix, the predecessor offering to the Business Performance Measurement Framework. I'm familiar with their model, so it makes a convenient example. This framework could be considered to have competitors that include Datasweep, Viewlocity, and others. These competitors to Gartner's framework have their own models for measurement, but their intention—enabling the exchange of detailed performance metrics between businesses—is comparable. (The presence of competition in this market for inter-enterprise measurement, of course, is just more evidence of a trend toward an end to secrets between businesses.)

Any two businesses sharing such information know a lot about each other. They know each other's capacities for *throughput*—production volume at a given level of quality—and for *responsiveness*—the ability to deliver the right stuff, on time, to the right location, with the right quality and documentation. They know in precise detail which parts of their own and others' organizations are performing up to acceptable standards and which are not.

That's a lot to know. Why would anybody give up so much detailed information about themselves? Given the choice, most businesses, like most

Gartner Business
Performance Measurement Framework

The list below describes the areas of supply chain performance that need to be monitored—in many cases, in real time—according to the Gartner Business Performance Measurement Framework. The model includes views of performance by location, by supplier, by product line, by business unit, and by a number of other "drill-down" factors. The result is that any performance metric can be precisely linked to any location in a monitored enterprise (or collection of enterprises). Because the model is shared, enterprises can compare performance precisely.

The measurements are broken out by the key aggregate measures defined in the Framework, starting with Customer Responsiveness.

These metrics are aimed at supply chain operations and are therefore mostly applicable to manufacturing companies, but the framework can easily be adjusted to apply to a service organization.

Customer Responsiveness

> Perfect Order
> > On-Time Delivery
> > Order Fill Rate
> > > Fill Complete
> > > Fill Accuracy
> > Material Quality
> > > Damaged Material
> > > Defective Material
> > Service Accuracy
> > > Order Accuracy
> > > Invoice Accuracy
> > > Documentation Accuracy

Operational Effectiveness

> Process Throughput
> > Rolled Throughput Yield
> > > Normalized Yield
> > > Throughput Yield
> > > First Pass Yield

GARTNER BUSINESS PERFORMANCE MEASUREMENT FRAMEWORK (CONTINUED)

Inventory Management
  Forecast Accuracy
  Inventory Turns
  Inventory Days of Supply
  Inventory Obsolescence
Capacity Utilization Index
Conversion Cost Index

Supplier Responsiveness

Perfect Order
  On-Time Delivery
  Order Fill Rate
    Fill Complete
    Fill Accuracy
  Material Quality
    Damaged Material
    Defective Material
  Service Accuracy
    Order Accuracy
    Invoice Accuracy
  Documentation Accuracy

individuals, would prefer not to. But there's no choice. The alternative is to abandon all hope of playing for the most successful teams.

Who Owns the Risks?

Wal-Mart carries an opportunity risk for the Coca-Cola products on its shelves. The shelf space might be better used if Coke™ doesn't sell fast enough. Coca-Cola shares that risk as well. If a particular line of beverages doesn't sell, Coca-Cola's production capacity and capital could have been better used elsewhere. The inventory risk of the Coke on Wal-Mart's shelves isn't shared; Coca-Cola owns it. Wal-Mart pays Coca-Cola for a bottle of Coke *when a customer buys it at a Wal-Mart register.*

Plenty of information sharing between Wal-Mart and Coca-Cola is required to reduce the risks to the point where the arrangement is workable. Wal-Mart has accurate sales projections by store, enabled by a very powerful data-mining operation. Accurate projections make it feasible for Coca-Cola to bear the inventory risk and manage its manufacturing costs and schedule. Wal-Mart's data also let Wal-Mart manage the shelf space devoted to Coke effectively—for example, by stocking shelves with Coke in the most popular container sizes, on demand, where needed.

Significant risks have already been displaced by Wal-Mart onto Coca-Cola. The obvious next step is for Coca-Cola to displace some portion of its risks farther down the value chain, to Coca-Cola's suppliers. It won't be long before everybody in Coca-Cola's value chain isn't paid until Wal-Mart's customer buys a six-pack of Coke.

A lot of trust is required to make that work, and trust is based in part on disclosure. Everybody needs to know what's been sold, when, and where, and who's going to get paid for it. When there's a problem, everyone needs to know who's going to fix it. *Nobody gets paid until everybody's done their job.*

Very soon, everybody in Coca-Cola's network will know who's delivering perfect orders (the right stuff, to the right location, with acceptable quality, on time) and who isn't. Without that kind of performance information, it's impossible to surface and resolve problems rapidly, wherever they occur, anywhere in the network.

Participation in this value chain will force the elimination of secrets. Everyone will know the capabilities of everyone else in key performance areas. Everyone will know everyone else's failures. As in professional sports, no one will tolerate a player who can't cut it and can't fix it.

The technology needed to make this kind of shared risk happen throughout a value chain is already available. All that's required is demand from dominant players. That demand is building now.

e-Business, 2003–2010

Large corporations around the globe are integrating electronically with strategic partners, customers, and suppliers, using mainly Internet-based technologies. The result is private exchanges of anywhere from a few dozen to a few hundred tightly integrated businesses. According to Gartner research, by 2003 there'll be 200 to 400 such networks, or hubs, linked at the edges to a few remaining horizontal, public e-marketplaces. (In February 2001, there were over 1,500 public e-marketplaces in the world. By the end of 2002, Gartner believes there will be fewer than 50.)

By 2010, participants in most private exchanges will have continuous, real-time visibility into each other's operations via shared performance metrics. Already, key suppliers and their customers in many industries have such visibility in order to manage just-in-time inventory systems. That visibility will extend all the way to the customer within a few years.

By then, companies that can't manage their performance to competitive levels will be detected immediately and pushed out of the network. In an Exception Economy, there are only two kinds of exceptions, and only one gets to stay in the game.

As they say in the CIA, *when three people know something, it's an open secret.* With so many businesses disclosing so much information to so many internal and external personnel, the details of core competencies will be as well known to competitors, customers, and partners as financials are now. In some cases, they'll be better known. Privately owned businesses can't be forced to disclose financials, but they can be forced to disclose performance metrics if they want to participate in a network that demands them.

Performance as a Leading Indicator

Because performance metrics like responsiveness and throughput get at the heart of a company's ability to satisfy customers, they're powerful leading indicators. Good throughput and responsiveness numbers indicate a quality product and perfect orders, meaning satisfied customers. Bad numbers, if not corrected quickly, indicate damage ahead.

Initially, these leading indicators will be used by partners in a value chain network to assess and predict each other's performance. Sooner or later, they'll be used by investors and markets for the same purpose. Instead of looking backward at financials, markets will look forward to the status of customer relationships predicted by performance metrics.

Even before then, they'll be known to the players—employees at all levels of the companies involved—and both virtuous and destructive team cycles will be operating at very high levels of intensity.

High Performance Attracts High Performers.
Low Performance . . .

We choose teammates carefully, even for parlor games where the stakes are low. *Over time, top performers move to the best teams.* A top performer in any game knows that his or her status ultimately depends on playing for the winning team, not just being a great player. When enterprise performance is an open book, a top performer knows whether his or her company is a winner, just as a professional soccer player knows whether the team he's playing for has a shot at the World Cup.

The reverse is also true. Poor performers seek (or are driven to) low-performing companies, where their poor performance is less of an immediate handicap. The performance of those individuals and the companies that choose them degrades further, faster.

What to Do in a Measured World

In sports, as in business, the numbers don't tell everything. Exceptional metrics are *one* of the things, not the only thing, that make a player stand

WATER IS EXCEPTIONAL? WELL, NO.

In "Bottled Water Ads Barely Make a Splash" (October 8, 2001), *USA TODAY* noted that:

> . . . water isn't about to take over [the soft drink business]. It still accounts for just 7.6 percent, or about $6 billion, of the overall beverage business. And the relative small size of the category may be one reason why waters have had trouble establishing strong brand names within the category . . . showing the brand-identity problem, the top-selling brand still has just 13 percent of the market.[3]

Unless it's thoroughly unavailable or unpalatable, what's exceptional about *any* water? You can't make it very exceptional in terms of color or flavor without making it *not water*. If it *is* water, it's the same color and basic flavor as *every other water*. If it's got too much flavor, people start wondering what's in the water, and that makes it either exceptional in the wrong ways (*What's in this stuff?*) or completely unexceptional (like tap water, which is unexceptional to the point that people expect to get it in restaurants for free).

I don't think it's the small size of the category that makes it difficult to establish a strong brand for water. Thirteen percent of a $6 billion market is a lot bigger than Antares's business, and they've got a very strong brand in their market. It's the unexceptional nature of the product. Water's water. And we *like it* that way.

out. Dennis Rodman and Mia Hamm didn't get all those endorsements just because they could play. Markets don't invest in companies simply because the numbers look good.

Businesses that haven't yet understood the importance of focusing all their attention and effort on the things they do very, very well should do so immediately. *When everything is known, no one knows everything.* People can always choose to ignore what they don't want to see and focus their attention on the things that excite them. But as the power of performance metrics as leading indicators is increasingly understood, companies will be asked to provide those numbers up front, and it will be harder and harder to explain—to customers, to capital markets, to prospective and current employees—if they don't look good.

Any musician knows that she'd better figure out what her best songs are, because if she doesn't, the audience will do it for her. Can there be any doubt that the audience knows, especially in a World Without Secrets?

ART IS EXCEPTIONAL, OBJECTS ARE NOT

Relationships matter. Networks matter. Context matters.

If your relationships are troubled, if the networks are bypassing you, and if the context is disruptive technological change, your industry is in trouble.

CHAPTER TEN

Art Without Secrets

The World Without Secrets is already flooded with intellectual capital, including artistic works of all kinds. The mass of intellectual capital will grow at an increasing rate in the next 10 years. For everyone who makes a living from the creation, sale, and distribution of original intellectual works—including journalists, painters, musicians, poets, novelists, directors, producers, television and film executives, record companies, music and video retailers, and many, many others—there are at least two problems. Not only must they struggle to be heard and seen in a World Without Secrets. They must struggle also to be *paid*.

WHO WINS AND WHO LOSES?

The effects of the World Without Secrets aren't the same for all the creative professions listed above, or even for all the players in a given intellectual property industry. Certain characteristics are key to the impact of digital technologies on the business of intellectual capital:

- Is the output of the creative process an *object,* or a *performance?*
- If the output is an object, can the object be *comprehensively* represented and distributed in a digital form?

Performers in general have much to gain, and little to fear, from digital technologies because digital copies of their work *aren't the same thing as the performance.* The value of the performance *rises* with widespread distribution of digital copies. The people whose business is *promoting and selling recorded works* have a lot to fear because *their revenue is based on the object, not the performance.*

Digital Objects Are at Risk

The most dramatic negative effects of unauthorized digital duplication and distribution are suffered by artists like writers and filmmakers, who create *tangible objects that can easily and completely be represented in digital form.* Such objects are basically collections of information—sounds, images, and text—in a fixed form. I'll refer to these from now on as "digital objects," even though they may exist in other forms (like a reel of film, or a book with paper pages) before they're converted to bits and bytes. In any case, because the forms are fixed, a "performance" of the work is indistinguishable from the work itself, and every performance is exactly the same.

For such works, sales or rentals of copies are usually the most important source of revenue for the entire industry value chain. Unauthorized duplication and distribution of digital objects damages revenues for everyone in the value chain, including artists, distributors, and supporting trades and disciplines. (Music *recording companies* are threatened in exactly this way, but *musicians* are also *performers.* I'll discuss the distinction in greater detail below.)

Pricing in an industry that depends on digital objects is *always* at risk, *even when there's zero unauthorized duplication and distribution.* Not only is a digital object at risk of theft. Even if it's never stolen, its price on the open market tends to zero over time, because digital objects are never scarce, and manufacturing costs are always near zero. Prices may decline all the way to zero if a "market breaker" competitor is willing to give a digital object away in order to sell something else.

The Value of Three-Dimensional Objects Increases

In a World Without Secrets, where copies of almost everything are common, authenticity and uniqueness are rare and valuable. Artists who create *tangible objects that can't be comprehensively represented in digital form,* such as sculptors and painters, are *positively* affected by digital duplication and distribution. The essence of a three-dimensional work—its existence in physical reality and its uniqueness—can't be digitally duplicated and distributed. Only *one* person in the world can possess an original painting or sculpture. It's easy to make and distribute digital *images* of a painting or sculpture, of course. Those images are like advertisements for the uniqueness and authenticity of the original, and they enhance its value.

Artists typically sell a painting or sculpture once, to its first owner; they never collect any money from resale of the work. It will soon be easy for artists to track sales of original works over time. The technologies of the World Without Secrets make it easy both to establish a work's authenticity via embedded digital signatures and to track a work's location, which can be used as a proxy for changes in ownership. Whether this capability translates into common business practice remains to be seen. In particular, artists at the beginning of their careers tend to have very little leverage over dealers and clients. If such practices take root in the industry, they're likely to start at the top and work down.

Performing Artists Gain

Certain arts, like theater or ballet, begin with a tangible artifact like a script or a score, but the art is ultimately expressed in a performance in front of a live audience. Even when the performance is filmed, the essence of the audience experience is missing from the recording. A performance is therefore a unique experience that can't be thoroughly duplicated and distributed, digitally or otherwise. An audience seeing a video or listening to a recording of the performance is always aware that *something is missing,* and they're willing to pay for that something.

Artists whose work is expressed in performance stand to gain from even unauthorized duplication and distribution of recordings of their work in the World Without Secrets (see Table 10.1). It's just like painting and sculpture (or, for that matter, professional baseball): The image of the real thing only increases demand for the real thing. Any performing artist whose work is worth seeing and hearing can arguably benefit from distribution of his or her art to everyone on the planet, free or otherwise. Such distribution effectively functions as advertising, and in the World Without Secrets it's more or less free. (No other form of worldwide advertising is even remotely close to free.) One of the arguable points, of course, is how much free distribution is maximally beneficial to the artist.

The same is not true of the players in a given industry who make their money selling recorded performances. They're selling digital objects, and their livelihood is deeply threatened.

TABLE 10.1   IMPACT OF DIGITAL DUPLICATION AND
DISTRIBUTION ON THE ARTS

ART	SUPPORTING INDUSTRY	ARTIST REVENUE	INDUSTRY REVENUE
Prose fiction	Publishing	Loss	Loss
Sculpture/painting	Galleries	Gain	Gain
Dance/ballet	Dance production	Gain	Gain
Poetry	Publishing	Loss (writing) Gain (performance)	Loss
Music performance	Music recording and distribution	Loss (recording) Gain (performance)	Loss
Film	Film production	Loss	Loss
Theatre	Theatre production	Gain	Gain

RELATIONSHIPS MATTER: THE FATE OF THE MUSIC INDUSTRY

We can see all these forces at work right now in the music industry. The structure of the industry includes artists whose essential business is performance; they stand to gain a lot in a World Without Secrets. Dealers in digital objects such as recordings—record companies, retail outlets, and many recording artists—stand to lose.

What's especially fascinating is how the arrival of digital duplication and distribution technologies has laid bare conflicts between the recording industry and the audience that buys the products. The crisis in this industry is partly about technology, but it's also a crisis in relationships. Rightly or wrongly, consumers are convinced that artists don't get paid enough and audiences pay too much, and the industry's relationship to the consumer is too weak to counter the perception. Dissatisfied consumers therefore believe they have a moral justification to circumvent the industry, and digital technologies provide the technical means to do so.

THE ECONOMICS OF LONG-PLAYING PLASTIC

The key to the crisis facing the recording industry is its dependence on long-playing formats. The industry's current dependence on the CD format is a case in point. The most important threat that digital music technologies pose to the industry is simple: They enable pricing and distribution on a single-song basis. *Single-song pricing is a stake in the heart of recording industry revenues, even if losses from piracy drop to zero.*

Suppose you went to the grocery store and you couldn't buy a box of your favorite cereal without buying 10 other cereals, at a cost of 10 to 15 times the price of the cereal you really wanted? The CD format (like the vinyl LP and the cassette before it) allows the industry to bundle one or two songs that are relatively expensive to produce (i.e., the hits) with others that are much cheaper to record, and sell the whole package at a price far greater than a single-song package could command (currently, $17 to $18 at retail in the United States). In 1999, over 60 percent of recording industry revenues in the United States resulted from CD sales. (Another 9 percent resulted from cassette sales—another long-playing format whose sales are converting to CD sales at a rate of about 20 percent per year.)[1]

The industry bears high up-front costs for promotion of recordings, most of which lose money in the marketplace. "An average music video at the moment costs $250,000 or more for a major label to produce," Miles Copeland, artist manager and former president of IRS Records, told me in an interview in August 2001.[2] "Some labels spend more. Independents spend less. Other marketing—such as radio promotion—costs about $200,000 per single. A major label has often spent $800,000 or more— sometimes much more—in marketing and promo by the time they've broken, or dropped, a new act." Most new acts don't justify the outlay. Four percent of all artists generate over 80 percent of all sales; most major-label releases sell a few thousand copies or less, and the break-even point is closer to 90,000 copies.

The growth of promotional costs more than offsets any reduction in manufacturing costs for CDs during the past decade. Retail demand for recorded music is apparently dropping. Unit sales of CDs have declined slightly on a per-year basis since 1995, when a major replacement cycle (CDs' replacing vinyl LPs) ended. No major label has tried to stimulate demand by significantly reducing retail prices across the board; it seems clear that the executives who run those companies don't believe that any resulting added demand will increase overall revenues.

If the industry can't afford to reduce the retail cost of a CD, what happens if pricing is by the *song?* Answer: Revenues drop. Assume that a few years from now, instead of selling 940 million CDs in the United States (the total for 1999) at $15 apiece, the industry sells *three times* that amount of digital songs at $2 apiece, plus 450 million CDs at current prices. The result is essentially zero revenue growth. If fewer CDs are sold in favor of single-song purchases, or if pricing pressure from digital downloads has caused CD prices to drop, or if consumers don't really want all those songs anyway, growth turns negative.

Digital Music as a *Disruptive Technology*

In his book *The Innovator's Dilemma,* Clayton Christensen describes the following characteristics of a *disruptive technology:*

- It offers a new value proposition that includes *less* functionality, a *lower* price, and *lower* margins than the established products.
- It has *different* features that appeal to a *new* market. It's not just a substitute for existing products when it's first introduced. Over time, it evolves to include more features, and eventually it pushes established technologies out of the established markets.
- It's marketed by a new value chain. The low margins, and the prices that go with them, don't appeal to the established value chain. The new market it appeals to isn't rich enough, at least at first, to excite established industry players. In fact, established players can't size the new market *at all* because there's no historical data to define the demand for the new product.

Single-song digital distribution qualifies, on all these counts, as a disruptive technology. A single-song digital download offers fewer features and functions than a packaged CD (and far less than a DVD). An MP3 has lower sound quality than a standard CD. The margins and prices are obviously much lower than they are for either current CD pricing or subscription pricing; in fact, they are so low that they're of no interest to established players. The established value chain of retail distributors and record companies can't make money on the single-song product. An upstart value chain of independent artists and record companies *may* be able to make money on it, even if they have to use the music as a loss leader for other products.

Disruptive technologies remake entire industries. The success of the recorded music industry in avoiding that fate depends on its ability to avoid single-song distribution. The problem is that, in a World Without Secrets, it's no more expensive or difficult to distribute music on a single-song basis, and everyone knows it. (One bundle of bits weighs almost the same as any other.) So, what do you do?

If you're in the recording industry, you try to convince consumers that they don't really want just the songs they want. You tell them they want more music for more money, not less for less.

Subscription Pricing

Let's go back to the grocery store. Suppose that I'm tired of buying 10 times the amount of cereal I want, just to get the cereal I really want. The people who make the cereal could just sell me the cereal I really want, but then they'd lose out on all the other cereal they've been selling me. The fact is: *Nobody* really wants the other stuff anyway, so the people who make it will have to write off a lot of cereal if I can buy only what I really want.

One day, I find out that I can get the cereal I want for *free*. The quality is slightly lower, but it's good enough. It's also *stolen* from the people who make the cereal, but *I don't care*. In my mind, those cereal makers have been charging me 10 times what the cereal's worth for a long, *long* time. I don't mind taking the money out of their pockets for a change. I've got a lot of sympathy for the farmers who grow the grain that goes into the cereal, but I believe they're getting screwed by the cereal makers, too.

The cereal makers figure they'd better do something quick. They can't give me what I really want; how can they make money trying to sell me what I can get for free? Then they come up with a great idea. Everybody loves all-you-can-eat deals! The cereal makers decide that they're going to charge me $10 a month for all I can eat of any cereal I want. They'll even throw in some other stuff, like pictures of the farmers growing the

---

THE REDUCED VALUE OF MORE IN A WORLD WITHOUT SECRETS

In a World Without Secrets, there's way too much information already, and music is just *more information*. Only the most uncritical listener wants *more music*, for example, teenagers want to see and hear everything Brittney Spears does. Everybody else wants better music, and they don't want to plow through everything in the world to get it.

It remains to be seen whether an industry-run subscription service can help an audience find *better* in addition to *more*. If they can't, the value proposition for the buyer becomes untenable very quickly.

grain, not to mention all sorts of useful recipes and hints for cereal-box arts projects. Everybody should be happy now, right?

Well, not exactly. There's a limit to how much cereal I can eat, and I still want only a certain kind of cereal. No matter how much is available, I'm not going to eat more of it. The $10-a-month tab is also at least one-third more than I was spending on cereal before, so it cuts into my budget for other food. The way the deal works out, I end up paying more for pretty much the same stuff I was getting before.

In a little while, I'm back to stealing cereal. How else do I get the stuff I really want without buying a lot of stuff that I don't want?

YES, IT REALLY WORKS JUST LIKE THAT

One current recording industry model for digital distribution is based on subscription pricing, pretty much as I've described it above, with an important extra value-reducing twist. Consumers will pay $10 per month for unlimited downloads of music and other artist-related materials, such as tour guides, lyrics, photos, and so on. The reduced-value feature is that downloaded music will no longer be playable when a subscription ends.

The average consumer now buys six CDs per year at a cost of $90. This scheme proposes that consumers will pay 33 percent more to *rent* the music that they would own if they made a conventional purchase. The deal is pretty clearly unattractive for even moderately sophisticated consumers. It may seem more attractive to the youngest teenagers and preteens. (In industrialized nations, the supply of teenagers is diminishing in proportion to the overall population, so the approach had better succeed quickly.)

It has been said that the recording industry is a $100 billion business hiding inside a $40 billion industry. But the major labels aren't acting as though they see tremendous untapped demand. They're acting like a mature industry that has essentially stable demand, and raising prices on the installed base is the only way to increase revenues. Another possible explanation is that the high pricing of subscription services is intended to avoid channel conflict with traditional—that is, nonelectronic—retail and wholesale CD distributors. High subscription prices reduce the conflict by encouraging most consumers—who really don't need all the extra stuff—to continue buying the old-fashioned way (see Table 10.2).

Either way, the survival of the industry in its current form depends less on collecting revenues for digital downloads than on controlling the

TABLE 10.2 MUSIC INDUSTRY MODELS, OLD AND NEW

MODELS	OLD	NEW
Format	CD	Digital download
Promotion	Recording company	Network Army
Product	Industry-configured bundle	Single song or personally-configured bundle
Distribution	Massive physical distribution network	Reduced physical distribution network

format in which the music is distributed. Control over the format equals control over price. And it's the format that digital distribution threatens most directly.

. . . of a Revolution, Indeed

O.A.R. (". . . Of A Revolution") is a rock band whose short expanding career shows how artists can bypass the record industry in a World Without Secrets and go directly to the audience. Since 1997, without either significant radio play or major label backing, the band has sold over 50,000 copies of three records. Its most recent release, titled *Risen,* sold 13,000 copies, via Internet dealer CDBaby, in its first month of sales.

Here's what members of the band said about their promotional techniques in an interview published in *Performing Songwriter* in June 2001:[3]

> We finished high school and we had this record we'd done for friends. We're very lucky that we have a lot of friends that go to a lot of different colleges. So we said, "Here guys, you take twenty, you take twenty . . ." Months later, they're calling and saying, "Hey, people like this shit." So we'd send more and say, **"Give away half, sell half."** [emphasis mine]
>
> . . . kids started going on the Internet and picking up new music there, and we came along right at the time that started getting popular. It really helped us out . . . we have a couple of guys who are really loyal to us who come down and tape shows and put them up on a server so you can go and get all these performances.
>
> These buddies of ours started taping shows and the next thing you know, all these kids are trading tapes and coming to shows and buying CDs. So, our show-taping policy has been to let people do whatever they want. **Tape whatever you want, just don't sell it. You can give it away to anybody.** [emphasis mine]

> . . . our fans are really loyal. Even though they have access to every live show we've played and to so much free stuff, they're still glad to buy the CDs—to support us and to have the complete experience.

This band illustrates perfectly the principle that, in a World Without Secrets, *the network is an amplifier.* O.A.R. built a Network Army, starting with their friends, and fed the army with free recordings. The Network Army grew, and it responded to the gifts by paying for recordings and attending performances. The relationship between the band and its audience is well on the way to being indefinitely self-sustaining, and it is *not* dependent on revenue from record sales.

The strategy is based on widespread recording *distribution,* not recording *revenues.* The obvious leader in developing this strategy was the Grateful Dead. Their nonchalance toward recording revenue was so extreme that they actively encouraged and supported their fans in making and distributing "bootleg" recordings of the band's performances. In return, the band enjoyed, worldwide, a 30-years-plus career of sold-out concerts at the stadium level. During that entire time, they never had a hit record. (Lead guitarist Jerry Garcia was once asked by an interviewer from *Rolling Stone* why the band never had a hit. "We're not good enough," Garcia explained. Aw, *Jerry.* It's *never* been about how *good* you were, man.)

The Grateful Dead have been followed by Phish, the Dave Matthews Band, the String Cheese Incident, and O.A.R. A performance-based revenue model is apparently viable—more so in a digital environment than in the world of analog tapes where the Grateful Dead began their career. In this model, maximum distribution of recordings—even at zero revenue, as in the case of bootleg performance recordings—maximizes opportunities for performance-related revenues.

A similar story is told by "The String Cheese Incident," a band that has grown since 1994 into a business with 50 employees and millions of dollars in annual revenue. In an interview in *Performing Songwriter* in June 2001, they said:[4]

> The Internet has definitely played a big role in getting our music out there. . . . People have been taping shows and trading tapes from the very beginning, and now people trade tapes online . . . there's a huge community of fans that's been built via the online trading of tapes.

The network is an amplifier. Increased distribution feeds the network. To work *for the artist,* the distribution doesn't have to be paid. In that sense, in a World Without Secrets, the interests of the *performing* artist are arguably more closely aligned with the interests of the audience than they are with the interests of a recording company. This is an important potential source of downward pressure on prices.

To say that a business model based on performance revenues is viable doesn't mean it's *viable for all*. All musicians aren't performers per se. "How are the Moody Blues supposed to make a living?" Copeland asked me rhetorically. "Back catalog sales are a big portion of their income. There are lots of songwriters whose *only* income is publishing and catalog sales." It's also not just about the musicians. "Record companies essentially break even on new record sales—if that," Copeland said. "They make money on the catalog. Growth in the catalog from year to year is what increases revenues. New record companies aren't profitable until the catalog has increased to the point that it generates ongoing revenues."

The clear implication is that independent record companies—more so than either performing artists or major labels—are terrifically vulnerable to the potential for lost recording revenues via digital downloads. If we assume that digital distribution will indeed reduce recording revenues—via single-song distribution, if nothing else—then a logical conclusion is that independents are significantly endangered. Not only will industry growth be flat or negative; the percentage of business going to the majors will increase. The industry will be smaller and more concentrated.

There may be implications here for artists in other media, whose work is distributed as a digital object. Homer wasn't a novelist; only after his death was his work delivered, in written form, to a worldwide audience. He was a singer. *The Odyssey* was his song. He *performed* it.

INDEPENDENTS: THEY'RE EVERYWHERE. ARE THEY DANGEROUS?

Independents currently account for 24 percent of the recording industry's sales worldwide—a bigger share than any of the majors. On June 26, 2001, Shawn Fanning of Napster announced a deal with the Association of Independent Music (AIM), a British trade group. AIM represents more than 25 percent of the U.K.'s music market, with over 150 independent labels and platinum-selling artists such as Moby, Tom Jones, and Tricky.

Alison Wenham, chief executive of AIM, made it clear that it was all about getting AIM's artists in front of the biggest possible audience. "We are neither culturally nor financially attuned to long litigation to protect copyright," she said. "But **this deal covers labels for whom access to the formal market is difficult.**" [emphasis mine].[5]

Members of the indie band Ash were even more blunt (as quoted at AIM's website, http://www.musicindie.org/intro/News/Press_Releases /aim_napster_press_release_26_06_01.asp): "Anybody that thinks Napster is taking sales away from artists and record companies is severely out of touch with modern contemporary culture. It is one of the best promotional tools in the world and we are very excited about it becoming a legitimate system for distribution of music." And if it doesn't, we may infer, it's still one of the best promotional tools in the world.

The meaning of this agreement could not be clearer: *Independents want access to the consumer.* It costs nothing now to give the music away, and if that's what it takes to get access to the consumer, they'll do it. But it's a significant gamble. There's no guarantee that access to the consumer at a price of zero will eventually translate into paid access. If it doesn't, independents have no alternative revenue stream. "If I question the viability of the majors, I have to double-question the viability of independents," Copeland told me.

Even so, the independents can go digital more easily than the majors. As per Clayton Christensen, established players in any industry are unlikely to adopt a disruptive technology. Everyone in the value chain depends on the established technology. In the record business, that includes wholesale and retail distributors. *They* are *more* dependent on the physical CD than the major labels. Not only does it provide the majority of their current revenues from sales of music, but their share of revenue from digital distribution will likely tend to zero unless they make drastic changes in their business model.

Established distribution channels are less significant to independents because independents tend to be crowded out of those channels. Independents therefore have greater potential to put significant pricing pressure on the entire recording industry via free downloads and single-song pricing, whether or not it's suicidal for independents in the long run. In the short run, it gets them access to the consumer that they don't have now.

On the production side, computer-based approaches to performing and recording music have dramatically reduced the cost of entry for independent production teams and musicians. In some dance-oriented genres, such as techno and house, hit records have been made by producers working in their bedrooms with a few thousand dollars' worth of equipment. The music industry's response is to drive mainstream commercial production values higher. However, digital distribution—especially single-song distribution—puts pressure on the industry to reduce the overall level of

THE ECONOMICS OF ARTISTIC INDEPENDENCE

For artists selling fewer than 100,000 units per recording, a contract with a major label may result in significantly *less* income. An artist selling 20,000 units in a year independently will gross $140,000 to $200,000 from those sales. By contrast, after Shawn Colvin sold hundreds of thousands of copies of her album *A Few Small Repairs,* the record had still not recouped recording and promotion costs, and Colvin had been paid nothing beyond the recording advance.

No independent will ever achieve the mega-sales that a major label can produce. But most independent musicians can live pretty well on $200,000 a year. When Aimee Mann went independent with her record "Bachelor #2," she was able to gross almost half a million dollars in a few months via sales of 50,000 digital downloads. That money is far too small to interest a major label, but to an artist it's an independent life.

production values, because raising production values for every recorded song to the level of a hit is far too expensive. Even if audience expectations for production values hold steady overall, the cost of bringing finished products to market will continue to drop, further reducing production costs as a barrier to entry.

WHAT ABOUT THE RELATIONSHIP?

What's Mariah Carey's current record label? What label initially released all of the Beatles' recordings? Whether or not you know—whether or not you consider yourself a Mariah Carey or Beatles fan—do you *care?* Does the name of a record company imply anything connected to your interests in the same sense that the brand of a car, a soft drink, or a lipstick does? Could you say that the brand of any of the five major recording companies stands for anything that's different from the others?

Everything starts with relationships. The recording industry doesn't have a direct relationship with the people who buy its products. With rare exceptions, the audience cares about the artists, not the recording companies that distribute their works. The public wouldn't care if the label on the recordings changed—or if there was no label at all, beyond the artist's name. Customer relationships are apparently so bad that a significant portion of the public thinks it's more acceptable, from a moral as well as a financial perspective, to download songs from Napster or MP3.com than to pay the record company.

In a World Without Secrets, people need help figuring out what's worth their time and attention. Amazon.com is capable of filling that role. It knows what people have bought, and it can reference other buyers' purchases to figure out what they might want to buy next. Record companies don't have that connection. They're three steps removed from the audience, behind artists, distributors, and media such as television and radio. Even if they weren't, they're not trusted.

The segment of the industry that has the closest connection to the consumer is the artist. That segment also has the most to gain from digital distribution.

Pricing and Customer Risk

The consumer bears all the risk of discovery when he or she buys music by an unknown artist, and, at $17 to $18 per CD, it's a fairly substantial risk. When consumers, on average, buy only six CDs a year, there's probably not a lot of experimentation going on, and the high price of a CD is a likely contributing factor. In a World Without Secrets, there's more and more material to look at, and consumers need a reason to take the chance.

Single-song pricing via digital distribution reduces the consumer's risk. *Free* downloads reduce the customer's risk all the way to zero. Independents present a bigger discovery risk to the consumer because, by definition, they're more often unknown. It makes sense that, for this reason also, independents will use digital distribution and free or near-free pricing as tools to create relationships with audiences.

STRATEGIES FOR RECORD INDUSTRY VIABILITY

Record companies don't have healthy relationships with consumers. The tide of technology is running against them, and there are plenty of people who can potentially use the technologies against them, legally and otherwise. High-bandwidth connections to the Internet—currently growing slowly, but sooner or later spreading rapidly—will only increase the pressure. What strategies might keep the industry viable in its current form? By extension, what strategies might work for *any* intellectual capital industry threatened by the technologies of the World Without Secrets?

STRATEGY 1: KILL DIGITAL DISTRIBUTION

Arguably, the best digital distribution strategy for the recording industry is to *kill digital distribution so that CD sales can continue indefinitely*. For the entire major-label value chain, it's certainly the strategy with the clearest payoff in the short term. Can it work?

The Legal Kill

The strategy the industry used against Napster was a legal variation of the kill-digital-distribution strategy based on property rights, as opposed to a marketing defense based on a superior value-add to the consumer. (Napster gave its customers exactly what they wanted at the lowest possible price, so its value-add was, in fact, superior.) It's definitely against the law to make and distribute unauthorized copies of recorded music without compensation to the owners, and Napster's business model, truly amounted to little more than redistributing stolen goods. The recording industry's legal strategy was morally justifiable as well as effective.

Legal strategies aimed at digital distributors are going to get harder to carry out. Napster had business offices and corporate officers to attack. They were trying to make money, of course, and a digital distributor motivated by something besides money—say, a bunch of college kids spread out over the entire globe—would be harder to find and sue or prosecute. A legal strategy wouldn't work at all in a situation in which artists and independent labels explicitly authorize a Napster-like service to give the product away.

Legal strategies against distributors are most likely to succeed in preventing *unauthorized digital distribution of a major-label* product. They're not likely to succeed completely, and authorized digital distribution of independent products will put pressure on the uniform pricing (for CDs and for other bundled formats) that has sustained major-label margins.

How Far Can It Go?

In May 2001, the industry pushed its legal strategy all the way to the border between privacy and property rights. The industry filed a lawsuit alleging that Aimster's instant messaging service promoted illegal exchanges of copyrighted music. Aimster responded that it had no "right or responsibility" to violate the privacy of its users, which it would have to do to know which messages contained copyrighted music.

Aimster's advertisements certainly implied that its service made it easy to exchange MP3s. The response may be disingenuous, but the argument's real. If the recording industry wins its lawsuit, a potential implication is that the industry has the right to examine any electronic correspondence—or to force the carrier to do so—in order to protect its intellectual property rights. That's a lot of power, and the industry's not likely to get it. Courts in the United States historically give greater weight to the public's right to privacy than to anyone's right to compensation. Even *with* that power, it's no easy technical matter to identify digital music files in a mass of instant messages. There are all sorts of technical ways to disguise the nature of a file, and many hackers will be glad to accept the challenge.

What can the industry do next, even if it wins? File suit against AOL for allowing e-mails that might contain MP3 files? If people don't want the government reading their e-mail, they surely don't want AOL or Sony doing it. It's impossible to calculate the resulting consumer hostility.

A wild card here is the recent change in public attitudes following the events of 9-11-01. If the recording industry can succeed in linking unauthorized digital distribution to secretive terrorist activities in the mind of the public, it may very well succeed in getting the authority to monitor communications for stolen content, or in enlisting law enforcement agencies to do it for them.

The Personal Kill

If you can't go after the people who distribute the stuff, you can always try prosecuting the people who buy it. If lawsuits against generalized carriers such as Aimster are unsuccessful in ending *illegal* digital distribution, this is a logical next step. But it's a high-risk approach.

To directly threaten individual users with capture and punishment, the industry would have to obtain their identities. Technically speaking, in a World Without Secrets, there are lots of ways to do that, *but almost all of them are deceptive.* For example, hidden functions could be planted in a "free" program or music CD to surreptitiously scan a user's hard disk or MP3 player for illicit copies. It's obvious, even from this brief description, that any such approach is deeply intrusive and damaging to relationships. (It may also be illegal soon in the United States.)

Most marriages in which one partner hires a private detective to spy on the other partner quickly end in divorce. However users are identified, it's hard to see how the industry will benefit if the people who buy music think they're being spied on by the companies that sell it. How many such users will ever buy any commercial recording again, from that company or from any other? How many such users will become active "terrorists" against the industry?

The recording industry might simply try persuading people that copying and distributing music is *wrong*, but I doubt that persuasion will work. The industry's relationships with artists and consumers are widely perceived as one-sided and unfair. When people think laws are unfair, they

PERSONAL KILL, INDEED

In August 2001, I wrote the piece of this chapter titled "The Personal Kill." When I wrote that "If you can't go after the people who distribute the stuff, you can always try prosecuting the people who *buy* it," I didn't dream that the industry would try anything *immediately*. "It's a high-risk approach," I said. It still is, but the industry is taking its chances.

On October 15, 2001, *Wired News* reported: "The recording industry wants the right to hack into your computer and delete your stolen MP3s . . . ." The article (by *Wired*'s Declan McCullagh) described in detail the RIAA's attempts to promote federal legislation that would give them the right to scan a computer user's hard disk, *without the knowledge of the user*, and delete unauthorized music files from the hard disk, *without the user's prior knowledge or consent*. The original language of the amendment was apparently intended as well to absolve the industry of any responsibility for unintended damages resulting from such actions (like, for example, damaging the user's hard drive):

> No action may be brought under this subsection arising out of any impairment of the availability of data, a program, a system or information, resulting from measures taken by an owner of copyright in a work of authorship, or any person authorized by such owner to act on its behalf, that are intended to impede or prevent the infringement of copyright in such work by wire or electronic communication.[6]

I can't believe that approaches like this will result in anything but damage to the industry's interests, but we may not have seen the last of them. It's easy to be punitive when you don't know your customers.

ignore them or actively try to defeat them. That's what they've done historically with laws aimed at controlling the use of drugs such as alcohol and narcotics. That's what many people clearly felt entitled to do when they downloaded songs from Napster. It's a reflection of the customer relationship problem, which isn't going away any time soon.

Ubiquitous Recording Devices Make the Problem Bigger

The problem for the recording industry will get much worse around 2005 to 2008, when button-size audio and video recording devices will be *everywhere.* At any given performance, half the crowd will probably be recording the show. (The other half could if they wanted to.) "Bootleg" recordings of virtually every artist with a following will be available, with or without the artist's blessing. Bootlegs will be an acceptable alternative to commercial recordings for many consumers, just as bootleg Grateful Dead performance tapes are preferred by many of their fans. (It's *better stuff* than the studio recordings, and the band said go ahead and tape. Okay?)

By 2006, long- and short-range high-bandwidth wireless networks will be in place, and they'll undoubtedly be followed by unauthorized live video broadcasts from concert halls. It's likely that broadcast "jamming" equipment will be installed in many public performance spaces. That won't stop on-site bootleg recording, but it will stop on-site streaming to the Internet.

Demand Makes Markets, Demand Sustains Them

Historically, no one has ever been able to completely shut down a market, legal or illegal, for a product that's in demand, whether the product is drugs, black market food and medicine, gambling, prostitution, or anything else. Where there's widespread lawbreaking, there are basically two choices.

First, you can criminalize the large segments of the population that are part of the market. That's what the United States did during the past two decades, in an attempt to control illegal drug use. We've criminalized a bigger percentage of the population than any other country in the world—about half for drug offenses—and the drug trade is still flourishing. When all is said and done, people really *want* the stuff, and the market won't go away.

Second, you can change the law to decriminalize the behavior. That's what occurred when Prohibition was repealed following the election of

President Franklin Roosevelt. I doubt that we'll decriminalize violations of copyright law just to make it possible for people to listen to stolen songs in peace.

I also doubt that most industrial societies will fine or jail large numbers of otherwise law-abiding citizens for listening to illegal copies of their favorite music. The implication is that digital duplication and distribution of music will continue to be widespread, largely uncontrolled, and at least occasionally illegal.

The Technical Kill

Can the industry prevent unauthorized duplication by technical means? The short answer is: Probably not, but the industry will certainly try.

We're talking about digital *duplication* and *distribution,* so a technical solution would prevent one, or the other, or both of those. It's very unlikely that the industry will be able to come up with a technical solution to unauthorized *duplication.* A collection of bits can always be copied. It's the essential nature of the medium. As of this writing, major labels are manufacturing and selling CDs using a Macrovision coating that generates noise that's supposedly inaudible to the human ear, but *very* audible once the music is rerecorded to a hard drive. Given the industry's relationships with its customers, it's regrettable, but not surprising, that the technical solution to the duplication problem is to degrade the product. Neither this nor other technical schemes are likely to work for very long. What one programmer can engineer, another can reverse-engineer. Further, much of the industry's valuable back catalog is already digitally recorded on standard CDs that can easily be duplicated.

Regarding technical approaches to preventing unauthorized distribution, we can state it simply: It's not easy, and it's probably not possible without massive violations of privacy in electronic communications. I wouldn't put it past the recording industry to try—Microsoft and Netscape have already engaged in similar invasions of consumer privacy, such as surreptitious communications and hard drive scans—but I don't expect it to succeed for long. I don't know how much damage to customer relationships any industry can tolerate and survive, but such practices would produce a lot of damage very quickly.

The software industry has faced this problem before, and it's instructive to see how it has been handled in that business. The industry's enforcement efforts are mainly aimed at businesses, not individuals. Very few software manufacturers still use elaborate copy-protection schemes or hardware devices aimed at preventing unauthorized copying. Software gets stolen, but the industry, overall, grows quickly—mainly, by delivering better products at lower costs to an expanding market. Innovation in delivery of "better products at lower cost" is clearly not a current recording industry strategy, though "better products at higher cost" (e.g., DVD) might be. It's also clear that the music industry hasn't expanded at the rate of the software industry, which may be the crux of the industry's fear of lower prices.

Strategy 1 Summary: No Can Kill

The Japanese were able to put the genie back in the bottle when gunpowder first appeared on their islands. Possession of gunpowder became a crime, and the Samurai maintained their monopoly on power for 200 years.

That's not going to happen here. The recording industry can't make the technologies of digital duplication and distribution go away. For one thing, those technologies are used in lots of applications besides music duplication and distribution, in lots of industries. They're not going back in the bottle.

By extension, the technologies involved will trouble every industry that sells a product that can be completely digitized. There are other strategies that may mitigate the effects; these too have significant flaws.

STRATEGY 2: MONOPOLIZE BANDWIDTH

If you can't make the competitors go away, perhaps you can make them invisible. Given the financial resources and promotional capabilities of the recording industry, it's feasible to crowd independents out of all paid—and some unpaid—channels for promotion. Neither market spaces nor mental spaces are infinitely expandable. Newspaper columns or radio airtime devoted to the Backstreet Boys are not devoted to Ornette Coleman.

Saturating bandwidth works best with young buyers, who are less price-sensitive and more crowd-conscious. They develop obsessive relationships with a certain performer, and, at that point, it's relatively easy to monopolize their personal bandwidth. The strategy also works to add differentiation and perceived value to artists and their recordings, to justify higher prices.

Is the Industry's Subscription Program a Deliberate Trap for the Unsophisticated?

The added-value features of the industry's subscription program are mainly of interest to young buyers, the kind who want *every* piece of information they can possibly get about their idols. It's possible that the subscription program is designed as a deliberate trap for such young, unwary buyers. I'm thinking in particular of the feature that makes downloaded music unplayable and useless when the subscription stops. A girl who discovers at age 14 that the subscription prices she gladly paid at age 10 are far too high may have no choice but to continue, unless she's willing to throw away her entire collection of downloaded music and start over.

One can imagine lots of consumer outrage and backlash. First, it's an *immense* incentive to steal. Most consumers would have no moral problem at all stealing music they'd already paid for. It's also an incentive for smart hackers to build software to decode the downloaded files. Once that happens, the subscription services provide no protection against price pressure.

The industry is already largely focused on selling child performers to a child audience; 9 percent of CD purchases worldwide are made by children between the ages of 10 and 14 years. Very young performers are selling well in almost every genre of recorded music, including classical. (The average classical release by an adult sells about 9,000 copies; the average classical release by a 13-year-old sells 14,000 copies.)

The industry's subscription program is, at least in part, a play to monopolize the consumer's personal bandwidth. The value-added features of the service will demand lots of time and attention from any user, especially until high-speed cable, satellite, or wireless connections become common (i.e., not before 2005).

It's Getting Harder to Monopolize Bandwidth

The effectiveness of the strategy in a World Without Secrets, where there's already too much information, is self-limiting. You can't monopolize bandwidth for more than a couple of artists or records at a time. Industry-wide, average sales per artist are declining, though the number of million-selling artists is increasing. A strategy aimed at monopolizing promotional bandwidth tends to increase industry concentration on a very few best-selling artists. That focus further damages relationships with other artists and creates incentives for them to become independent.

There's also a danger, in this strategy, of further damaging relationships and credibility with new buyers. Bandwidth saturation on the Internet is hard to achieve—and risky. The cost of entry is lower, meaning more alternatives are available for the consumer and independents. Anyone who knows how to navigate can find lots of information about alternatives, including price. Acculturation to online buying, and its accompanying information gathering and analysis, happens quickly. Children who, without a thought, paid $18 plus shipping for a CD at age nine may be outraged, at age 15, when they see the difference between the CD price and the cost of a digital download from a peer-to-peer site.

In short, monopolizing bandwidth works best in the traditional media that major record companies know and love. In the networked environment of a World Without Secrets, it may backfire.

STRATEGY 3: PROHIBIT ALTERNATIVE BUSINESS MODELS

A final strategy for reducing or eliminating the impact of digital duplication or distribution is to somehow force all the players in the industry, independents included, to abandon digital distribution channels or maintain uniform pricing. Antitrust law prevents this strategy from being effective. Beyond that, you can't threaten people who think they have nothing to lose, and some independents may think they have nothing to lose by abandoning traditional industry models and relationships altogether.

New Models for Indies in a World Without Secrets

For most of the twentieth century, production was a choke point for the industry. Records cost a lot to make, and most artists couldn't pay the bill without help. Thanks to digital recording technologies, that's no longer true.

For the past two decades, promotion and distribution have been the choke points. Selling lots of records meant manufacturing, moving, and advertising lots of physical product, which only majors could handle effectively. Thanks to digital duplication and distribution technologies, that's no longer true either.

Promotion and marketing remain significant barriers to mass market sales, but they won't prevent pressure on prices and margins from digital technologies. Business models that maximize the direct relationship between the artist and the audience will contribute to that pressure. We can expect to see such models emerging in full force when high-bandwidth connections become common. That's when *digital distribution as advertising* becomes fully feasible.

New business models for independents might include the following characteristics:

- Explicit focus on recordings as a loss leader/advertising medium designed to stimulate revenue from other sources (performance, publishing, licensing, and so on).

- Digital-only distribution more or less direct from the artist to the customer, supplemented when necessary (e.g., on customer demand, or for sale at live performances) by physical media such as CDs.

- Single-song pricing scaled to duplication and distribution costs (one-tenth or less of current standard retail CD prices) and/or to demand. Pricing might include customers' configuration of value-added elements such as accompanying artwork, artists' notes, lyrics, MIDI files, sheet music, and so on.

- Packaging and features aimed at discouraging unauthorized copying via higher value-add for authorized copies, including elements conferring higher levels of authenticity or personalization.

- A high proportion of revenues from recording sales accruing directly to the artist. Although overall per-unit revenues from recorded music sales would be low compared to revenues derived from CD sales at inflated prices, *artist* revenues could easily be comparable or better, on a per-unit basis, to typical major-label deals.

- A brand that stands for a lifestyle or philosophy that includes, and is expressed through, music. (Former Indigo Girl Amy Ray's Daemon Records describes itself as a *regional* company focused on new Southern rock bands.) This has previously been a successful approach for independent labels like Windham Hill, which began as a vehicle for a single artist (solo acoustic guitarist Will Ackermann). In most cases (like Windham Hill's), the focus is ultimately diluted through expansion of the label's roster. An implication is that the business model may have limited scalability. An extreme implication is that such a brand may be limited to one, or a very few, artists; in other words, the artist *is* the brand.

▪ A focus on customer relationship management that may ultimately include multiple products (besides music) that express the company's and customers' philosophy or lifestyle.

▪ Value-added relationship management services to the artist and the audience, such as customer database management, artists' Web site and bulletin board management, artists' tour publicity and management, and so on.

The model above has major limits. First, it's less capable of generating volume record sales than the major label model. (It's intended to stimulate revenues from other sources.) Given the low value-add (compared to traditional models) for record companies and distributors, the likeliest parties to initiate and sustain this model are artists themselves. Ani DiFranco, whose views on artists' independence (and success in building an independent outlet for her recorded music) have recently influenced the far better-selling artist formerly known as Prince (or is that the artist formerly known as The Artist, formerly known as Prince?) is a prime example. She has built a record company that employs eight people, without heavy support from either radio or a major label. Other likely parties to initiate such models are dedicated members of an artist's audience, especially those with entrepreneurial instincts, and castoff executives from the major labels, of which there will be plenty within the next few years. (You don't need 100 percent of the people in five major labels to support the 5 percent of the acts that are generating profits.)

A Two-Tier Industry

In a World Without Secrets, digital objects are anybody's to own. The price of digital objects can only go down from here; the price of an artist can easily go up. Artists and the value chain that supports them will shift from *selling objects* to *selling the presence of, and relationship to, the artist.* The artist is the authentic thing that the audience wants most; the objects are ultimately just souvenirs of the relationship. Independent artists stand to gain the most from this new reality. Dealers in digital objects, including current independent record labels, stand to lose the most.

In 5 to 10 years, the industry will have changed in several important ways:

- For all players, per-unit recording revenues will decrease.

- Independent artists will make a better living over a longer period of time; widespread digital distribution will be supporting increased performance and publishing revenues.

- Major labels will face declining revenues, even with higher unit sales.

- Independent record companies will face severe declines in revenue.

- The current distribution system for physical product will be dramatically reduced and potentially eliminated.

If it seems outrageous to predict the demise of the distribution system, remember that no one needs warehouses to handle a product that's made of bits and bytes and is delivered via a communications network.

The industry will evolve into a two-tier model over the next 10 years. At the upper tier will be major-label-supported artists, relatively few in number, selling large but steadily declining numbers of physical CDs as high-bandwidth delivery makes it harder and harder to justify bundled formats and pricing. The major labels may very well ride CD sales all the way down, in order to avoid channel conflicts with traditional distributors. The farther digital pricing declines, compared to CD pricing, the harder it will be to avoid those conflicts. As performance and publishing revenues increase in proportion to CD sales, major labels will demand a higher share of those revenues from their artists.

On the lower tier will be independent artists. Their revenues will be fueled by performances, supported by low-cost or free digital distribution of recorded music, often on a single-song basis. (This suggests the next choke point for the industry: access to performance venues.) Over time, these artists will put increasing price pressure on the upper tier of the industry, and especially on its distribution network, which is geared to physical product.

The middle tier—independent record companies—may disappear entirely.

SUMMARY: THE FATE OF DIGITAL OBJECTS

The future of intellectual property industries lies in selling performances and relationships, not digital objects. Attempts to sell digital objects at increasingly higher prices can only succeed when the seller has a de facto monopoly. (Microsoft has successfully used its monopoly power to increase prices, for business users of its Office products, by tens or hundreds of percent over the past few years, via changes in the terms and conditions of use.) For anyone else, prices decline over time, tending (like costs) to zero.

Revenues for manufacturers and distributors of digital objects will drop steeply in the next 10 years in the World Without Secrets. It's a good time for those players to think about how they're going to make a transition to a new business. They might start by thinking about what makes a company *exceptional,* or not, beginning with its relationships.

POWER AND KNOWLEDGE

Hunter's Second Law:
When everything is known, no one knows everything.

Fifth Corollary:
It's impossible to calculate the full value of a given piece of information to all the people who might possess it.

Power corrupts. Knowledge is power. Right.

CHAPTER ELEVEN

Crime Without Secrets

In 1983, one of my colleagues at Gartner was refused entry to a National Security Agency (NSA) office in Washington, D.C., because he was carrying a portable tape recorder. In April 2001, the same colleague visited the same building carrying a laptop computer and a Palm Pilot, either of which was capable of copying huge amounts of data from any computer in the place.

An NSA security guard barely looked at the Palm Pilot, even though it's got plenty of storage capacity and the ability to communicate wirelessly. The laptop got his attention. "You can't bring a personal computer into the building," he said.

"Oh, it's not a *personal* computer," my friend said. "It belongs to the *business.*"

"Oh. Well, that's fine," said the guard.

My friend was issued a visitor's badge, and he walked in with his massively dangerous—but obviously ordinary to the point of inconsequence—machines.

This episode illustrates a couple of important points. First, businesses—even businesses that are all about security—take bigger risks than they used to when it comes to exposing themselves and their information. *No one wants to be left behind.* You need computers, we need computers, we *all* need computers. So bring the computers, just so long as it's *business.*

Second, the boundaries are down. You don't always need technical skills to get inside. Sometimes a good line of patter is all it takes. *Human beings don't change.* Humans can be baffled, bamboozled, buffaloed, and beaten. Kevin Mittnick (who now refers to himself as the "winner of the scapegoat sweepstakes"), the most infamous cracker of the 1990s, talked his way into systems far more often than he hacked his way in. That was only a few years ago. Talk still works.

A third point, not so evident from the NSA episode, is that it's not always, or even usually, the people on the outside who are the most dangerous. After all, the ones on the inside know where everything is. They don't have to bring anything in at all, and they can take plenty of stuff *out*.

Buying In

In 1997, the Charter Pacific Bank of Agoura Hills, California, a legitimate business, offered Kenneth Taves, the owner and operator of a Web-based pornography business—also legitimate, if less prestigious—the opportunity to buy a list of about four million credit card numbers belonging to Charter Pacific customers. Charter Pacific apparently believed that the list would be used by Taves to guard against fraudulent purchases of his web site services.

Taves paid Charter Pacific $5,000 for the list. Then he, his wife, and a partner fraudulently billed over 800,000 of the people on the list $19.95 each—some more than once—for access to various porn Web sites. (As if pornography—a $10 billion industry worldwide, with the lowest imaginable barriers to entry—isn't profitable enough! It's clear that this guy just did *not* know how to run a business.) The take from the scam ultimately exceeded $49 million. When the Federal Trade Commission (FTC) figured out what was going on, Taves was arrested and had to give back most of the money. He was convicted of multiple counts of fraud as well.

Taves had previously been convicted, in California, of being an accessory to murder, a fact that apparently didn't alter the Charter Pacific Bank's decision to sell him its list. Hunter's Second Law says: *When everything is known, no one knows everything.* Perhaps Charter Pacific didn't know about the conviction, even though it was a matter of public record in the same state. Perhaps the bank didn't ask, or asked but was lied to. (The bank's current owners did not respond to repeated requests for information on this point.) The Fourth Corollary to Hunter's Second Law is: *Information only matters when someone is looking.* Until then, it's just more information, and *everybody's* already got *way* too much information to look at. In any case, Charter Pacific was an unwitting enabler for Taves's crime. The bank was his "man on the inside."

In 1999, when the story first appeared, this fraud was widely described by the press as an "Internet fraud scheme," but the Internet was almost completely tangential to the operation. Taves didn't use the Internet to get the card numbers, he didn't use the Internet to generate the charges, and he didn't use it to collect the money. The core of the fraud was the list, period. That's what gave Taves access to the money. All he had to do to get the list was write a check to Charter Pacific Bank. What Taves charged the owners of the cards *for* is really beside the point. He happened to own and operate several Web sites that happened to offer porn, but he might as well have charged the victims for video rentals or pizzas. We could argue that it was inherently more plausible to charge people who lived hundreds or thousands of miles away for access to a Web site than for pizza, and that's true. But Taves should have known that *whatever* he charged them for, it wasn't ultimately going to be *plausible*.

YEAH, IT'S ABOUT TECHNOLOGY

There *is* an important technology angle in this scam, but the technology was there all along, and Taves used it just like any other business. It's the technology infrastructure—networks, databases, and processing—that credit card companies have built to support the ease of using what Visa calls *the closest thing there is to a universal currency*. Once Taves had the list in hand, all he had to do was bill those numbers. Visa and Mastercard did the rest. Without that technology, Taves could never have defrauded over 800,000 people so quickly.

Taves and his crew were easy to catch. They had no apparent exit strategy. Many of their victims complained to their credit card companies, something Taves had assumed wouldn't happen because of the embarrassing nature of the charges. (But wouldn't it be more embarrassing if you didn't complain? Wouldn't that imply that you *did* buy the porn?) Many of Taves's victims didn't even have Internet access, and therefore couldn't possibly have used a porn Web site. But Taves and his crew succeeded in collecting the money. They might have held onto it if they'd had an exit strategy, like *running*.

Taves and his criminal cohorts were convicted and sentenced to various inconveniences, including repayment of the money he stole from his victims. Jail time was not part of the sentences.

THE LESSONS

This story carries a few important lessons. The first is: Lots of criminals think opportunistically. They get a tool and they do a crime, right away, without even thinking about anything as strategic as an exit plan. (If I'm ever stupid enough to steal $49 million, I hope I will be smart enough to change my name and leave town with no forwarding address immediately afterward.)

The second lesson is: *Information has value,* and different people see the value differently, depending on their plans for the information. This is perhaps the most important thing of all where cyber-crime is concerned. It's important enough to repeat. *Information has value.* We all know that fact intuitively, but most of us don't calculate the value of information in the precise numeric way that a criminal does. A banker doesn't see that four million credit card numbers represent $49 million in almost immediate revenue, because he doesn't imagine that you're instantly going to fraudulently convert 20 percent of those people into paying customers for your service.

Some businesses understand the value of their information to a competitor; most businesses don't understand the value of their information to a criminal. But a criminal sees information and understands immediately how it can generate money or trouble. The most important cyber-crimes, the most deadly cyber-attacks, are all about stealing information.

The third lesson is: There are many ways to acquire and use electronically stored information, regardless of the intention of the person acquiring it. All that's needed are sufficient resources, time, and skills. *Skills* doesn't necessarily mean *technical* skills. In many situations, technical skills are irrelevant to acquiring information. Plenty of information can be bought openly and legally. If you can't buy it, lots of other tricks can be tried before you have to learn how to actually crack anything. And using it only requires access to the technology that others have already built.

The fourth lesson is: Existing technology infrastructures enable crimes that are massive and nearly instantaneous. How do you get access to the infrastructure? With the *keys,* of course. That's exactly what Charter Pacific sold to Taves: a set of four million credit card account *keys.*

PLAN B

People have committed and will commit crimes forever. Internet crime—crime conducted anonymously via a computer plugged into a network—is new, though, and I guess that's why we think it's so fascinating. (Exceptions are fascinating, and what's new is exceptional.) But the crimes that account for the vast majority of all cyber-crimes aren't committed by a stranger operating from an unknown location on a network.

Gartner research says that, on average, over 70 percent of all unauthorized intrusions on information systems are committed by companies' own employees. The Defense Security Service's report, *2001 Technology Collection Trends in the U.S. Defense Industry,* which describes the means used by foreign states and nonstate actors to acquire protected defense-related information from American companies, lists "Internet activity (hacking)" *sixth* among the most common approaches, accounting for only 4 percent of all such activity.[1] It's about 15 times more common for a foreign entity to either simply request the information or to attempt to get it by hiring, or being hired by, American companies. It's three times more common for a foreign company to try to buy either the technology or the company that makes it. All these approaches are attempts to use insiders, *not cracking*, to get the goods.

If someone really wants to steal information, it can sometimes be done over a network. But there are easier ways that can be managed by people who aren't technical enough to operate a digital bathroom scale.

Here's an example. I want to know something about your company—for example, the buyer names and phone numbers for your 50 largest customers, plus the amounts they pay you for particular products and services. I find out who manages your company's databases. I befriend him and take him to Atlantic City for the weekend. (You can substitute Las Vegas, Rio de Janeiro, or Cannes if you like, but Atlantic City is so delightfully *sleazy*.) I get him thoroughly drunk and introduce him to a prostitute or two, and a card game—all very friendly. On Sunday morning, as his head spins and pounds painfully, I present him with a set of compromising photographs (use your imagination here; I recommend that you pull out *all* the stops) and a debt equivalent to five years of his salary. I follow that with a pointed request for assistance in looting his company's databases.

This approach is simpler, more foolproof, and less expensive overall, not to mention more fun for everyone, including the database administrator. The theft that results is less likely to be detected, and there's a good chance that it will continue over a longer period of time. It may continue when the database administrator changes jobs and companies, even if the reason for the job change is that the theft was finally detected. Many companies don't like to reveal when an employee is fired for cyber-crimes against the employer. It makes *so* many people look bad.

Insiders have access. They've already got the keys. In April 2001, Daniel Wiant, the Chief Financial Officer for the American Cancer Society of Ohio, pleaded guilty to charges of bank fraud, money laundering, mail fraud, and illegal use of a credit card. His crimes had netted him almost $7 million. He had worked for the Ohio chapter of the American Cancer Society for seven years; he began stealing from them in 1997. Before he was employed by the American Cancer Society, it turned out, he had been convicted three times of theft-related offenses. The Ohio chapter didn't check for a criminal record before hiring him into its information systems department.

It's usually pretty hard to break into a computer and steal $7 million. It can be done, but most crackers don't have that kind of skill. It's easier for an insider. It's *very* easy if the insider is the Chief Financial Officer or is employed in the internal information services department. And it's easiest of all if no one else in the organization is taking care of business, like checking references on the new hires.

Humans make mistakes and, in a heavily networked world, criminals quickly and easily act to take advantage of mistakes.

WHAT WE FEAR

Gartner researcher Laura Behrens wrote, in May 2001: "Consumers are simultaneously concerned about the security of their information and transactions online and unable or unwilling to take active security measures themselves."[2] Gartner research shows that fear for the security of online transactions is the most significant factor inhibiting online buying.

It's unclear whether consumers understand that information *in transit,* in most cases, isn't at risk. The tools and skills needed to intercept information in transit are very demanding—well beyond the capabilities of all but the most talented cyber-criminals. (Or of the FBI, whose Carnivore program is specifically designed to intercept information in transit. But the FBI has the assistance of the Internet Service Providers (ISPs) on whose servers Carnivore is installed.) *Information at rest*—information stored in databases—is far more at risk. The odds that a transaction will be intercepted on the Internet are much lower than the odds that the database where the transaction is stored will be stolen or copied, and much, *much* lower than the chance that the business that owns the information will sell it to someone else.

Are you worried about using your credit card on the Internet? It's the wrong question. Ask yourself whether you want to use the credit card *at all*.

It's Not the Transaction, It's the Database

To say that *information at rest* is the issue is to define targets as well as circumstances. For businesses, *information at rest* means any of several things. It might refer to proprietary information, like a new product design or a contract bid. It might refer to structured data, like customer credit or transaction information. It might refer to stored e-mail communications. Any or all of these could be converted to money by a thief or a buyer.

For a consumer, the threat of stolen information is summed up in the words "identity theft." Identity theft is nothing more than impersonation via stolen credentials. In other words, it's a kind of fraud with multiple victims, including the person who's impersonated and the business on whom the impersonation is practiced. Identity theft is apparently increasing; I say "apparently" because conflicting reports have been issued from multiple sources, and reporting standards aren't clear. Cases reported by American financial institutions more than doubled from 1999 to 2000, according to the Treasury Department's Financial Crimes Enforcement Network.

It's not the transaction, it's the database. The Financial Crimes Enforcement Network says that "the most common ways to become the victim of identity theft are through the loss or theft of a purse or wallet, mail theft and fraudulent address changes." Those aren't cyber-crimes. The first two are *muggings*. *Mail theft* is about as nontechnical as you can get, but it's effective. Credit card bills come in the mail. Student loan bills, which often contain Social Security numbers, come in the mail.

It's not a bad idea to be wary of the potential for Internet-based identity theft, or any other kind of Internet-based crime. But it's important to keep in mind that it's the *information* that's really dangerous, not the vehicle. If you've got the key, *you can unlock a lot of money.* You don't even need to know how to turn a computer on to *get that key*.

MASS VICTIMIZATION

In at least one important way, the Internet offers the potential for a new class of crimes. *A network is an amplifier,* and by taking advantage of the power of a network to amplify the messages that go into it, it's possible to change the basic economics of crime. Instead of dangerous attacks on heavily defended targets, a criminal can use a network to attack thousands or millions of lightly defended targets. Each target yields a relatively small score, but, in the aggregate, the volume is impressive.

That's what Taves did. A banker gave him access to a network, and Taves used it to generate masses of relatively small fraudulent orders. The network in question wasn't the Internet; it belonged to the credit card companies. But the *means of access* isn't the point. The point is the availability of all those *victims.*

Ways in which the Internet *could* be used to carry out such mass attacks have already been demonstrated by legitimate businesses. As an example, consider Netscape's SmartDownload, a program that improves the speed and ease of Internet downloads. Early versions of this utility, supplied free by Netscape via Internet download, also had a covert function. It surreptitiously tracked, and reported to Netscape, what was downloaded from which Internet sites by the program's users. In other words, the program spied on the people who used it.

SmartDownload reported very specific information to Netscape, including the IP address of a user's machine that could be used to find the machine again on the Internet. No user who didn't know how to analyze inbound and outbound Internet traffic could have known what Smart-Download was doing. It would be easy to create a program (like Smart-Download) that worked to covertly scan users' hard drives for passwords, account numbers, and other useful information. It would then be just as easy to quietly transmit that information to a location somewhere on the Internet, as SmartDownload did.

Such programs are feasible right now for crimes on a mass scale, even in cases where target machines are protected by firewalls. The program could be delivered as a virus, maybe hidden in something *nice,* like a pretty picture. (Viruses usually enter a victim's machine as an e-mail attachment, and firewalls don't stop e-mails.) Viruses in general are discovered quickly only because their creators insist on making their effects visible. (Vandals like to see their vandalism. We're not talking about vandals.) If a virus never announced itself, most users would never know it was there. In fact, absent overt signals, it's unlikely that even antivirus software vendors would know about it for some time. In that case, even a user who diligently performed regular virus scans could be victimized.

Days, weeks, or months might pass before discovery of such a virus. In the meantime, a perpetrator would have plenty of time to use or resell valuable information. Many individual victims might have limited resources available to steal, but that's unimportant to potential criminal profitability. *The network is an amplifier.* Taves's payoff was collected $19.95 at a time, and he didn't have to confront a single bank guard to do it.

It's important to remember that each of Taves's *victims* lost a relatively small amount. No one's life or livelihood was destroyed; it's hard to see how it could have been. Taves used credit card numbers, and there are strict limits on how much any victim of credit card fraud pays. In some mass victimization scenarios, those limits wouldn't hold. A thief who had access to *all* the information on a victim's hard drive might find enough there to ruin the victim.

In general, such attacks succeed because they're surreptitious, not because they're overwhelming. If you don't want to be a victim, make it a point to understand the basics of self-protection. In particular, be careful with passwords, put a firewall on any Internet-connected machine, and don't accept e-mail from anyone you don't know, especially if it's got an attachment. Don't accept free software unless you know enough about the company offering it to be sure it has no criminal intent. If you don't know, assume the worst. Remember that *Saturday Night Live* routine about the woman who opens her door and gets eaten by a shark? *Don't open the door.*

"Consumers are simultaneously concerned about the security of their information and transactions online and unable or unwilling to take active security measures themselves," said Laura Behrens. If you're going to worry, you might as well do something about it, or just turn off the machine.

Crime as State Enterprise

Certain cyber-enabled crimes—such as crimes enabled by data-mining—demand the resources and attitudes of a state. The resources are available to lots of criminal organizations, but the attitudes aren't. The vast majority of criminals think opportunistically, just like Taves did. It's beyond their abilities to plan and carry out certain classes of crimes, with or without computer support.

As an example, suppose that I wanted to identify criminal markets for a new designer drug, or for development of kidnapping revenues. If I had access to the right databases and computers, I could use data mining technology to construct demographic models of the target countries. I could look for cities that had a certain set of winning characteristics, such as population density, wealth (high or low), and age distribution; access to multiple means of transport, such as air, rail, sea, and highways; lower-than-average funding for police—street presence as well as investigative facilities such as access to various technologies; and relative lack of penetration for competing products and criminal networks. I run the model, and the candidate locations appear.

This kind of stuff is easy for lots of businesses because businesses think ahead. (Or die.) Criminals don't. Taves didn't even do enough research to know which of his targets had an Internet account. *States* think ahead, and states have the resources to execute such crimes. Corrupted or hostile states, or those under the control of criminal organizations, are potential candidates for such approaches to cyber-enabled crime.

Already there have been reports from Colombia of rebel military forces using advanced technologies in the field. According to the U.S. Immigration and Naturalization Service, the Fuerzas Armadas Revolucionarias de Colombia (FARC) "maintains computerized databases of potential kidnapping and extortion victims—including people's citizen identification numbers, bank records, and credit histories. It also utilizes laptop computers at roadblocks to check detainees against its lists of preferred victims and potential targets."[3] This level of planning for use of information technology in support of organized criminal activity is well beyond the capabilities of most criminal organizations, now or ever.

I discuss issues related to state support of cyber-crime in more detail in the next chapter, "War Without Secrets."

WHY WORRY?

People worry, often about the wrong things. We worry about data in motion instead of data at rest. We worry about having our credit cards stolen when no credit card theft can cost us more than $50, and our bank accounts are waiting to be looted by anyone with the *key*. We worry that our names are in too many databases, and we download any software offered for free by parties unknown to us who make no guarantees.

Bad things happen on the highway to people who don't know how to drive. That doesn't mean everyone should stop driving. It means that the people who want to should *learn to drive.*

CHAPTER TWELVE

War Without Secrets

As I write this, the United States is preparing to fight its first war against terrorism. It's not a new kind of war, but it's new for us. We have big armies, big weapons, and tactics that are designed for use against other big armies with big weapons. That stuff works against such enemies, sometimes spectacularly. (We defeated the Iraqi armed forces and forced them out of Kuwait in 1991 at a cost of fewer than 100 American lives.) That approach doesn't work so well against enemies who are scattered among a population of innocents (including our own people and our friends all over the world), who strike against undefended civilians (not military targets), and whose goals are about jihad—capturing *souls,* not territory or markets.

Guerrilla wars have been *won*—the British won in Malaysia in the 1950s, for example—but this is a *terrorist* war. A terrorist war has never been won by any nation, if *won* means that the enemy surrenders or is destroyed and never troubles the victor again. Some governments—Syria, Egypt, and France among them—have succeeded in reducing terrorist activity within their borders to very low levels, mostly via systematic, brutal reprisals against terrorists and the communities that support them—including, in some cases, entire families. The Israelis succeeded in destroying Black September, but certainly didn't succeed in ending terrorism against Israel.

We've been attacked by an army of terrorists, and we've announced our intention to strike back with the full might of the world's largest Engineered Society. We may not succeed. The British have been trying to win against the IRA for a long time, and they've got it to the point where they can live, more or less, with the level of disruption the IRA causes. The British, of course, aren't at liberty (morally or otherwise) to assault the IRA the way Syria's Hafez Assad assaulted the Islamic fundamentalists who troubled him in the 1970s. But the IRA never killed over 3,000 people in a single attack. No nation can live with that level of disruption.

It may work for us, but I don't think it will unless we start thinking about war in a different way. I'm sure that the tactics that worked against Iraq won't produce a quick victory this time.

Big weapons need big targets. These targets are *exceptions*.

ARE TERRORISTS A NETWORK ARMY?

In the Network Army scenario, a wide variety of value systems are expressed via communal activism. The result is rapidly shifting alliances of activist communities aligned on value systems, *not* territory. The communities tend to be nonhierarchical and they communicate openly via the Internet.

Terrorists share certain characteristics with the Network Army. Like the Network Army, their value systems are various, intersecting on one or more planes (for example, opposition to Israel or the United States) where they exercise significant power. They're international and are united by ideology, not geography. But the Internet is only *one* of the means they use to communicate, and they don't communicate openly. (That is apparently changing. Web sites now exist where one can contribute money to terrorist causes.) Their organizations are definitely hierarchical, and authority is reinforced with sanctions that include death. On the other hand, a terrorist cell in the field is highly autonomous once its mission is defined.

A Network Army need not be very large, and terrorists are relatively few in number—perhaps a few thousand worldwide. They're still able to project lots of power, as per Hunter's First Law: *The power of a network in a given context equals the square of the number of people on the network, times the intrinsic power of those people in that context.* The context in which terrorists operate is destruction, and their intrinsic power in that context is *very* high.

ENGINEERED SOCIETY WARFARE AND THE TERRORIST

Since at least the nineteenth century—the industrial era, the age of mass *production*—the wars of Engineered Societies have been about mass *destruction* of soldiers, civilians, and industry. The apex of Engineered Society warfare in that sense (God willing) was World War II, in which nations were systematically bombed into rubble, entire populations were massacred on and off the battlefield, and a single bomb, in a few seconds, killed tens of thousands of people in a medium-size Japanese city. That was a bottom-up kind of war; heads of state were insulated from battles, and privates and civilians were directly in the line of fire. You had to kill thousands of privates to get a shot at one general, and dozens of generals to get a chance to kill the Fuehrer.

That's not an effective approach to killing terrorists. They work alone or in small teams, often autonomously—not in big armies of uniformed men. The masses of people surrounding terrorists aren't terrorists themselves, or even necessarily terrorist sympathizers. Because terrorists live for extended periods of time among their victims, the masses surrounding them may even be *your people.*

Engineered Society wars, like all other activities of the Engineered Society, have *rules.* For example, you're not supposed to starve or shoot prisoners once they're under your control. War is messy, and the rules get broken frequently, but Engineered Societies are increasingly fastidious about upholding them. Soldiers know that most of the time, in a World Without Secrets, camera crews follow soldiers into battle and *truth will out.*

Terrorists don't follow the rules. (Rogue states like Serbia under Slobodan Milosevic don't either, but that society was far too fragmented to be thoroughly *Engineered.*) Terrorists don't care. They don't expect to be tried or executed for their crimes. They expect, in many cases, to die *committing* them. Their ideology makes no distinction between military and civilian victims; they're all *enemy,* and the civilians are easier to kill. If that truth is exposed, so much the better for the terrorists.

The Terrorist as Exception

A terrorist war is an Exception Economy war waged by a Network Army. Terrorists are an exceptional handful of the most extreme zealots in their

GUERRILLAS AND TERRORISTS

Mao Tse Tung described a guerrilla as *a fish who swims in the ocean of the people*. The guerrilla draws strength, literally and figuratively, from a particular place and people. He operates among them, fighting *for* them and *with* them against a shared enemy, typically an army of occupation. He usually has a program for social justice and the rebuilding of the nation, once the war is won.

No guerrilla war has ever been won by anyone who didn't treat the problems of the people among whom the guerrillas operated as the paramount issue. Because guerrillas are rooted in a specific place and time, defeating guerrillas requires tactics specific to that place, time, and people. The British in Malaysia relocated whole populations and succeeded. Americans tried the same thing in Vietnam and failed.

Terrorists aren't guerrillas. They're not grounded in a specific territory; they operate internationally. They live among their victims, not their people. They don't fight armies, or even soldiers. They kill undefended civilians. The problems of the people are completely secondary to the destruction of the enemy. Terrorists have no program beyond warfare, or the program is strictly ideological.

Both guerrillas and terrorists are difficult to defeat, but guerrillas only threaten opponents *within their territory*. Terrorists strike at ideological opponents *anywhere* in the world.

Conventional armies used against guerrillas can be at least temporarily successful. Conventional armies apparently don't work well against terrorists, at least not if the experience of the British and the Israelis is any guide.

societies, people who use death in battle—their own and their victims'—as a *tactic*. The targets are exceptional, potent *symbols:* the White House, Camp David, the World Trade Center, the United States' homeland. Terrorists choose those targets because they know that it takes something exceptional to get the attention of a world full of Distracted Consumers. (When I saw the second plane hit World Trade Center Tower One, I assumed that it had been timed—15 minutes or so after the first strike—to ensure that *everyone* in America would be watching.) In Israel, terrorists explode bombs on buses. In the United States, their attacks are scaled to be exceptional in a nation that has theme parks almost the size of Israel.

Because terrorists are *exceptional,* counterattacks aimed at *masses* of soldiers, civilians, and industry can only fail. The terrorist is a *super-empowered angry man* enabled by ideological hatred and by *knowledge* of how to use the powerful tools and weapons provided by any industrial society. As long as one such man exists, deadly attacks can occur. Counterattacking against masses of people only produces more such men. If terrorists are exceptions, then successful tactics have to focus on the exceptions by finding the *few* deadly people within the crowd, isolating them, and destroying them.

In general, these are the traditional tactics of law enforcement, not warfare. But the line between crime and war is deeply blurred in a World Without Secrets. One important remaining difference is that, in warfare, preemptive defense—the kind where I take you out before you can act against me—is permissible; in law enforcement, it's generally not.

The description above implies that it will be soon. The investigative techniques of law enforcement will be wed to the proactive defenses demanded by warfare. It's already been done by the Israelis. The result is *warfare against exceptional terrorists, prepared via investigation, conducted via assassination.*

LEADERS ARE EXCEPTIONS

Engineered Society warfare makes some sense when the enemy is an entire nation *united.* Does it make sense when the enemy is an entire nation subjugated and forced into combat by a mad king or the modern equivalent, a Pol Pot or a Saddam Hussein? What was gained by killing Iraqi soldiers in the Gulf War that would not have been gained by killing Saddam Hussein and a few dozen people working directly under him? What was lost, besides the lives of those Iraqis who couldn't refuse Hussein's orders, by leaving Hussein alive when the war was over? One possible answer is: the lives of over 3,000 people in the World Trade Center.

In a corporate war, markets and the business press focus on the CEOs. It's understood that their actions and decisions matter most. Why take the bottom-up view in a *shooting* war? Why not acknowledge that a very few people are the exceptions that matter, and take a top-down approach to *them?*

(Some) Infrastructure Is Exceptional

If terrorists are indeed a Network Army, then destroying resources—like factories—that are essential to the functioning of an industrial Engineered Society has little effect on them. Such resources are territorial, and terrorists are international. In any industrial society, they find the resources they need to cause havoc in abundance.

The resources required by a terrorist Network Army are *communications*—the basic enabler of any Network Army—and *money*, which buys the local resources needed to carry out local acts of destruction. Because these resources are also required for human activities of all sorts, it's not practical to eliminate them, except on a local basis in countries that make a practice of harboring terrorists. Doing so may drive terrorists out of those countries; at least, it will make it more difficult for them to operate there.

CRIME IS WAR, WAR IS CRIME

Boundaries blur in the World Without Secrets. The personal becomes public. National markets are subsumed into world markets. The lines between soldiers and civilians and crime and warfare blur to the point that they disappear too.

Table 12.1 compares some of the traditional differences between crime and warfare; it's clear that many of these have *already* disappeared. The actors in terrorist attacks may be allied with states, but are often not states themselves. Terrorist attacks, like traditional crimes, are carried out in the places where ordinary citizens live, work, and play, not on the

TABLE 12.1   CRIME VERSUS WARFARE

	CRIME	WARFARE
Objective	Personal/financial gain	Advance ideology Annex territory Protect or annex markets
Actors	Nonstate	State
Setting	Civilian	Battlefield
Target	Lives and property	Lives and territory
Horizon	Tactical/immediate	Strategic/generational

battlefield. (We might also say that at least since 1864, when General William T. Sherman made his March to the Sea and, along the way, laid waste to civilian property in Georgia, Engineered Societies have explicitly waged war directly on civilians in civilian settings. However, such attacks are aimed at overcoming an army; damage to civilians *per se* isn't the primary purpose.)

The most significant operational difference between crime and warfare is the difference in planning horizons between states and criminals. In October 2000, when I ran a Gartner workshop on the effect of the Internet on criminal business models, I asked a member of the Secret Service in attendance what percentage of criminals think strategically. "Zero," he said without hesitation. Criminals think opportunistically. States think strategically. *Terrorists* think strategically. The attack on the World Trade Center likely took over two years to plan and execute. That's longer than the planning horizon for many businesses, and certainly longer than the planning horizon for almost any criminal enterprise.

Other than that, the differences seem less important than the similarities. Criminals seek personal gain; states seek to protect or annex markets, which equals financial gain both for national entrepreneurs and for the rulers of the states. *Markets* increasingly substitute for *territory* as a target for state acquisition in the World Without Secrets. Markets mean wealth, which territory alone can't provide.

Acquisition of wealth by cyber-theft, cyber-espionage, or other cyber-crime is less likely to provoke warfare between Engineered Societies than annexation of territory, at least for now. And in a World Without Secrets, it's much easier to pull off.

All this implies that certain classes of cyber-crime, especially those that require significant capital investment, planning, and support over long periods of time (such as cyber-crimes enabled by data mining) will be largely carried out by states, not nonstate actors like professional criminals.

I'll return to the issue of cyber-crime as a surrogate for cyber-war later. In the meantime, let's examine new models for explicit warfare in a World Without Secrets.

NETWORK-CENTRIC WARFARE

Network-Centric Warfare is an explicit attempt to apply the principles of the e-business economy to the conduct of war. In his article, "Network-Centric

Warfare: Its Origins and Future" (Naval Institute Proceedings, January 1998), Vice Admiral Arthur Cebrowski (U.S. Navy, retired) gets right to the point:

> Society has changed. The underlying economics and technologies have changed. **American business has changed** [emphasis mine]. We should be surprised and shocked if America's military did not. . . . Network-Centric Warfare and all of its associated revolutions in military affairs grow out of and draw their power from the fundamental changes in American society. These changes have been dominated by the co-evolution of economics, information technology, and business processes and organizations. . . .
>
> We are some distance from a detailed understanding of the new operations—there is as yet no equivalent to Carl von Clausewitz's "On War" for this second revolution—but we can gain some insight through the general observation that **nations make war the same way they make wealth.** [emphasis mine][1]

I wonder. I mentioned that comment to Ken Watman, Director of the War Gaming Department at the U.S. Naval War College, in the course of our interview, and he responded immediately. "Well, a note of skepticism is appropriate regarding nations making war the way they make wealth. In World War II, German military procedures were *much* more decentralized than their industrial procedures. Their military mentality of command didn't correspond to their industrial mentality. In contrast, in our country we value individualism, but in point of fact our organizations don't value it at all."[2]

"Perhaps it's more true that nations fight wars the way they play *sports*," I said.

"There's something to that," Watman said. "Look at football. *Very* centralized decision making. The Germans make that argument when they compare soccer and football. Football has rigidity and authority. Only the quarterback talks in the huddle, and even *he* doesn't have the authority he used to. Plays are called on a statistical basis from off-field. The preparation's very rigorous, very good, very *American,* there's lots of attention to detail. But soccer can't be prepared for that way. It's very fluid, there's no pause, you can't regroup. The players have to make the decisions on the field."

"It's interesting," I said, "that lots of American kids are playing soccer now."

Watman laughed. "But we've brought all the heaviness of American football to soccer!" he said. "Everyone wears a uniform, everyone pays attention to the coach!"

Perhaps the real truth is that character isn't compartmentalized. Like Eric Raymond, we're all ourselves, all the time, unless we're trying not to be. If that's so, then it's probably true that Americans make war the way they make wealth, just as it's true that they make war the way they play football.

War as Increasing Returns

Admiral Cebrowski demonstrates an acute understanding of how business in the Internet Economy works, and it's clear why he wants to apply the principles to warfare:

> . . . a product or product standard achieves such a dominant position that consumers drop competing products. . . . Locking-out competition and locking-in success can occur quickly, even overnight. **We seek an analogous effect in warfare . . . .** [emphasis mine]

He spells out exactly how that can be achieved, again by using Internet Economy business models as reference points:

> Network-Centric operations deliver to the U.S. military the same powerful dynamics as they produced in American business. At the strategic level, the critical element for both is a detailed understanding of the appropriate competitive space—all elements of battlespace and battletime.

This "detailed understanding" is supplied by what Cebrowski calls the *logical model for Network-Centric Warfare,* which consists of three *grids:* the *information grid,* the *sensor grid,* and the *engagement grid.*

> The entry fee is a high-performance information grid that provides a backplane for computing and communications. The information grid enables the operational architectures of sensor grids and engagement grids. Sensor grids rapidly generate high levels of battlespace awareness and synchronize awareness with military operations. Engagement grids exploit this awareness and translate it into increased combat power.

The net result is:

> Network-Centric Warfare . . . is analogous to the new economic model, with potentially increasing returns on investment. **Very high and accelerating rates of change have a profound impact on the outcome, "locking-out" alternative enemy strategies and "locking-in" success.** [emphasis mine]

This is organized Engineered Society warfare in a World Without Secrets: massive deployment of technology to feed every detail of armed force and battlefield intelligence to all our fighters in real time, transforming the *rate of change* on the battlefield in ways that leave the enemy gasping for the air that *we* have sucked instantly from his lungs.

It's worth asking whether it's really possible to ensure accuracy and security for those information and sensor grids, and for the communications that make them usable in combat. How would a combat unit know for sure that the communications were secure and accurate, and what would the unit do if they weren't?

"Don't get locked into Cebrowski's definition," Watman advised me. "There's lots of ways of thinking about what a definition does. It could be descriptive or operational. In a descriptive sense, Network-Centric Warfare means that a group of formerly relatively disconnected entities suddenly becomes networked to the point where the entire collective knows what any one of them knows. *Then* you ask how that would be done. In my opinion, the definition is amorphous at this point, and it's difficult to know whether, for example, a sensor grid is the way to do it."

Cebrowski describes his model as a *logical* definition, so there's plenty of room for interpretation. Because the *physical* model doesn't exist yet, there's no way to tell whether it can actually work in an operational sense.

If it does work, it's still important to ask what it works *for*.

Roots

I asked Watman whether Germany's World War II model for tank warfare—what we call *Blitzkreig*—was a predecessor to this approach.

"That's an interesting idea," Watman said. "In many ways, the point is pretty solid. That approach was developed by a small group within the German Army with a tough tactical problem: how to avoid the outcome of World War I. They had to avoid the trench lines. So they came up with this combination of inventions, a wedding of motorized vehicles and radio, plus a tactical approach that stressed fluid avoidance of points of resistance. When you do that, a motorized unit can move a very long way very quickly. It's physically very destructive. It's very demoralizing for the resistance."

Sure. They're stuck in place, cut off from all their support, with enemy tanks racing around them and behind them. If you're manning a fixed fortification like the French Maginot Line, you can't even take your weapons to the battle. The basic assumption behind any fixed fortification is that the battle will come to the fortification.

In an Engineered Society, adherence to the dominant value system (in this case, *fixed fortification is strength*) is a kind of litmus test. There's always a tendency to accept it completely at face value; to do otherwise is to risk being thrown off the team (as Winston Churchill and Charles de Gaulle were, in the 1930s, for questioning the dogma of their respective governments). If the other side has a better idea—like detouring tanks around your guns and cutting off your supply lines—there may be no fallback position.

"I hadn't thought before of *Blitzkreig* as an early model for Network-Centric Warfare," Watman said. "But certainly the presence of a radio in every vehicle provides a kind of situational awareness. In the Russian armor at the time, only the *leader* had a radio. But really what we're talking about is down at the tactical level, at the level of individual tanks, as opposed to the operational level of planners, or the strategic level of an entire theater. Cebrowski might say, 'Imagine how well it would have worked if in each tank you automatically got a screen full of information from the sensor grid that told you everything about where the enemy was and where he was going. You could see over the next hill, which the Germans couldn't do, and you'd be able to make much better decisions.' "

So fast gets faster, and smart gets smarter. But who's making the decisions?

Who's in Charge?

"Military operations are enormously complex," Cebrowski says, "and complexity theory tells us that such enterprises organize best from the bottom-up . . . bottom-up organization yields self-synchronization, where . . . combat moves to a high-speed continuum."

The implication is that Network-Centric Warfare pushes decision making down the military chain of command and puts it at the level of the fighting unit. I asked Watman whether that was so.

"I could imagine people saying decentralization is embedded in Network-Centric Warfare," Watman said. "Others might say it enhances hierarchical control. That's one of the central tensions in Network-Centric Warfare. It's like the definition of a railroad. It runs in *both* directions. The idea of networking things together opens up prospects both for greater centralization and greater decentralization. Historically, in the American system, these developments have been used to increase *centralization*.

"Look at the way we use AWACS [airborne warning and control system] both for sensing and operational capabilities. AWACS uses radar to sense what's going on in a big airspace, so it lets you direct big collections of forces in an optimal way. Operationally, radar transmissions *from* the AWACS go back *to* the AWACS. There's a command and control system in the AWACS, so the guys in the AWACS direct all the other aircraft in the space. But you could do it differently. You might just have sensors mounted in the AWACS, and every airplane in the space could get a direct transmission."

"Why don't we do it that way?" I asked.

"There's a variety of reasons," Watman said. "Looking at the problem in a traditional cost-benefit way, at least on paper, there are powerful incentives to centralize. Otherwise you'd have to build an AWACS receiver into every plane, which is expensive and challenging for the pilot to deal with.

"The problem is in the question of time and effectiveness, as opposed to efficiency. What you underestimate with the centralized AWACS is the amount of time it takes to run information into the AWACS and then out again, instead of sending it directly to all the planes. Also, the people sitting in the AWACS are farther from the tactical situation than the people in the attack planes. It might be better to put more power into the hands of the people closest to the problem. But the other point of view is that it's better to put the power in the hands of the person with the overview."

That's the Network Army versus the Engineered Society. Right there.

Network Army, Not

One thing is very clear: Network-Centric Warfare is *not* a Network Army at war. It's an Engineered Society adaptation. It changes the dynamic of war by speeding up the rate of information flow, ideally making information simultaneously available everywhere on the battlefield. But it doesn't distribute the decision making. That's still centralized; it's just *faster*. It's still assumed that a complex fighting force *can't organize itself.*

"Americans have always had the communications equipment, but we've never divested ourselves of the centralized approach," Watman said. "There've been attempts to give local commanders more authority, but they've met with only partial success. It's surprising in an individualist country."

Not if football is the model for how you play, and Microsoft is the model for how you do business.

"Promotion in the American military is exceedingly competitive," Watman said. "If you, as an officer, mess up in any way other than trivial, you very likely have ruined your career. That breeds micromanagement to the *max*. Senior officers do *not* want to leave their careers in the hands of some lieutenant. Numerous officers have been dismissed because they were victims of acts of God, because they were sound asleep and something happened on the ship. With some exceptions, a captain of a ship is responsible 24 hours a day, no matter what. It takes a very secure individual to delegate under those circumstances.

"It's not as if we're a bunch of 'droids shuffling mindlessly," Watman added. "If you talk to the people who favor centralization, they've got good arguments. The weapons are capable and powerful. We don't have unlimited numbers of them. The forces are varied in their characteristics; they have to be carefully blended to get the right results. You can't do that in a decentralized way. It's like an orchestra with a conductor."

"A conductor has a score," I said. "He knows what's coming next." It's an interesting simile, though. If you want an example of a rigid, hierarchical Engineered Society, a symphony orchestra works pretty well. The biggest difference between Stalin and Leopold Stokowski, the legendarily dictatorial conductor of the Boston Symphony Orchestra, is that Stokowski didn't actually kill people when he purged them. (And Stokowski had talent, of course, for something besides purges.)

"Sure," Watman agreed. "You can compensate in battle by having redundant plans and coordinating carefully. Read Field Marshal Montgomery. He used to talk about 'tidying up the battlefield.' Don't rush off everywhere; keep everybody coordinated, well-organized, under control. The Germans, if one unit ran ahead of the others, they'd swing their resources behind the unit that was in the lead and let them run. It's another way of coordinating."

So the centralized army of an Engineered Society responds to the unexpected, flexibly and effectively, as long as the unexpected is another Engineered Society army. But a centralized army can't be everywhere, even if surveillance *is*.

On September 11, 2001, as on every other day, the North American Air Defense Command (NORAD) was thoroughly prepared for any threat to American airspace originating *outside* North America. Between them, NORAD and the FAA had complete radar visibility over most of the world. But they weren't prepared to deal with an airborne threat originating *inside* the United States, like American jetliners turned into flying bombs. (It's something like the French and the Maginot Line; NORAD was facing

DO YOU NEED A NETWORK ARMY TO FIGHT A (CRIMINAL) NETWORK ARMY?

The following testimony by U.S. Secret Service Deputy Special Agent in Charge—Financial Crimes Division, James A. Savage Jr., before the Senate Committee on the Judiciary, Subcommittee on Technology, Terrorism, and Government Information, July 25, 2001, illustrates how a Network Army model is already being deployed in support of cyber-law enforcement. [All emphasis is mine.][3]

> The Secret Service has found a highly effective formula for combating high tech crime—a formula that has been successfully developed by our New York Electronic Crimes Task Force. While the Secret Service leads this innovative effort, **we do not control or dominate the participants and the investigative agenda of the task force.** Rather, **the task force provides a productive framework and collaborative crime-fighting environment in which the resources of its participants can be combined to effectively and efficiently make a significant impact on electronic crimes.** Other law enforcement agencies bring additional criminal enforcement jurisdiction and resources to the task force while representatives from private industry, such as telecommunications providers, for instance, bring a wealth of technical expertise.
>
> Although based in New York City, the task force provides assistance and conducts investigations, **which span the country and often lead overseas, harnessing disparate repositories of resources and expertise from the academic, private and government sectors.** It is not uncommon for the New York Task Force to receive requests for assistance directly from foreign law enforcement representatives based upon its reputation for responsiveness and as a center of excellence. The result is a significant impact domestically, and occasionally abroad, as well.
>
> **Within this New York model, established in 1995, there are 50 different federal, state and local law enforcement agencies represented as well as prosecutors, academic leaders and over 100 different private sector corporations.** The wealth of expertise and resources that reside in this task force coupled with unprecedented information sharing yields a highly mobile and responsive machine. In task force investigations, local law enforcement officers hold supervisory positions and representatives from other agencies regularly assume the role of lead investigator. These investigations

DO YOU NEED A NETWORK ARMY TO
FIGHT A (CRIMINAL) NETWORK ARMY? (CONTINUED)

encompass a wide range of computer-based criminal activity, involving e-commerce frauds, intellectual property violations, telecommunications fraud, and a wide variety of computer intrusion crimes, which affect a variety of infrastructures.

Since 1995, the task force has charged over 800 individuals with electronic crimes valued at more than $425 million. It has trained over 10,000 law enforcement personnel, prosecutors, and private industry representatives in the criminal abuses of technology and how to prevent them. **We view the New York Electronic Crimes Task Force as the model for the partnership approach that we hope to employ in additional venues around the country in the very near future.**

forward while the enemy was already behind them.) NORAD sent combat jets up to intercept the hijacked jetliners as soon as the FAA told them the planes had departed significantly from the planned flight paths, but they were too late in every case. NORAD was definitely ready to carry out its mission. It just wasn't ready to deal with something totally new. The trackers could see the planes detour from their planned flight path, but they didn't know what it meant.

The passengers on the planes knew what it meant before anyone else. The only jetliner hijacked that morning that didn't destroy its intended target is the one the passengers fought for. They delegated the job of defense to themselves.

All Engineered Societies are an attempt to impose order, one way or another, on an unruly universe. The Network Army *is* an unruly universe. Maybe you need a Network Army to fight a Network Army.

One thing is certain: If you don't know who's going to come in contact with a terrorist next, and a terrorist might appear anywhere, then anybody might have to be prepared to handle a terrorist. That's very different from deciding to let the authorities *watch everything all the time,* which is what Americans apparently think is required. On the morning of September 27, 2001, NBC advised that, in a recent poll, 84 percent of the Americans surveyed were willing to submit to constant e-mail wiretapping in order to improve security against terrorists. That's reliance on a system, on a *few* people with power and guns watching *everybody else*.

In America, we'd rather *make the cars smart* than *train the drivers*.

CRACKERS AT WAR: THREAT OR MENACE?

CRACKER REMINDER

For the purpose of this book, when I use the term *cracker*, I'm referring to a person who uses computer skills for destructive purposes, not an ignorant redneck with a bad attitude. *Hackers* are the good guys; *crackers* are the bad guys. It may be hard to learn, but you'll have much more credibility with serious cyber-types once you do.

Crackers make trouble. War is trouble. Does that mean that crackers make war? Yes, of a sort, but so far not of the sort where people die, even if they do lose lots of money and get *very* annoyed.

In the spring of 2001, a U.S. bomber on a reconnaissance mission over the coast of mainland China struck a Chinese fighter plane in midair. The resulting tensions between the governments of the People's Republic of China (PRC) and the United States were expressed and ultimately resolved via a variety of traditional, official channels. The conflict also played out in a series of exchanges between crackers based in the PRC and the United States, who assaulted each other electronically, defacing and launching distributed-denial-of-service (DDoS) attacks on Web sites in both countries. That conflict eventually petered out, but it was never officially resolved in the way that a dispute between governments is usually resolved.

While it was going on, lots of Web site operations were disrupted. The September 22, 2001, report from Dartmouth's Institute for Security Technology Studies, titled "Cyber Attacks During the War on Terrorism: A Predictive Analysis" (referred to hereafter as *The O'Neill Report,* after John O'Neill, the career FBI agent and law enforcement professional who died in the World Trade Center attacks on 09-11-01, and to whom the report is dedicated), notes that about 1,200 Web sites based in the United States, "including those belonging to the White House and other government agencies, were subjected to DDoS attacks or defaced with pro-Chinese images over one week in 2001."[4] That's certainly a lot of defacing and denying. "It should be noted that a number of recent Internet worms, including Lion, Adore, and Code Red, are suspected of having originated in China," the report adds. Code Red is estimated by some sources to have caused over $2.4 billion in damage.

This stuff is clearly *malicious.* "Former Republic of Yugoslavia and Serbian attackers repeatedly disrupted NATO's communications infrastructure" during the bombing campaign against "targets in Kosovo and Serbia during the spring of 2000," The O'Neill Report observes, adding: "The attacks periodically brought NATO servers to a standstill over a number of days." Yes, *but:* ". . . services directly related to coordinating and executing the bombing campaign are believed to have been unaffected . . . ."

So we have to ask: What critical war-making functions were affected by all that cracking? I doubt that resolution of either the Chinese-American incident or the NATO action was even delayed by cracker activity, much less that the outcomes were changed in any substantial way.

I can see how this kind of cracking might become dangerous. Intrusions into information systems carry the possibility that somebody will eventually bring down a system that's running a critical war-making (or civilian infrastructure) function. If we were in a Network-Centric Warfare scenario, then messing with NATO servers might involve disruption to the Information Grid or the Sensor Grid, and the result would effectively be a lot of combat units running blind. The point is, though, it hasn't happened yet, and it's apparently not for want of cracker effort. Perhaps it's simply that crackers, however antisocial they may be, aren't killers. People *are* what they *do.* (That implies that things may change, probably for the worse, as the cracker population changes to include people—like terrorists—who *are* killers.)

Is it possible that all these Web site defacements don't really amount to much more than annoyance—part of which is the associated expense—and *cosmetics?*

Follow the Data

Cracking systems to extract *information* is clearly a lot more dangerous to the owners of systems that get cracked, even if the extent of the danger is unpredictable. The Fifth Corollary to Hunter's Second Law is: *It's impossible to calculate the full value of a given piece of information to all the people who might possess it.* This is especially true when information from multiple sources is combined to yield new insights. When somebody steals your information, you don't know why that person wanted it or what he or she is going to do with it. If the thief is very creatively destructive, the answers might be surprising as well as catastrophic.

The value of a given piece of information might be very high to a criminal or an enemy, *whether or not the information is used to launch cyberattacks*. In terms of the potential for harm, it seems clear, at this point, that the most dangerous information is that which can be used to launch successful attacks against targets in the *physical* world, not in cyberspace. "The theft of money or credit card numbers, proprietary information, or sensitive government information can have devastating consequences," *The O'Neill Report* says. And how. You might not even know how devastating for a while. Criminals are opportunistic; they get a credit card number and they use it, right then. Terrorists and nations at war plan ahead.

There's lots of evidence that attempts to gather information that could be used against the legitimate owners—both in commercial competition and in competition or war between nations—are increasing. The U.S. Defense Security Service (DSS) report, *2001 Technology Collection Trends in the U.S. Defense Industry*, notes that the number of "countries with identified collection involvement" related to U.S. defense technology has increased from 44 in 1996 to 63 in 2000. The report adds that ". . . foreign technology collection efforts will continue to address force modernization, **economic competition, and commercial modernization, and will frequently target technologies with dual-use applications** [emphasis mine]."[5]

Is this crime or war? The targets are commercial as well as military—markets perhaps *more* than territory. What's very interesting is that, except for the *targets*—"Information Systems was the most widely sought militarily critical technology category in 2000, as it was in 1999," the DSS says—in most cases, these are not *cyber*-crimes. The DSS lists the three most common approaches to illegally gathering information as "unsolicited requests for information," "soliciting and marketing of services," and "acquisition of U.S. technology/company." "Internet activity"—cracking—accounted for only 4 percent of all attempts to acquire restricted information.

The means for dealing with the relatively few cyber-attacks were described simply by the DSS:

> In one example, a network attack originated in Europe. The attack lasted over a period of a day. . . . All attempts were logged by the firewall monitoring software and no malicious activity was encountered. **The facility had the appropriate level of protection in place to repel such an attack.** [emphasis mine]

There's a simple message here: *Crackers mostly get inside systems that aren't protected, or aren't protected very well.* Like most simple messages, it's too simple. There are certainly crackers with enough skill to get past even very strong security. In his testimony to the Joint Economic Committee of Congress on February 23, 2000, Stephen E. Cross, Director of the Software Engineering Institute at Carnegie Mellon University, cited a few very troubling examples:

> In a case of cyber-extortion, an intruder stole 300,000 credit card numbers from an online music retailer. The intruder, who described himself as a 19-year-old from Russia, sent an e-mail to the *New York Times* bragging he had accessed the company's financial data through a flaw in its software. . . . Security experts still do not know how the site was compromised or the full extent of how the break-in affected the site's customers.
>
> Intruders gained unauthorized access to proprietary information on the computer network of a major U.S. corporation. The company was not able to identify the techniques used by the intruders to break through the firewall.
>
> Just last month, in the most serious systematic breach of security ever for British companies, a group of intruders based in the U.K. broke into the computer systems of at least 12 multinational companies and stolen confidential files. . . . Scotland Yard and the FBI . . . believe the group is highly professional and may be working for information brokers specializing in corporate espionage.[6]

Note that in every one of these examples, the intruder stole valuable *information*. The motive in every case was apparently financial, but as per the Fifth Corollary, *It's impossible to calculate the full value of a given piece of information to all the people who might possess it.* It's impossible as well to know how many people might eventually buy the information stolen in those attacks, or what they might use it for.

Other kinds of attacks, besides intrusions, may also be difficult or impossible to handle. Cross cites distributed-denial-of-service (DDoS) attacks as an example: ". . . there is essentially nothing a site can do with currently available technology to prevent becoming a victim of, for example, a coordinated network flood."

That said, most attacks—particularly the ones that are about stealing information—can be repelled when there's *an appropriate level of protection in place.* We'll return to that point later; it's important when we're talking about how to deal with cyber-crime/cyber-war threats, however serious they may be.

Warrior-Gamesters

In *A History of Warfare,* John Keegan describes:

> . . . war without beginning or end, the endemic warfare of non-state, even pre-state peoples . . . in which there was no distinction between lawful and unlawful bearers of arms . . . a form of warfare which had prevailed during long periods of human history and which, at the margins, still encroached on the life of civilized states . . . .[7]

Keegan is talking about armed warfare waged by irregulars, but the passage seems appropriate. What's more like a *non-state people* than an army of crackers? What cracker would distinguish between *lawful* and *unlawful* bearers of arms? Who would contest that crackers, *at the margins,* encroach on the life of civilized states? (They're certainly not yet encroaching on the life of civilized states at the *core.*)

In cyber-war, the lines between *amateurs and professionals* and *combatants and noncombatants* are blurred on both sides. The U.S.-based crackers involved in the unofficial USA-PRC cyber-war were certainly not under the command of any official U.S. government agency; the Chinese crackers may or may not have been. The victims—none of whom was seriously injured in any sense this time around—included both military and civilian Web sites.

Barriers to entry and exit for members of a cracker Network Army— at war or elsewhere—are practically nonexistent. There's no distinction between *home* and *battlefield.* Like modern office workers, who are "at work" when they're *paying attention to work,* not when they're in the office, the cracker Network Army launches attacks and games from the same place, maybe in the same hour. Their attacks *are* games.

Even more than a bombardier who drops explosives from miles above a target, the members of a cracker Network Army will never see their victims, and will never face a violent counterattack. A cracker is an odd kind of warrior who is emotionally and physically removed from opponents and victims. Given the nature of the weapons used, it's even impossible for the cracker to predict who—friend or foe—will ultimately be harmed by some cyber-attacks.

Like most Network Armies, crackers (at war or otherwise) have few *leaders* per se. They wage war on their terms and schedule, and for their own reasons, potentially including profit. War provides a convenient cover for all sorts of crimes, just as a cyber-crime may eventually provide a convenient smokescreen for the launching of a war.

What's the Difference?

When I talked to Len Hynds, the first Director of the United Kingdom's new National Hi-Tech Crimes Unit (NHTCU), in September 2001, he minimized the distinction between war and crime in cyberspace.[8]

"Cyber-crime and cyber-warfare are terms that have been widely used within the media," he told me. "They're not born out of discussion by law enforcement, in the U.K. or elsewhere. My view is this. The nature of the activity could be the same in both categories. A denial-of-service attack could be cyber-*crime,* but could also be an act of cyber-*war.* So we're not talking about the modus operandi. We're talking about the underlying *motive.*

"And there could be primary and secondary motives. The *underlying* motive may not be immediately apparent. For example, we might identify a group of organized criminals involved in some kind of Internet fraud. We might not know that the money is going to be used to support terrorist activity.

"In a denial of service attack, the obvious motive is the first result of the cracker's actions. He simply brings a Web site to a halt because he can. The underlying motive may not be apparent."

"Maybe to cripple a competitor," I suggested, "to reduce or eliminate his market share."

"That's one possibility," Hynds said.

And what if the perpetrator is a government and the salvo against this competitor is just one step in eliminating competition worldwide for an important national industry? Is that crime, or war? Protecting interests in

TERMINOLOGY FULL DISCLOSURE

I've quoted Len Hynds as using the term *cracker* to refer to a cyber-criminal. In fact, Len used the term *hacker,* as per common practice in the press and among the public at large. In the interest of consistency, and to avoid confusing the reader, I've put the word *cracker* into the mouths of my interviewees when they've used the word *hacker* to mean the same thing.

I trust that the reader will forgive me for wanting to avoid confusion. I trust my interviewees will forgive me for swapping two consonants for one.

a market, captive or otherwise, was one of the classic rationales for war, well into the twentieth century. Money is *still* worth fighting for, much as we might like to think otherwise. (It's not yet an acceptable rationale for murder, of course, at least not for murderers acting on behalf of their *personal* interests.)

There are *so* many layers of possible motives. If a terrorist brings down a building, or destroys a factory, is the intent to make a statement, or kill all those people, or to make a fortune by shorting the stock of the insurance companies or manufacturers affected by the attack, or eliminate a competitor for a certain company in a certain nation (and get paid for it by the company in question), or all of the above?

Criminal Network Army

"In the real world, we recognize the boundaries within which we live," Hynds said. "In the electronic environment, you can live within a cybernation, a cyber-world where you live among like-minded people who think and act the way you do, wherever you live."

He's just described a Network Army.

"It's one of the ways in which criminal activity is revitalized," Hynds said. "For example, organized pedophilia. A pedophile has to know how to make contact with other pedophiles. He has to know he's not alone in his beliefs and views. On the Internet, he can find a chat room where he's surrounded by pedophiles."

He's just described the Lost and Lonely *becoming* a Network Army.

"The most obvious example is within the cracking groups," Hynds said. "It's fascinating to see these groups. They come from all over the world, and they're drawn together by their common purpose. Crackers share tools. They have a commitment to making cracking easier. You can identify similar traits in other groups, too. We see fraud techniques discussed within the Internet environment. Trade secrets are shared. The potential for being *captured* is discussed."

"Do you see criminals *working* together?" I asked. Sharing information is one thing. Network Armies take communal *action*.

"In Italy, there was a case last year where a group of pedophiles came together over the Internet to take action against the people investigating them. They aimed to cause violence to the prosecutors and investigators pursuing them."

That's action.

"That's not common in the U.K., is it?" I said. "No," Hynds said.

Nor in the United States. "But as the cultural norms of the real world spread through Network Armies in the cyberworld, that kind of attitude could spread too," I said.

"It's possible," Hynds said.

WHAT'S POTENTIAL AND WHAT'S REAL?

Speaking of what's possible, *no one has yet offered a scenario for large-scale cyber-assault that is both credible and deadly.* Period. Aside from thefts of information, which in every case are as serious as the information that's stolen, there hasn't been a cyber-assault yet that has caused serious harm *to human beings,* although plenty of money has been spent to fix viruses and other cyber-problems. No assault to date has killed anyone, or even wrecked anyone's national economy.

I repeat: *No one has yet offered a scenario for large-scale cyber-assault that is both credible and deadly.* There are people who claim to have such scenarios. The most widely reported of these was an exercise that was run by the National Security Agency (NSA) in 1997. Called "Eligible Receiver," the scenario aimed to simulate a full-scale cyber-attack on U.S. military and civilian infrastructures. Eligible Receiver, said numerous NSA officials, proved that the United States was wide open to catastrophic cyber-attacks. Press Mentats have generally accepted those claims at face value.

But the Eligible Receiver report was never made public. It's impossible to tell how well-conceived or well-executed it was, or even whether the people talking about it have, inadvertently or otherwise, misrepresented its findings. Certainly the press has misrepresented its findings, since the basic facts about Eligible Receiver—how many crackers were involved, what the targets were, what cyber-techniques were employed, where the software used by the crackers came from, and what the crackers were able to do in terms of disabling systems—vary widely from one press report to the next. In some reports, there were 20 crackers; in others, 35. In some reports, the crackers were able to take down telecommunications and utility systems; in others, NSA officials like John Hamre are quoted as saying they just showed that they *knew how to do it.* (What that means isn't explained. At what point was the demonstration of *how to do it* considered solid enough to prove that *it could be done,* short of throwing the switch?) Some press reports claim that the crackers took out 911 systems. That was flatly contradicted in testimony to Congress by NSA representative Ellie Padgett, in June 1998. (Padgett states plainly that 911 systems were never subjected to cyber-attack, simulated or otherwise, as part of the exercise.)[9] One press report says that the crackers got all the software they needed off "hacker Web sites"; another says that the crackers used commercial off-the-shelf software.

They can't all be right. Maybe none of them is. A look at the Eligible Receiver report would clear up a lot of the confusion. The NSA has chosen not to make the report public, so we're being asked to take its word that it accurately represents how successful a large-scale cyber-attack on our civilian infrastructure could be.

I'd rather not take their word. I'd rather ask the question that any self-respecting Mentat *should* ask: *Why? Why* does nobody seem to know exactly what Eligible Receiver really proved and how? This exercise was supposedly staged and conducted with great success by a team of moderately skilled crackers using widely available software. That's about as far from *secret* as anybody can get. Why is that report classified? If the exercise proved that it's easy, that any cracker can just go in and *do all that damage* at any time, from whom are we hiding this information?

Not the crackers, that's for sure. That leaves *you* and *me*. (And, of course, any credulous Mentats who happen to be listening—the ones who've forgotten to ask *why* and *how,* let alone *what, where,* and *when.*) You might figure that *we're* the ones who need to know. We're the ones who need to protect ourselves. And I do mean protect *ourselves*. Lots of computer attacks, like viruses, are spread via a network from machine to machine. *You can't stop a virus from a central agency like the NSA,* any more than you can stop a virus in the real world by circulating an order from Washington. *Every* infected machine has to be treated *individually. Every* machine owner has to know how to avoid infection.

In cheap science fiction movies from the 1950s, the President and the Joint Chiefs of Staff decide not to tell the population that flying saucers (or giant ants, or giant anything—I really dig the giant octopus in *It Came from Beneath the Sea;* hail Ray Harryhausen!) are real, because that news would cause a whole lot of panic. In those movies, the population eventually finds out that the flying saucers are real *anyway,* because they land in everybody's backyard and begin ray-gunning everything in sight. This situation is kind of the reverse. We're being told that the flying saucers have already landed, and we'd better freak out and do something *right now.*

If the flying saucers have landed, they're largely invisible. So we have to rely on a secret report that supposedly proves that the flying saucers are real. And to a certain extent, they *are* real. *Some* sightings have occurred. Cyber-attacks *happen*. They *will* happen more frequently.

They're just not deadly. Not yet; maybe never.

But we're acting as if they already are deadly. And the solutions that are being proposed *are*, definitely, *deadly*.

Not Digital Pearl Harbor *Again?*

Here's *Newsday, Inc.* describing Representative Rob Andrews (D-New Jersey) on May 2, 2000, announcing his "Cyberterrorism Prevention Act," which was later enacted into law as an amendment to the Defense Authorization Act of 2000:[10]

> "We are here to talk about preventing an electronic Pearl Harbor."
>
> Those ringing words may seem out of place, coming as they do from a politician in a suit and tie as he stands inside a windowless electric power switching station some 8,000 miles east of Hawaii. But that's the point that Rep. Rob Andrews, D-N.J., is trying to make: The next big attack on the United States could hit anywhere, even the South Jersey suburbs of Philadelphia.
>
> Indeed, it's quite possible that the attackers could be Americans and that their weapon of choice could be a computer. In March 1997, for example, a Massachusetts teenager hacked into a telephone company computer system and knocked out telecommunications for the western part of the state. For six hours, air traffic controllers at the Worcester airport relied on cell phones and battery-powered radios to direct planes to safety.
>
> In February 1998, two California teens, working with a third hacker in Israel, broke into a Pentagon computer that was managing U.S. troop deployments to the Persian Gulf.

This story has several things in common with almost all the writing done so far about cyber-warfare. First and foremost, it's *ballistic* from the start. We're not just talking about a cyber-attack, we're talking about the *next Pearl Harbor*. There's a pervasive sense of dread. The next attack could take place anywhere, even in South Jersey, a suburb of Philadelphia, for God's sake! (W. C. Fields, whose tombstone supposedly bears the legend "On the whole, I'd rather be in Philadelphia," would ask, at this point, where he might find a cracker or two, and whether their services come cheap.)

The examples cited to prove how dangerous this stuff is—not *could be*, but *is*—are all about potentials. "Two California teens, working with a third hacker, in Israel, broke into Pentagon computer . . ." Well, that's bad—absolutely *no* doubt about it—and it's got to be stopped. (In fact, it can be stopped. I'll discuss how later.) It could have been very bad. The crackers might have stolen information that could have been used to hurt people. If there'd been a shooting war going on, information about troop movements could have hurt a lot of people.

But what's *really* bad is that there weren't enough controls on a Pentagon computer to keep two teenage crackers out of the system. It's usually *not that hard.* As I said before: *Crackers mostly get inside systems that aren't protected.* It's like stealing a car that's sitting at the curb, idling, while the driver is talking to somebody a block away. *Any* punk can do it.

Congressman Andrews thinks these cyber-crimes demand immediate, dramatic action, more than turning off the ignition and locking the doors for sure. The article continues:

> . . . Andrews would allow the Defense Department to immediately investigate cyber-attacks against itself; current law requires the Justice Department to determine that an attack has come from outside the United States before the Pentagon's security services can get involved.
>
> But, as Andrews observes, "Computer crime is instantaneous . . . it ignores both distance and borders." Indeed, a Hacker Internationale of sorts already exists. The 1998 attack on Persion Gulf troop deployments began in California, but it was simultaneously assisted by a citizen of another country.

So—two California teenagers plus one guy from Israel equals a "Hacker Internationale."

Let's call in the troops.

Rob Andrews Says . . .

I spoke to Congressman Andrews via phone on the morning of September 28, 2001. The interview had been rescheduled from earlier that week because of Congressional meetings related to the attacks on September 11. I started the interview by asking Andrews what he considered to be the likeliest scenarios for a deadly cyber-attack.[11]

"There are three basic threats," Andrews said immediately. He's clearly well versed in the subject. "First, corruption of the systems that run the power grid. Lots of confusion would follow that. It would include bringing down communications systems prior to a conventional attack.

"Second, disruption of the air traffic control system, either by shutting off power to the system or by corrupting the data.

"Finally, masking of a physical attack. For example, pouring arsenic into a reservoir, then corrupting the data that monitors water quality to mask the attack."

The list sounds plausible, but it's not as straightforward as it seems. The introduction to *The O'Neill Report* says that:

> American and allied military strikes are likely to lead to further terrorist strikes against American and allied citizens and interests, both in the U.S. and abroad. This aggression will likely take a variety of forms and may include cyber-attacks by terrorist groups themselves or by targeted nation-states. Even more likely are **cyber-attacks by sympathizers of the terrorists, hackers with general anti-U.S. or anti-allied sentiments, and thrill seekers lacking any particular political motivation.** [emphasis mine]

No one doubts any of this. The report continues:

> The specter of an unanticipated and massive attack on critical infrastructures . . . has been raised in a number of reports on national security and by the NIPC. **The degrees to which these infrastructures are dependent on information systems, and interrelated to one another, are still not understood. Neither is the extent to which these information systems are exposed to outside entry from the Internet.** [emphasis mine]

So we don't really understand how an external attacker would get into these systems, or how that attacker could coordinate an attack against multiple systems to bring the infrastructures down. In other words, we don't really know that our critical infrastructures are so vulnerable to cyber-attack. (Wasn't Eligible Receiver supposed to demonstrate that?)

The O'Neill Report goes into details about some of the infrastructures involved. Financial systems, it turns out, run mostly on private networks, so they're fairly hard for crackers to crack. "Voice communications systems" like "911 and emergency services telephone exchanges" are vulnerable to "proprietary software attacks from **insiders familiar with the technical details of the system**" [emphasis mine].

That's a telling statement. An insider like that isn't a cracker coming in over a network. Protecting the *network* while that guy is around is like guarding the road while murderers set up shop in your house. He's not any kind of *generalist* cracker, either. He's a trained mole, planted well in advance of an actual attack.

Electrical infrastructures, water resources, and oil and gas infrastructures are more vulnerable, but it's not just the cyber-stuff that's vulnerable there. For water resources, the report says, "Physical security, in addition to heightened cyber-security awareness, must be followed during the impending conflict."

It's the Devil You Know

Even more important is this comment, which follows up on the report's observation about the dangers to voice communication systems:

> **Malicious insiders are the greatest threat to our critical national infrastructures.** Insiders armed with specialized knowledge of systems and privileged access are capable of doing great harm. [emphasis mine]

That's twice they said it: The most dangerous attacker is inside the system, not in a cyber sense, but physically. He's not an intruder. He works there.

There's no doubt that *any insiders armed with specialized knowledge of systems and privileged access* are capable of *extremely* serious damage. Gartner estimates that more than 70 percent of all cyber-crime is the work of insiders. We're constantly warning clients to *watch out for the people who have legitimate access to the system already*—the people who work for the company that's going to be victimized.

Of the three basic attacks Representative Andrews describes, the example he provides of the third type—masking arsenic in a reservoir by messing with the sensor systems—absolutely requires that kind of insider knowledge. How would a cracker without such knowledge know what to do, even if he got external access to the systems? What's the chance that those sensor systems are accessible via the Internet, given that: *the degrees to which these infrastructures are dependent on information systems, and interrelated to one another, are still not understood, and neither is the extent to which these information systems are exposed to outside entry from the Internet?*

This is very serious stuff. But it's also very different from the idea that a cyber-hacker will come in via the Internet, from thousands of miles away, to take out our infrastructures.

Do we still need to bring in the military?

How about checking resumes when we hire people at the Water Works, and being a little more careful, at the Immigration and Naturalization Service, about who gets into the country, and maybe taking the necessary steps to implement effective security on the information systems?

Isn't It a *Problem* to Turn the Military Loose on the Rest of Us?

"You're talking about overriding the Posse Comitatus Act," I said to Congressman Andrews. (That's the 1878 law that forbids policing, within the borders of the United States by U.S. military forces.) "Isn't that dangerous?" Not that it hasn't been done already—military involvement in the destruction of the Branch Davidian compound at Waco, Texas, in 1993, was one of the things that made Timothy McVeigh decide to blow up a building full of federal government employees. But why make it *legal*? "Isn't involvement of the military in domestic investigations a slippery slope?" I asked.

"Yes," he said, "but it's a slope we have to traverse." From the way he said it, I was sure he'd heard the question delivered in exactly those terms before, and delivered the same answer. "Take the example of the attack on the reservoir. We could leave it as an FBI—a *criminal*—matter. Or we could treat it immediately as a *military* matter and bring in military intelligence. The third option is to balance the approaches. If you treat it simply as a matter of criminality, suppose the perpetrator was trained by a terrorist in Egypt? You could have a lot of dead people by the time you find that out."

Yes, you could; no question. I fear you *would*, and it wouldn't much matter where the perpetrator was trained. If a reservoir is poisoned and water quality sensors are disabled or manipulated, people will certainly die. *Any* investigation will be after the fact. The only hope of avoiding that is to stop it before it starts. Does that mean we bring in military intelligence *before any crime is committed*? That's a preemptive defense. This is a war, so preemptive defense is allowed. But wouldn't it be more effective to check the resumes of the employees at the Water Works? Or even put armed guards around the reservoir?

"On the other hand," Andrews said, "this could lead to the militarization of everything."

Definitely.

It's the Target, Not the Motive

"That's not what we want either," Andrews said. "So the way to solve it is to look at context. If there's any evidence to suggest that it could be part of an attempt to destroy the country, you have to invite involvement by the defense and military community. Involvement should stop when evidence shows that there's no involvement of terrorists."

Well, anyone who tries to poison a reservoir is trying to destroy part of the country. I guess the *context* is the *target*. This is a very different approach from the one described to me by Len Hynds of the U.K.'s NHTCU. "We're not talking about the modus operandi. We're talking about the underlying motive," Hynds said to me. "And there could be primary and secondary motives. The underlying motive may not be immediately apparent."

What was the motive for the break-in that those two California teenagers and their Israeli pal pulled on a Pentagon computer in 1998? "The obvious motive is the first result of the cracker's actions," Hynds said. "He simply brings a Web site to a halt because he can." Teenagers are always doing stupid and daring things just to prove they can. This was really stupid, but was it war? Certainly it would be now. No matter how stupid you are, you can't attack a military facility during an actual war and claim you were just playing.

"This *is* a slippery slope," I said. "We didn't override Posse Comitatus during the drug wars. Then, as now, there was fear that foreign powers were harming the United States, and there was, in fact, significant damage to the human infrastructure. The military resisted involvement in the drug wars. Why override Posse Comitatus now?"

"Because the acts that have been done are much more damaging and much more immediate," Andrews said.

Leap of Faith

Something bothered me in that statement. "Congressman, you used the past tense," I said. "These are *prospective* acts."

"I would have said so on September 10," Andrews said.

"September 11 was a physical attack," I said. "I've seen no evidence of cyber-attacks, nor even any evidence that attacks that could kill people are possible."

"There's classified material, war gaming, that shows the potential," Andrews said.

There it was. The big leap.

The *potential* for a deadly cyber-attack is the same as an *actual* attack. The *actual* physical attack on September 11 somehow demonstrates that the *potential* cyber-attack is real.

And the *potential-actual* attack justifies using *every resource possible* to prevent the *potential* damage. That includes using the military to police U.S. citizens.

So What?

A lot of the people who read this chapter will ask themselves why I care. Here's why. If we're justified in calling in the military to police *every potential attack* that could occur, then we are on a *really* slippery slope, an 80-degree incline coated with petroleum jelly. A lot of potential attacks—most of the really dangerous attacks—have nothing to do with cyberspace and *everything* to do with physical space.

Poisoning a reservoir is not a cyber-event. If we have to protect every reservoir in the country from physical attack—and we might—we're soon going to need troops on every corner in the country. And we'll have them there indefinitely because that's how long we're going to have terrorists.

Maybe that's the way it has to be. That's the way it is in Israel and Northern Ireland. In Israel, the military can stop anybody on the street, at any time, for any reason. That's what you do when the next guy to get on the bus could be carrying a bomb; you see a guy with a bulky coat, and you ask him *What's under the coat?*

But if we've got to go there, it ought to be because there's a *real* threat.

"On the public record, Operation Eligible Receiver showed the effects of attacks on public facilities," Andrews said.

But Eligible Receiver *isn't on the public record.* And Eligible Receiver was a war *game,* not the real thing. And there's no way to argue about what's in a classified report. We don't really know *what* it showed.

Is that the idea?

"In many cases, in that game, the victims didn't know for some time that they'd been attacked," Andrews said.

Well then, I guess they didn't *die.* And since the games were apparently a simulation, why would they know anyway? And where did that simulation run? On the victim's systems? Or on a computer running a model in an NSA office?

We were out of time. The Congressman had to leave. "Emphasize this," Andrews said. "There's an awful lot of *I told you sos* going on. I'm not doing that. The issue isn't *if* this will happen, it's *when.* We have to make sure it doesn't happen by doing something about it now."

I agree, but I don't. The issue *is* if, *and* when. And I agree that we have to do something, but I disagree that turning the military loose on U.S. citizens is the thing to do right now.

The primary goal is to stop attacks before they start. Military cyber-policing isn't the right tool for that. First, it won't work. Second, it takes up time and resources that could be spent on the things that *do* work.

Let's talk about both those things. Most of all, let's talk about the things that stop cyber-attacks before they start.

Maybe we'll learn something about stopping some of the *physical* attacks—the *really* dangerous ones, the ones that are known to kill people—too.

WHAT TO DO, RIGHT NOW

I appreciate that knowledgeable observers—some of them are my colleagues at Gartner—disagree with me about the nature of cyber-threats. I appreciate that this stuff matters. I appreciate that if we get it wrong, people might get hurt or killed.

I take some comfort from the fact that I've looked at the to-do lists for cyber-security produced by people who clearly disagree with me, and what I see there is similar to the advice Gartner gave its clients before 9–11–01. For example, *The O'Neill Report* proposes the following.

First, put the nation "on high cyber-alert during the war on terrorism." That means watching traffic in cyber-space for activity that might indicate an impending attack. That traffic information is there now, but relatively few people are paying attention to it. It's expensive to monitor because it requires smart people, but it's not difficult in a technical sense. It's even subject to automation, in the sense that we're talking about masses of factual data—what traffic is moving where, when—that can be analyzed via data mining. That takes money, too, but it's well within the state of the art.

Second, follow standard "best practices" for computer and physical security, including things like installing antivirus software and firewalls, and keeping all of that, plus the operating systems and software, up to date. The only impediment to that is more money, again to hire skilled personnel to do the job.

Did You Say *Basic?*

Lots of systems administrators aren't taking these basic steps now, and that's a prime reason why their systems get cracked. "Any credible vulnerability assessment will find that two out of three Web servers connected to the Internet are vulnerable to simple attacks that can at least result in changing the content of the Web server," my Gartner colleague, John Pescatore, said in early September 2001.[12] Consider the "Moonlight

Maze" cyber-crime, in which dozens of Web sites in the United States and Canada were cracked by Eastern European crackers over a period of *years*. Most of those sites hadn't applied known security patches for their server operating systems, months after the patches were available. They left the door open. They were easy marks.

Third, the report says, "Secure critical information assets." You might take them offline, for example. If you did, they'd still be vulnerable to dangerous *insiders,* but that's a different problem.

Fourth, implement "Ingress and Egress Filtering" to ensure that incoming Internet packets—collections of bits—are bona fide messages from bona fide sources, and to slow them down if they're not. "These preventive measures are well within the capabilities of most Internet service providers," the report advises.

The Cost of Doing Business

"The White House Office of Science and Technology estimates an annual cost of $100 million for U.S. losses of proprietary information," Stephen Cross said in his testimony in February 2000. "The American Society for Information Science (ASIS) estimates that the losses may exceed $250 billion." Well, that's a range of about 25,000 percent, and it doesn't even include losses resulting from viruses and distributed denial of service attacks, which we've estimated at Gartner to be in the low billions-of-dollars range annually. I guess we can take our pick. I'd bet that $100 million for *losses of proprietary information* is on the low side. But who knows? Lots of businesses don't like to report their losses from cyber-attacks, internal or otherwise. It's something like having syphilis in the 1940s. Plenty of people did, but nobody wanted to admit it. It wasn't just embarrassing; it was, like, *really* embarrassing. That was the Lost and Lonely scenario for venereal disease. Sexually Transmitted Disease sufferers are now a Network Army, and ads for herpes medications run on network television. Pretty soon we'll see ads on TV for cyber-security services, and they'll start with a scene in which a calm consultant in a nice dark suit reassures a troubled, vaguely guilty CEO that the very *best* companies get cracked *all the time.*

A single loss of proprietary information can cost hundreds of millions of dollars, as it did for a Gartner client, a leading manufacturer, whose bid for a major contract was stolen and then beaten—barely, suspiciously barely—by a competitor. Given the choice between moderately high predictable costs and potentially catastrophic, unpredictable costs, most people choose the predictable costs. That's why everyone reading this has some kind of insurance.

This is all straightforward and practical, isn't it? There's a problem. There's a pretty good solution. It's just another cost of doing business, really. It's more than you wanted to pay, but costs are like that.

So why are we all *freaking out?*

I Didn't Say It Would Be *Easy*

The O'Neill Report offers straightforward advice, but it's a misrepresentation to say it's optimistic. It closes by warning that while "the vast majority of previous politically related cyber-attacks have been nuisance attacks . . . the potential exists for much more devastating cyber-attacks . . . ." The mood is dark. There's trouble ahead.

Cross sees trouble, too. "Internet attacks in general, and denial-of-service attacks in particular, remain easy to accomplish, hard to trace, and a low risk to the attacker," he says. "The intruder technology is evolving, and future tools may be more difficult to defeat." He adds:

> There is little evidence of improvement in the security features of most products; developers are not devoting sufficient effort to apply lessons learned about the sources of vulnerabilities. The CERT Coordination Center routinely receives reports of new vulnerabilities. We continue to see the same types of vulnerabilities in newer versions of products that we saw in earlier versions. Engineering for ease of use is not being matched by engineering for ease of secure administration. . .

Cross is talking about systemic issues that go beyond responding to attacks. He's talking about the basic principles behind commercial software design, construction, and testing.

At the Core

"We continue to see the same types of vulnerabilities in newer versions of products that we saw in earlier versions," Cross says. It takes time to engineer security into software, and it's most effective when it's done at the level of basic architecture. That means you have to think about security from the start. If you don't, you get trouble. Security in Microsoft's products has always been an *add-on,* a *feature,* never part of the basic architecture of the software. The result is that Microsoft's products get cracked all the time. Microsoft's not unusual in terms of its approach to design. Very few software

companies build security into their basic architectures. But because Microsoft's products are so widely used, and because they perform such basic, powerful functions on any computer, they're very attractive targets for crackers who want to get the biggest possible effect for their efforts.

It's a tremendous change from current software industry practices—from conception-to-design-to-coding-to-testing-to-installation-to-maintenance-to-*everything*—to focus on security first. The short history of computing since the earliest days of the personal computer has been about erasing boundaries and getting *more people into the driver's seat*. The vehicles built for that purpose look good, even if they don't have the equivalent of a horn or brakes. But no one seems to care, so far. Brakes are for people who want to stop. We want to *go*.

In 1998, I predicted, in research published by Gartner, that widespread software failures resulting from the Y2K bug would produce a backlash against faulty software. At that time, it seemed likely to me and my colleagues that Y2K was going to produce at least some seriously ill effects for a number of people. I expected that software development would become a regulated industry by 2002—the way pharmaceuticals are regulated now, and for pretty much the same reasons.

Y2K didn't happen—at least not in the form of a big public catastrophe. Software's not a regulated industry. New software that breaks is introduced every week. Anyone who owns a computer owns software that breaks. But the stakes seem to be higher now. Maybe they're not, but they seem to be. If terrorists and cyber-criminals are just waiting for your software to screw up so they can come in and hurt you, then faulty software isn't just annoying, or even infuriating. It's a *menace*.

Does that mean that software is more likely to be regulated now? "Technology evolves so rapidly that vendors concentrate on time to market," Cross says, "often minimizing that time by placing a low priority on security features. Until their customers demand products that are more secure, the situation is unlikely to change." So it's up to us, the people who buy the stuff. Are *we* ready to demand products that are more secure?

We're a little scared, maybe getting more scared, but this is a big change. We're not used to thinking of security first. We're Distracted Consumers. We pick up strangers in bars, and we barge into the Internet with our credit cards, and we figure if it was really dangerous, somebody would stop us. So sexually transmitted disease (STD) victims are a Network Army, and we have an Internet that any teenager with an average IQ and a personal computer can crack, even if *cracking*, for most of these intruders, is like spray-painting their names on the side of a subway train in cyberspace.

I wonder how scared we all have to be before we're ready to slow down.

The weird thing is that so many people seem to think we need to be scared out of our wits—scared into believing a cyber-catastrophe is coming—just to make sure we take care of the basics.

Maybe they're right. Relatively few people have been taking care of the basics until now.

1, 2, 3

It seems like the first thing to do is to plug the holes that should've been plugged all along. That's pretty simple. We might have to spend a little more, but we know how to do it.

The second thing to do is to change the way the software industry works, from an emphasis on innovation to an emphasis on quality engineering. You can have both, of course, if you're set up to do it that way, but the industry isn't set up that way now. That'll take some time. Maybe forever.

What's left?

What about teaching the drivers—you and me—to drive?

Can You Teach the Drivers How to Drive?

Cross's testimony to Congress recommended a few steps toward improving Internet security. The first two were all about gathering information:

- Support an established center for collecting, analyzing, and disseminating information assurance information.
- Support the growth and use of global detection mechanisms.

The third step was: *Support education and training to raise the level of security.* The audience for that training, as he put it, is basically everybody:

> The combination of easy access and user-friendly interfaces has drawn users of all ages and from all walks of life. As a result, many users of the Internet . . . have no more understanding of the technology than they do of the engineering behind other infrastructures. . . .
>
> There is a critical need for education and increased awareness of the characteristics, threats, opportunities, and appropriate behavior in cyberspace . . . in particular, support programs that provide early training in security practices and appropriate use. . . . Children should learn early about acceptable and unacceptable behavior when they begin using computers, just as they are taught about acceptable and unacceptable behavior when

they begin using libraries. Although this recommendation is aimed at elementary and secondary school teachers, they themselves need to be educated by security experts and professional organizations. Parents need to be educated as well and should reinforce lessons in security and behavior on computer networks.

Well, that's *almost* everybody. Let's include the professionals too:

Similarly, many system administrators lack adequate knowledge about the network and about security. . . . Invest in awareness campaigns that stress the need for security training for system administrators, network managers, and chief information officers. . . . In the short term, the greatest need is for short "how to" and "what to be aware of" courses. In the long term, there should be undergraduate-level or master's-level specialties in network and information security.

So, first we put the mechanisms in place, to figure out what's really happening. Then we teach the drivers to drive. Then everybody drives. Safely.

Anyway, that's the plan.

Solid Engineering

It's a good plan. It's an *engineer's* plan. Cross leads the Software *Engineering* Institute. Engineers are taught to define a problem, gather information, define the solution, and implement. It's neat and it works for them, consistently.

The Software Engineering Institute promotes a program for managing software development that's based on something called the Capability Maturity Model, which is all about how *consistently* an organization behaves in the process of developing software. The Capability Maturity Model is very structured, very clearly defined, very *engineered*. We've estimated at Gartner that it takes a typical information services organization located at the bottom rung of the Capability Maturity Model—that *is* typical, by the way—over two years to get to Level 2, and another one to two years to get to Level 3, where it's executing the development process as consistently as, well, an engineer. It costs an organization about $8,000 per developer to get to that point.

The Software Engineering Institute isn't afraid of training. It's not afraid to prescribe it to other people, either. It's sure that the big payoff justifies the big effort.

Some of my colleagues have doubts. Here's Mike Zboray—formerly an analyst on Gartner's security research team, and currently head of systems security for Gartner—commenting on security training programs in an internal Gartner debate in October 2001:

> "Education" [in security policies and procedures] is a waste of time. It hasn't worked in the past and won't work now. If you want to feel like you're doing something, then do an education program. If you want to accomplish something, then invest in technology and back-office processes to accomplish specific security goals.

I get Zboray's point. It's like Driver's Ed. You get a few hours of orientation when you're age 16—here's the gas, here's the brake, here's the wheel, *let's go!*—and then you never hear about it again. If you've got a talent for driving, you figure out how to do it, more or less on your own. If you don't, you're a bad driver, maybe a dangerous one. Either way, the training doesn't have much of an effect. It especially doesn't have much of an effect on drivers who have neither talent nor interest.

Real training—the kind airline pilots get—assumes that some people are going to wash out. The ones who wash out *don't get to fly*. Driver's Ed isn't about washing out anybody. The assumption is that everybody, more or less, is going to drive sooner or later, whether or not they learn anything in Driver's Ed. They can flunk Driver's Ed and still get their license. They just don't get whatever Brownie points the Driver's Ed certificate might have gotten them with their insurance company or high school.

If all those kids in the classes Cross proposes *don't get it* about Internet security, are they going to be banned from the Internet? Are their parents going to be banned if *they* don't get it? *Teaching the drivers to drive* means that the ones who don't get it *don't get to drive*.

It seems like the drivers in this case are the *system administrators, network managers, and chief information officers* Cross mentions as candidates for how-to training now and university degrees later. They're the ones who learn how to drive or get off the road. But I see why Cross wants to train everybody. The problem touches everybody.

Distributed Problem, Distributed Solution

Cyberspace is distributed. Even physical space seems more open in the World Without Secrets. The boundaries are *down*. "[Control] is in the hands of users, not in the hands of the provider; and use cannot be administered by a central authority," Cross says. "The security of each system on the Internet depends on the security of **all other systems on the network**" [emphasis mine].

Like Cross, *The O'Neill Report* describes a distributed threat, and it proposes countermeasures that rely on a distributed response. Item one on the report's list—put the nation on high cyber-alert—might be handled centrally, though not with current infrastructures for monitoring. The rest of the list—implement standard best practices for security, secure critical information, install ingress and egress filtering—*must* be handled by systems and security administrators and Internet Service Providers at the local level. That's where the computers are. If the biggest danger is insiders, then you've got to watch the insiders, and you can't do that anywhere but on the scene.

If Cross is right—if the security of every system does depend on every other system—then we're done for. An infinite number of points to launch an attack equals an infinite number of chances for success. But we ought to keep in mind that the purpose of security is to limit the damage a cracker can do. You really don't have to provide bulletproof protection for every computer on the network. You have to protect the ones that have something, or do something, that, in the wrong hands, would be potentially damaging.

Nobody's going to take down a refinery by cracking you and me. Nobody's going to find the plans for the Stealth bomber on my home computer. If what we're worried about most is cyber-war, then ordinary citizens' getting cracked doesn't seem like such a big problem. It's certainly not enough of a problem to justify calling in the troops. We wouldn't do that even if those citizens were mugged.

We haven't discussed some of the more radical solutions, like building multiple Internets. *The O'Neill Report* said that banks were relatively secure because they're on private networks. Why wouldn't we use the same solution for everyone else? Why should everybody have access to every Internet?

But why go that far? Can you imagine what we'd have to do to make any part of the world *perfectly safe*?

What Is *Safe Enough*?

The systems humans create always have noise in them. The real question is: *How much noise can we tolerate?* We tolerate 40,000 people dying on U.S. highways every year, and over 1,000,000 dying worldwide. That's a lot of noise, man. But it's not exceptional anymore, so *we can handle it*.

Cyber-space is exceptional. Nobody—**nobody**—has ever been killed in cyber-space, but already we seem to think the noise there is unbearably loud. Cross seems to think we can't tolerate *any* noise in cyber-space. *The security of each system on the Internet depends on the security of all other systems on the network,* he says. What will it take to engineer all the noise out of the system? Will training every school child, every teacher, and every parent do it? What about every systems administrator, network administrator, and chief information officer? When is it safe enough?

It may already be safe enough, if by *safe enough* we mean that *nobody gets killed.* If by *safe enough* we mean *no critical information gets stolen, and no critical infrastructures are harmed,* we can do it—more or less successfully—with tools that are available to us right now. If by *safe enough* we mean *no one gets robbed or seduced, ever,* then we're never going to get there. Our streets aren't that safe, even the ones with cameras all over them. Why should cyber-space be the only completely safe environment ever built by humans?

I guess we're still virgins in cyberspace, and maybe that's why we act like shocked virgins whenever someone commits a crime with a computer, or when anyone suggests to us that a crime *might* be committed, *could* be committed, *almost certainly will be committed* some day by a *very bad man in cyberspace.* I think the anxious patter is a little tired. When the people telling us that there's so much danger out there say in the very next breath that we can protect ourselves by taking the routine maintenance seriously, I have to wonder what the real problem is.

Here's What I'd Do

If I were in charge of cyber-security for everyone reading this, here's what I'd do.

I'd tell everybody—especially the systems administrators who know how to do the job—to make their systems secure. "Secure" means secure *in proportion to the importance of the system in ensuring public well-being.* I'd tell everyone that there's a remote chance of a cyber-attack that could do serious damage to people, but we can handle the threat if everybody takes a few precautions. (I'd avoid calling those "common sense" precautions, because if they were common, you wouldn't have to tell anybody about them.)

I'd invest in the straightforward technologies and procedures that make it harder for crackers to get in. I'd check the bio and resume of every worker in an infrastructure industry who has access to a computer. Then I'd recheck the bio and resume of every worker in an infrastructure

WHAT'S SECURE ENOUGH?

For those who want to get technical, here's John Pescatore's description of what kinds of technology are needed to ensure various levels of Internet security.[13]

- *Level 1*—All Web servers should be protected by a simple firewall that limits the ports and services the Web server exposes to the Internet, and monitors the state of connections to the server.

- *Level 2*—The operating system under each Web server should be configured according to common security checklists. Security processes should be established that ensure that all security patches are tested and promptly applied to all Internet-exposed Web servers.

- *Level 3*—Network-based intrusion detection sensors should be deployed on the network segment hosting the Web servers.

- *Level 4*—Installing host-based intrusion detection software on Web servers requires more operational expense but can provide detailed indication of attacks against high-value servers.

- *Level 5a*—Policy enforcement software acts as a layer between the Web server operating system and all applications. These products prevent hackers from subverting vulnerable applications to take control of the operating system.

- *Level 5b*—Deploying additional firewalls as proxy servers that focus on HTTP (and future protocols such as SOAP) in front of Web servers can prevent the vast majority of attacks without requiring software to be installed on every Web server.

- *Level 6*—The most secure approach to Internet-exposed Web servers is to only deploy nearly invulnerable Web servers. By running Web servers on trusted operating systems, or using Web server appliances that are based on trusted operating systems, enterprises can achieve the highest level of security but at a very high cost of ownership.

All enterprises should implement at least Levels 1 and 2 as a minimum level of due diligence. Any enterprise storing sensitive information on Web servers should add Level 3. Enterprises using Web

(continued)

WHAT'S SECURE ENOUGH? (CONTINUED)

servers as front ends for external access to applications should add Level 4, 5a, or 5b, depending on a realistic assessment of the organization's ability to control the configuration of security software on Web servers. Organizations that have problems controlling the actions of Webmasters should stick to Level 4. Those that have more control over Web server software configurations should choose Level 5a or 5b, depending on cost and extranet architectural issues. Enterprises in regulated environments or life-and-safety applications should budget for the cost of implementing and managing Level 6 security configurations.

industry who has access to a computer. When that was done, *I'd re-recheck the bio and resume of every worker in an infrastructure industry who has access to a computer.*

I'd release the Eligible Receiver study to the public, so we can all see whether we've got to protect ourselves, and against what. I'd recognize that you can't protect a world full of networked computers from any single point on the network, *wherever* it is. I'd start teaching people to make their own machines secure. I'd tell them as much as possible about what crackers might realistically do, so they'd know, when they saw a cracker at work, what they were looking at. I'd keep in mind that most of the people I talked to wouldn't remember much of what I told them, and that's probably okay (for everyone besides them) as long as they're not in charge of a system that's managing important data or functions.

I'd start thinking about more radical solutions to the problems of life in a world full of superempowered angry men. I'd consider acting quickly when leading indicators show that a leader anywhere thinks murder is the way you solve problems.

I'd teach the drivers to *drive,* and I'd try to remember that not everybody you see on the road is a *driver.*

And I certainly would not call in the military to police U.S. citizens in cyberspace. I might need them to guard the reservoirs, but I certainly don't need them reading everybody's e-mail.

CHAPTER THIRTEEN

Digital Pearl Harbor

You've got to be very careful if you don't know where you're going, because you might not get there.

—Yogi Berra

On December 8, 2000, Richard Clarke of the National Security Council, then President Clinton's national coordinator for security, infrastructure protection, and counterterrorism, warned the United States of the potential for an event that he called "Digital Pearl Harbor." As reported by the Associated Press, Clarke said:

> "It may be improbable that cyberspace can be seriously disrupted, it may be improbable that a war in cyberspace can occur, but it could happen."
>
> "On coming to office, the next president will find that several nations have created information-warfare units," Clarke said.
>
> "These organizations are creating technology to bring down computer networks. Some are doing reconnaissance today on our networks, mapping them," he said.[1]

Clarke's warning seems very serious on its face, especially if you're one of the people to whom the subject of computer networks seems complex and frightening to start with. The comparison to Pearl Harbor is especially scary, because a lot of Americans died at Pearl Harbor, and the strategic balance of power in the world shifted, at least for a while. (When it shifted back, America was more prominent and stronger in world affairs than ever, but lots of things had changed.)

When I began researching Digital Pearl Harbor, though, it became apparent that no one has a clear idea of how an attack on cyberspace could produce those kinds of results. In the public discussions of cyber-terrorism to date, it's impossible to find a single scenario of anything remotely approaching that magnitude. Here's a fairly typical example—the testimony of Dr. Dorothy Denning, of Georgetown University, to the House of Representatives Special Oversight Panel on Terrorism, on May 23, 2000:

> . . . to qualify as cyberterrorism, an attack should result in violence against persons or property, or at least cause enough harm to generate fear. Attacks that lead to death or bodily injury, explosions, plane crashes, water contamination, or severe economic loss would be examples. . . . To the best of my knowledge, no attack so far has led to violence or injury to persons, although some may have intimidated their victims. . . . My personal view is that the threat of cyberterrorism has been mainly theoretical, but it is something to watch and take reasonable precautions against.[2]

Dr. Denning cited, as examples of attacks that have occurred, such nonterrifying incidents as Spanish protestors "bombarding" the Institute for Global Communications (IGC) with e-mail messages, and Serbian "hacktivists' . . . blasting" NATO computers with "e-mail bombs" (which apparently carry a harmful payload, if not exactly an explosive one) and denial-of-service attacks. As Dr. Denning noted mildly, "While the above incidents were motivated by political and social reasons, whether they were sufficiently harmful or frightening to be classified as cyberterrorism is a judgment call."

Indeed.

I'm reminded of movie critic Pauline Kael's scornful comment that a certain horror movie ought to be titled *The Amityville Nuisance*. Most modern nations would gladly trade a world teeming with enemies exactly like these for the ones they've suffered until now.

I came to the conclusion, after researching the issue, that Digital Pearl Harbor is a vague menace at best. The result of repeated warnings about Digital Pearl Harbor is an equally vague fear, and I began to wonder whether that was really the point of all those warnings: to create enough fear to justify the building of an elaborate military-industrial complex in cyberspace. There's already plenty of computer crime out there, and more is arriving faster every day. But the general population, along with most businesses, wasn't yet alarmed enough even to take simple precautions like installing a firewall on every computer that's attached to the Internet. That's so, even though a machine that's not so protected, especially one with an always-on cable or DSL connection, is certain to be cracked. People were dumb and happy where cyber-security was concerned.

Without a Digital Pearl Harbor to scare them into action, most citizens simply wouldn't care to foot the bill for strong security in cyberspace. And it didn't look to me like a real Digital Pearl Harbor—a single cyber-event deadly enough to change attitudes everywhere—was likely. I wondered whether someone—maybe a software security manufacturer who needed triple-digit sales growth—wouldn't try to fake one. It's a paranoid scenario, but it has been done. Hitler faked the Reichstag fire; some people think. Lyndon Johnson faked the Gulf of Tonkin incident. It wouldn't be very difficult to fake a cyber-attack that wasn't immediately traceable to the real source, specially if you helpfully planted clues leading to one of the usual suspects. (The Second Corollary to Hunter's Second Law says that in a World Without Secrets, people mostly see what they want to see.)

It didn't occur to me that there was another scenario that would scare everybody enough to justify massive spending on cyber-security and every other kind of security available. If I'd thought about it, perhaps I would've realized how plausible it was, but, by definition, nobody thinks about the unthinkable.

The *unthinkable* in this case means a real Pearl Harbor. The kind where people, not computers, get killed—lots of them, all at once—and everything changes, right away, forever.

ON THE MORNING . . .

. . . of September 11, 2001, I was working on research for this book when my wife, who watches the *Today* show almost every morning, called loudly and urgently to me to come downstairs *right away*.

I went to her immediately, and I saw what had excited her. The television was showing live images of the World Trade Center. One of the towers was on fire.

"A plane hit it," my wife said, talking fast in a high, tense voice.

"A plane?" I said. I wondered whether it was an accident.

"A *big* plane, a 737."

It still might be an accident.

"Rebecca works in one of those towers," my wife said.

Rebecca is my wife's brother's only daughter.

"She works at Fiduciary Trust," my wife said. "She's on the ninetieth floor."

I knew that the building wasn't much more than 100 stories tall, and the plane had apparently struck well below that. I could see that anyone on the ninetieth floor of that building was in very grave danger.

"Which building is she in?" my wife said. She trembled all over: her hands, her voice, her face. "Oh God, which building is she in?"

"I'll find out," I said. I ran to my computer and tried to get Fiduciary Trust's Web site. It took a couple of anxious minutes to find out that the site was down. I thought that was a bad sign. I ran back to my wife.

"I couldn't bring the site up, "I said.

"Maybe she was late for work," my wife said. "Maybe she's not there."

I didn't say anything. My niece is an ambitious young woman working in a big New York City office full of ambitious young people. Only day trippers show up for work there after 8:00 A.M.

"I hope so," I said.

My wife called her brother at work to ask him which building Rebecca worked in. He didn't know the tower had been struck by a plane. He hung up so he could call his wife and son.

A few minutes later, when a second plane struck the other World Trade Center tower, I realized that it was a terrorist attack. It no longer mattered which building my niece worked in. It only mattered whether she'd gotten to work on time.

Then the first tower hit fell apart and fell down while we, and everyone else in America with a television set turned on, watched.

My wife called her brother, crying. I went back to work. There wasn't much I could do, and it was easier than dealing with my feelings.

On the morning of September 11, my niece Rebecca was sleeping over at her boyfriend Matt's place in Manhattan. Normally, she'd have stayed at her own place in Hoboken, but they'd gone to a Yankees-Red Sox game the night before, and the game was called because of rain, so they went out for a drink, and then it got late, and she ended up staying over.

The alarm clock went off well before 8:00 A.M., but Matt was tired, and he hit the snooze button while Rebecca kept on sleeping. When the alarm went off again, and again, he kept hitting the button. By the time Rebecca woke up, it was almost 8:30, and she was already a lot later than she'd wanted to be. She yelled at Matt for another 15 minutes while she dressed and combed her hair, and then she took off at a run for the subway.

She couldn't take her regular subway, which would have deposited her on a platform in the basement of the tower where she worked in the World

Trade Center. She tried to get on the first arriving train, but a well-dressed woman in her mid-thirties got on before her and pushed her back onto the platform as the doors closed. The woman smirked at her through the window as the train pulled out of the station. Rebecca had to wait five minutes for another train; she cursed her boyfriend and that woman all the while.

When she emerged from the Fulton Street station 10 minutes later, she walked quickly toward her office. She had a block to go when she noticed people looking up and pointing, and she saw the fire in Tower One, the first tower hit. She stopped in her tracks and stared in disbelief. A few minutes later, the second plane struck Tower Two, the building where Rebecca's department was located, just below the floor that contained her cubicle. People trapped in Tower One were jumping from windows 80 floors or more up, to escape the flames. She saw them fall.

She turned and ran with the World Trade Center at her back, and she didn't stop until she reached the East River, where she began to hyperventilate and vomit. A young woman from Queens named Angela stopped to help her. Tower One collapsed behind them on the street they'd run from a few minutes earlier.

At about 11:00 A.M., Rebecca succeeded in finding a working pay phone, and she called her father, my wife's brother, at his office where he was waiting for her brother, to tell him she was unhurt. She wasn't calm. She'd seen a lot of people die, and she figured all the people she'd worked with were dead, too. Her father called my wife, and she told me, and I felt a sudden wave of relief and joy, followed immediately by a wave of sorrow for all the people who had died in the buildings I'd seen collapse on live television.

Almost all of Rebecca's department's coworkers survived the attack. Her boss understood what was happening when the first plane hit Tower One. He'd been there in 1993, when the World Trade Center was bombed for the first time, and he knew a terrorist attack when he saw it. The public address system in Tower Two was advising everyone to stay calm and stay where they were, but he wasn't having any of that. He gathered his entire staff and left Tower Two immediately. They, all but one, were out of the building before the second plane hit.

I wonder what happened to the woman who pushed Rebecca off the train, and whether that woman was on her way to the World Trade Center, too. She's not very nice, of course, but I hope she didn't die for it. She saved my niece's life.

Rebecca and Angela talk on the phone now, every day.

It's not over, and it won't be over for a very long time—perhaps not ever. It's hard to think of a modern terrorist war that ended.

In the meantime, all the cyber-security that a Digital Pearl Harbor might have justified is apparently justified, and then some.

WHAT HAPPENED AFTER PEARL HARBOR

The Japanese attack on Pearl Harbor on December 7, 1941, had a deep and lasting effect on how Americans perceived the importance and necessity of military spending. In 1996 dollars, America's military budget in 1940 was the equivalent of about $25 billion. After a relatively short period of demobilization immediately following World War II, Americans began to spend to counter the growing threat of Communist totalitarianism. By then, Americans understood what it might mean to be unprepared. We were willing to spend huge amounts to ensure that we would never, ever be blindsided by a military assault again. Between 1950 and 1995, American military spending, in 1996 dollars, averaged over $300 billion a year, an increase by a factor of 12 over pre-World War II military spending.

Pearl Harbor—and the war that followed—permanently changed attitudes toward the military. American society was militarized to an extent never seen previously in peacetime, and rarely in war. For 25 years after the end of World War II, the military services were highly respected, even revered in this country. Universal military conscription was introduced, and lasted—like reverence for the military—until the Vietnam War threatened to tear the country (and the military) apart. An extensive national security apparatus was created and empowered to operate in secrecy, sometimes in violation of Federal laws—for example, by spying on American citizens engaged in legal political activities. Those violations, and other military excesses, were generally treated by the American body politic as regrettable but tolerable side effects of an absolutely necessary commitment to defense. Certainly no official in charge of those security forces ever received serious punishment publicly for such violations. One of the officials who headed the CIA in that era was even elected President.

The Cold War ended, and the United States remains heavily militarized. We now spend more on defense than the next 12 nations combined. President George W. Bush's first proposed military budget was initially set at about $318 billion, and even before the assault on the World Trade

Center, there was no reason to think it would go anywhere but up in the next four years.

In short, Pearl Harbor and the Cold War pushed the United States strongly in the direction of an Engineered Society. This attack will, too, for some of the same reasons and a few new ones.

A PEARL HARBOR FOR THE NEW CENTURY

The World Trade Center attack is similar to Pearl Harbor in several ways. The casualty list is long; hundreds more people were killed at the World Trade Center than at Pearl Harbor. The enemy was known, and known to be dangerous, but the scale of the attack was unprecedented and unimaginable. The enemy is based in foreign lands, and is ethnically, religiously, politically, and economically very different from mainstream U.S. society—hence, easily demonized. (To the credit of everyone involved, American leaders have so far made strenuous efforts to avoid demonizing the enemy on any other than political grounds.) The United States is shocked, anguished, and ready to do whatever is necessary to defeat this enemy and gain revenge.

This war may be more protracted than World War II because the enemy is harder to find and identify. Like a Network Army, there may be no single person among the terrorists who could surrender his entire force, even if he wanted to. The fight may go on until every super-empowered angry man is dead. The British have been fighting the IRA for most of the past century, and the bombings there go on and on.

The boundaries are gone, in physical space, economic space, and cyberspace. The scope of what must be controlled to make an environment secure in this scenario is potentially limitless. Unlike World War II, the enemy in this war wears street clothes, carries concealed weapons, targets unarmed civilians instead of armed soldiers, and *intends to die* in the execution of his mission. In a globalized economy, enabled by global communications, anyone anywhere can be a terrorist, and anyone can be a victim.

It's a perfect setup for a security "arms race" in a paranoid society, which of course is consistent with the enemy's goal: to terrorize the society to the point of dysfunction and collapse.

And in a world in which there are no boundaries between us and a dangerous enemy, it's very tempting to watch everything, all the time, whether it's paranoid or not, whether or not it even *works.*

The Return of Friction

Before 9-11-01, the global economy aimed to be frictionless. To a large extent, it still is. Our credit cards, networks, and Internet-and-phone-based just-in-time 24–7 systems are all designed to make things happen on demand, anywhere. Credit cards are zero liability, so consumers won't hesitate a second before picking up the phone or the keyboard to make a purchase. Shippers put the goods on your doorstep within a day, even if the package is coming from thousands of miles away. It's *smooth*.

Our economy—not to mention our personal agendas—is dependent on maintaining that forward momentum. When things slow down—for example, when travelers have to arrive at an airport two hours ahead of time instead of half an hour ahead, and wait while their bags and their persons are checked from top to bottom—the economy slows down, too. Our agendas slow down. We feel the friction, and it's literally *a drag*.

The security we've lived with until now is intended to be frictionless, too. When it's perfect, it keeps *bad people out forever* and lets *good people in instantly,* and the good people don't even know it's there. Any friction, even for security's sake, is hard for us to tolerate. We want to be safe and secure, but we want to keep our choices and lifestyles intact, too. It's not easy to do both. It's very hard to do both when the threat that security is supposed to prevent suddenly becomes much larger, more dangerous, and close by.

We want to protect ourselves, but we don't want to slow down.

What happens next?

If you're American, you bring in the biggest, most powerful technology you've got, and you wire it into a smart and powerful system that controls everything. In other words, you *make the cars smarter.*

The drivers may just be strapped in for the ride, but at least they're moving.

A Dream of Electronic Handcuffs

On September 18, 2001, the *New York Times* carried an article titled "Technology's Role to Grow in a New World of Security," by William Glaberson. Among the solutions described in the article were the following:

> Security experts say technology has presented almost limitless possibilities, including national electronic identification cards. "Each American could

be given a 'smart card,' so, as they go into an airport or anywhere, we know exactly who they are," . . . .

Such cards, with computer chips, would have detailed information about those they were issued to and would identify them when read by a computer. The cards could be coordinated with fingerprints or, in a few years, facial characteristics, and be programmed to permit or limit access through turnstiles to buildings or areas. They could track someone's location, financial transactions, criminal history and even driving speed on a particular highway on a given night.[3]

It's fascinating to see the kind of controls technology vendors and some law enforcement officials would like to put in place. This stuff is a control freak's heart-pounding, sweaty dream. This card would give its possessor—any police officer, any *security guard,* any *petty thief*—immediate access to an extraordinary range of details about anyone's life.

The card is just a *key,* of course. I've talked already about the fact that keys with the power to open lots of databases are available now, and more are on the way. I've talked enough about the technology of surveillance to make the point that much of the stuff described by the *Times* is technologically feasible, now or soon.

Whether all that technology would work to prevent terrorist attacks is an open question. In the short run—meaning within the next three to five years, the answer is simply No. Having the technology is only the first step, and it's the easy part. The technology only works when people use it, and they can only use it when a supporting infrastructure of people, process, and facilities is in place. That part of the solution takes years and billions of dollars to build on a national, let alone an international, scale. I've previously noted that scanning technology is likely to be widespread within 5 to 10 years; I can't imagine the circumstances that would make it happen overnight.

Let's take a straightforward example. If we're all going to get a smart identification card something like the one described by the *Times,* we've first got to achieve a meaningful consensus, throughout the society, that we really want it. (Do *you?*) Assume that we do. Now we've got to decide what technology we're going to use. That takes at least a little time—more time if we change our minds at any point about the functions the card is supposed to perform. We've got to design technical and human systems for making the cards and controlling their distribution. We've got to design and build the identification reference databases. (They're still just empty vessels at this point; loading them up comes later.) Anyone who needs to read the cards has to acquire and install the necessary equipment. We've got to test the system for function and capacity. (Suppose the stuff doesn't work, or doesn't work all the time, or works very, *very* slowly? Friction, man.) We've got to set up the facilities to make and distribute the cards. We've got to figure out how to protect everything in the system, too, because you sure don't want a terrorist or a criminal getting into the card factory or the ID database. (Imagine the price a terrorist or a drug dealer would pay for a half hour alone with the machine that makes the cards.) Next, we've got to establish the facilities and procedures for people to get their cards. Then we've got to start lining everybody up to get their pictures taken or their fingerprints scanned or whatever it is that makes the card a bulletproof form of ID.

I presume that it's clear by now that this stuff won't be helping us to stop terrorists a year from now. Even after it's introduced, you can figure that there'll be gaps and noise in the system. Whenever you make 250 million of anything, it's tough to control them all. It's not true that when the database is up and running we'll know exactly who everyone is, as the Times says. We'll know exactly who all the law-abiding citizens are. With everyone else, we'll know who the card *says* they are.

Fake electronic IDs are not much harder to produce than any other kind. *Any set of electronic bits can be hacked;* it's a basic principle of the World Without Secrets. Hardware can't be hacked, but it can be bought or stolen. We can make it against the law to make or carry a fake or altered card, just as laws have been proposed to make it illegal to defeat an electronic security device or reverse-engineer a computer program. So what? No one who's planning to commit mass murder is going to balk at making a false ID.

As to whether cards like this will prevent terrorist attacks in the longer term, my guess is that the answer is still *No,* but it depends on what you mean by *prevent.* We can't prevent prisoners from assaulting, raping, and killing each other in a maximum security prison, where everybody's under observation almost all the time. (Some observers believe that the brutality of American prisons is a matter of official policy, not policy failure, but we'll put that issue aside for now.) If *prevent* means *zero attacks,* I doubt it can be done. Even if we watch everybody, all the time, how do we stop a terrorist, who's ready to die, from killing people with weapons that are easily found everywhere in an industrial society?

But the intention is clear. If we just let the machines do the work, we can at least get the friction down, and we can all keep moving.

We won't be moving in quite the same way, though.

UNDER OBSERVATION

Heisenberg's Uncertainty Principle says that the act of observing a thing changes the thing that's observed, even if the observer does nothing *but* observe. That means, I guess, that the mere fact of ubiquitous electronic surveillance changes the way people behave.

In August 2001, I interviewed anthropologist Dr. Susan Anderson, formerly a member of the research team at Xerox PARC, and now an adviser to Gartner.[4] I was specifically interested in how people act when they're being watched and know it.

"When I worked at PARC," Anderson told me, "we had a ubiquitous computing project that included everything from active badges on up to handheld stuff like PDAs. People had location sensors and communications devices on watches and keychains. They had badges that opened doors, and there were sensors planted all around the building to track all the devices. There were basically two reactions: *Oh, cool!* and *Oh, my God, get me out of here!* The issue is control. How much control do I have over my own environment?

"The science fiction on this subject is pretty thoroughly dystopian. It's almost always about establishing a secret place in a totalitarian society. The more surveillance is distributed along authority and class lines, the more we would see that kind of subversion. It's not good for our society.

"We've always had class issues in America. Ubiquitous surveillance pushes those issues to an extreme. Suppose the technology for monitoring and control was applied along class or race lines, for example: as they already are, of course."

I wondered immediately how it could not be so. Everyone knows that racial and ethnic profiling are already part of police operations in many cities, and must be part of the war against terrorism. If all you want to do is stop street crime via video surveillance, you'll wind up putting cameras in the neighborhoods where there's lots of street crime. That's where poor people live. It's not Wall Street, even though lots of money gets stolen on Wall Street on a fairly regular basis. (I guess we'll take care of everybody on Wall Street via monitoring of e-mail and financial transactions. But they won't be so aware of it.)

"People outside the mainstream already don't trust the mainstream," Anderson continued. "Add this to the reasons, and trust may break completely. It's a much more extreme kind of disenfranchisement than we've seen so far. The technology is always in the hands of the few. It easily leads to subjugation, control, subversion.

"You can imagine that local monitoring tuned in to local mores could be acceptable to people. In some societies, life is lived publicly, and everybody knows what everybody else is doing all the time anyway. But that's direct access, not technology-mediated access."

That's the way America was when the Puritans ran the colonies, of course. If you had an affair with somebody, they dragged you into the middle of town and pinned a big scarlet letter "A" on your chest.

When I moved to Vermont in 1991, I had a hard time getting to know people. Everyone seemed so *withdrawn*. I mentioned that one day to a singer whom I'd accompanied on piano on a few gigs. "It seems like the state motto is 'It's none of your business,'" I told her.

"No," she said seriously, "the state motto is 'It's none of *my* business.'"

It's a good motto, but for how much longer? If safety is everybody's business and the world is a very unsafe place, where does the boundary between my business and yours end?

Well, that's easy. It ends when my business will make you unsafe. But how do we know when *that* is? Especially if we want to know *before* it happens?

You see? That's why we have to watch *everything*.

WATCHING EVERYTHING IS NOT KNOWING EVERYTHING

The Second Corollary to Hunter's Second Law—*When everything is known, no one knows everything*—says: *People see only what they want to see, and that's usually what lies on the path of least resistance.* That's true even of people whose professional lives are spent gathering and assessing information. It may be especially true of those people because they're continually swamped in data, and the temptation to assume that most of the data are the same as they ever were is very strong.

Consider this report in the September 19, 2001, *Los Angeles Times:*

> . . . in 1998 . . . computer hackers tapped into a NASA Jet Propulsion Laboratory computer in Pasadena and accessed data about the commercial air traffic system. "The FAA had to shut down communications for several live flights going on at the time," said [Tom] Talleur, then chief of NASA's cybercrime unit. This intelligence could have told hackers the configuration of GPS navigation satellites and allowed them to jam the system during a war, he said . . . because NASA officials did not understand the implications of the hack, they refused to allow [Talleur] to install an "intercept box" needed to track the hackers immediately. . . . [5]

Is it significant that someone wants to know privileged information about the location of GPS satellites? NASA officials didn't think so. Maybe they should have. It's information that could be used to do significant damage. If something had happened right away, like jets or satellites falling out of the sky, it would have been obvious that it was important. But nothing did, so it wasn't. The NASA officials saw what they wanted to see: a cracker came and left, and nobody got hurt.

It's not a very good test of significance, but it's not surprising. How do you react to a theft of information that might be used against you at some unspecified point in time, by an unspecified enemy, for unspecified purposes? Freak out? Then what? Move all the satellites? Stop all flights everywhere?

Recently, I saw a news report on NBC to the effect that a couple living in Virginia reported directly to the CIA, about a year ago, that their neighbors were acting suspiciously and ought to be investigated. The CIA apparently didn't think so. Two of those suspicious neighbors died on September 11, 2001, when the plane they hijacked crashed into the World Trade Center. The information from the Virginia couple was apparently good, and certainly timely. Would it have been better information—more worthy of attention—if it had been pulled off a Carnivore sweep? Could it have been pulled off a Carnivore sweep?

If we don't know what's important now, why will we know what's important when it's surrounded by even *more* information that's mostly not important?

IF AUTOMATED SURVEILLANCE WORKS, WHOM DOES IT WORK ON?

Immediately following the attack on the World Trade Center, U.S. Senators Orrin Hatch (R-Utah) and Dianne Feinstein (D-California) proposed legislation that would allow any U.S. attorney or state attorney general to order a 48-hour installation of the FBI's Carnivore surveillance system on an Internet Service Provider's systems.[6] "It is essential that we give our law enforcement authorities every possible tool to search out and bring to justice those individuals who have brought such indiscriminate death into our backyard," Hatch said.

Senators Hatch and Feinstein don't know whether more Carnivore surveillance will help catch terrorists, because no one knows that. They think it might help—if you read everybody's e-mail, maybe you'll find something written by a very careless terrorist, the kind who uses the word "bomb" and the name of the target in the same e-mail, and then addresses it directly to Osama bin Laden. It's a long shot, of course. Terrorists aren't stupid. If prisoners in maximum security prisons and American POWs in North Vietnam can find effective ways to communicate secretly under the noses of attentive captors, terrorists can write e-mails that don't trigger Carnivore's alarms.

Terrorists are sophisticated. Sophisticated people know how to hide. Here's an example.

ZeroKnowledge was one of the companies that, until recently, offered Internet "anonymizer" services. For a fee, the company would set up your Internet access so that no one—not even ZeroKnowledge—would know who you really were. (ZeroKnowledge abruptly announced that it was exiting this business about a week after 9-11-01. A few days earlier, I'd predicted to a colleague that ZeroKnowledge would make such an exit, or be forced to do so by law enforcement authorities, within six months. It's hard to stay ahead in the predictions business in a World Without Secrets.) I proposed the following approach to finding ZeroKnowledge's subscribers to Bill Spernow, a former cyber-cop and Gartner analyst who now works as a high-tech security consultant:

> I deposit a worm on ZK's servers. The worm simply attaches itself to any machine that logs in, burrows into the machine, extracts an IP address *(which uniquely identifies a computer attached to the Internet),* user information, and anything else it can find on the hard drive, and then exits, erasing any trace of itself. The worm takes pains to avoid alerting anyone involved to its presence (e.g., it lives only in RAM, does not execute when the machine is otherwise silent). Would it do the job?

Here's Spernow's reply:

> Realizing that your technique was possible (but difficult), I would loop through two or three anonymous service providers before I did my nasty deed—whatever that might be. Making your worm's task that much more difficult is the timeline analysis that would have to be done to get back to the originating IP address. In the end it would do you no good, because it would probably be a legitimate account that I compromised at some local ISP using a local dial-up phone number. (Phone companies don't keep records of local calls, nor do they have the ability to do so at the generic level.)
>
> Bottom line: If I don't want you to find me, you won't![7]

If it was easy to track e-mail to its source, a substantial number of the thousand or so highly skilled and dangerous crackers in the world would already be in jail. The people who track crackers have already come to that conclusion, and they're relying on human intelligence—networks of people, not machines—to find the most dangerous crackers.

Suppose that terrorists can get phony ID cards when they need them, and can code their messages so automated analysis software can't figure out what they're really talking about, and can manage electronic communications so that they're effectively anonymous. All of these suppositions are very probably true. Then the people who will be controlled by massive surveillance are law-abiding citizens like *you* and *me*.

We're the ones whose real names and addresses and photos and fingerprints and bank accounts and driving histories are stored on a hundred different databases, tied together with our faces or our credit card numbers or our national ID numbers. We're the ones whose apparent lives are the same as our real lives.

We're the ones without secrets. Or the ones who'll have them stripped away.

THE ISSUE IS CONTROL

When I'm under constant surveillance, who's in control? Like Anderson said: *How much control do I have over my own environment?* If I can't control the external environment—what people *see*—I can try to control the internal environment—*what I present*.

"It's very hard for people to project a mask," Anderson said. "But people can have different personas at home and at work. You can imagine putting on a different persona as you go out the door. There's a different way of behaving in a public space when you're under surveillance. You're less honest, less authentic, less authentic, less different from others. It's the 'homogenization' of public behavior.

"You may not know who plants surveillance devices, but you know the kinds of people who do it and why they do it, so you're concerned about control issues. People can be ignorant of what's going on around them, but everybody knows stuff and suspects stuff. People might know that individuals plant these things sometimes, but suspect that they're all planted by the government."

That's a paranoid attitude. But it's probably accurate.

"Political discourse, religious discourse, private feelings, disagreement, argument all go underground. It's very difficult for a democratic society."

I can sum it up briefly. The society gets Engineered.

THE RETURN OF THE ENGINEERED SOCIETY

War—especially a war with popular support, like this one—turns any society into an Engineered Society, where *values are widely shared* and *action is channeled through communities organized around the dominant value system*, like the military, or the Red Cross. There's more respect for traditional authority, more control, less tolerance for anyone outside the mainstream.

That's where the United States is right now. We're all willing to support the defeat of the enemy by any means necessary. Hatch and Feinstein have proposed powerful new controls. More will probably follow in cyberspace and physical space. The Bush Administration is debating the reintroduction of military conscription, which was a key element of the shared experience that produced shared values in the United States during the 1950s.

Ken Watman told me, "In the USA, we approach problems as if they were all about engineering. We're a very hierarchical society, not in the official sense—we're suspicious of federal authority—but in our business and in the military, we're very top-down. We have greater faith in the power of organization than in the power of the individual."[8] Now more than ever. Who can stand alone against terrorists who hijack commercial jetliners and ram them into buildings?

There are a lot of reasons why Network Armies everywhere might be driven to the defensive by this war, but there are good reasons to think that Network Armies will survive. The Network Army thrives on open Internet communications, and the openness of the Internet is certainly threatened by this war on terrorism. But this is an international war, perhaps even a new kind of World War. Americans are carefully framing it as an international war against terrorism, not *Muslims*. Information will continue to flow freely worldwide. It must, to create the global trust that's necessary to avoid a religious World War.

If information moves freely, people may not. The Network Army thrives in a world without physical borders. Because terrorists also thrive in a world without physical borders, governments will be keenly sensitive to international activists of any kind. It may be more difficult for the Network Army to gather and exert its power against the Engineered Societies it opposes. Without the ability to project power, Network Armies may splinter, or revert to a Lost and Lonely scenario.

The Network Army thrives on diverse and intersecting political and social agendas. In wartime, political and social agendas that conflict with the dominant agenda are put under intense pressure. Striking workers, for example, might be jailed if their industry is critical to the war effort. To the extent that the war is an all-consuming effort, it simply drives other agendas out.

The two-part question that's impossible to answer is: *How long will this war last and how much destruction is yet to come?* The longer it lasts and the worse it is, the likelier it is that Network Armies will face suppression by angry Engineered Societies.

WHO'S NOT ON THE TEAM?

The TV running next to me as I write this in late September 2001 is showing a Fox TV report on the World Trade Center attacks. Over the reporter's head, Fox is broadcasting a banner that reads "America United." I've seen lots of banners on TV news in the past week, with similar messages. As I flip the channels to check on what else is running right now, I see "America on Alert" on MSNBC and "America's New War" on CNN. One of the local news stations has a banner that reads "America Rising." E! is running a prerecorded show called "Hollywood Unites"; two E! correspondents are interviewing the woman who plays Ray's mom on "Everybody Loves Raymond." (Some of the things you see in the Exception Economy are just a little *too weird,* man. *Hollywood Unites?* Like a sitcom actress knows something about this stuff that *we* don't? Like it's our *entertainers* that are going to lead the war against terrorism?)

I've heard God invoked frequently this week, too, not just by politicians with conservative religious agendas (or religious leaders with conservative political agendas). I've heard God invoked by professionals for whom detached objectivity is one of the professional requirements, like TV news reporters. I don't blame them. The events are overwhelming. If you've got faith (95 percent of Americans, I was advised by NBC News, believe in God, and 80 percent attend church regularly), this is when you use it, even if it's not very professional.

Some professional Mentats seem to have given up, at least temporarily. The reporters on one local TV station in New York City have spent a lot of the past week yelling and waving their hands. One of their reporters explained unapologetically, on-air, that she's so caught up in the events that she can't *not* shout sometimes, and she figures it's okay because it brings her closer to her audience. I don't think she really gets it. Professional Mentats are supposed to *lead* the audience, not *sit in it*. But what we all want, right now, is to come together. It's scary to be alone; right now, it's like being Lost and Lonely. (I don't suppose I need to explain that, in a society under constant electronic surveillance, things get more difficult for lots of the Lost and Lonely.)

Our President has made the message to foreign leaders and nations very clear: You're with America, or you're with the terrorists. That's a message for everyone in America, too. *Everybody's on America's team.* We all really do want to be on the team, and we're willing to sacrifice to make the team win.

That might even include having our e-mail read and our phone conversations tapped and our movements tracked with a national electronic ID. We're willing to go that far because we think it might help, but there are a few questions. The first is: Will it really help? The second is: Can anyone roll it back if it doesn't? The third question is: How will we know?

The stats from Ybor City don't show that the crime rate changed during the four years after the cameras went in, but the cameras are still there. They've even been augmented with software. Even if you can't measure the impact, you wonder how much worse things would be if you didn't have the technology.

Once you start, you tend to keep going.

PEARL HARBOR IN THE BORDERLESS WORLD

Pearl Harbor changed everything for Americans, suddenly and forever. The events of 9-11-01 have done the same, though the change is still forming. You can see it coming in this paragraph from the *New York Times:*

> Some security officials said Americans had yet to focus on the more difficult questions most likely to follow tighter airport security. Once airports and airplanes are more secure, they said, the country will have to consider extending many restrictions to other public places like stadiums, train and bus stations, universities, elementary schools, parks and reservoirs.[9]

In a World Without Secrets, where the boundaries between private and public are eradicated, the boundary between public spaces and war zones is the next to fall. We're on the verge of an armed, guarded, monitored society, and we don't know yet whether all those elements are needed to ensure the safety and security of the nation. I don't know what the final outcome will be, or how deeply surveillance of ordinary citizens will be entrenched in American life.

We want to eliminate the friction, and eliminating secrets seems to be a part of it. Most of the secrets involved are the harmless secrets of ordinary citizens, but the technology can't make that distinction. Only the people working the technology could distinguish the harmless secrets, if they care to.

It will be the business of all of us to make them care, and it will be our business for the long and indefinite future.

CHAPTER FOURTEEN

The Last Secrets

There's little to add to what I've already said. The most important thing is this: In a World Without Secrets, many of the secrets we lose are those that we give away freely, without thinking, in return for the elimination of some small friction. Whenever we use a credit card, we expose ourselves. The price we pay for ease and simplicity in our daily business is the erosion of the distance between us and every commercial entity in the world, transaction by transaction. We can gain some of that distance back by reintroducing a little friction into our lives.

We can slow down the relentless accumulation of information about us.

But regardless of any efforts we might make to slow down that accumulation, it will occur. In the era of global information access, the thinking of our societies about the ways in which businesses and governments are allowed to handle information is foolishly, dangerously inadequate. It's based on the mental habits of a world in which information moved in physical containers at the speed of a train, and geographic boundaries were effective in separating states from each other. All that has nothing to do with a global commerce-enabled world. We need a new social compact that specifies the responsibilities that go with owning information, and the importance of protecting it. If the goal of commerce is to support a frictionless global marketplace, then all the players in the marketplace, worldwide, must play by the same rules. Those who don't must be invited to leave. Disregard for the sanctity of information must be treated as seriously as disregard for borders once was.

The drivers have to drive: to take responsibility, to ask *why,* to seek explanations and demand accountability, to install effective human oversight in recognition of the absence of limits on the capabilities of our technologies. Such oversight demands that the boundaries created by policy be treated as if they were made of granite 100 feet high and 10 feet thick. Businesses must take the lead in setting and publicizing those boundaries, for the sake of their relationships above all else.

It may work, meaning it may succeed in maintaining the distance between us and others that is our privacy. Maybe not. The legal definition of a right to privacy is barely older than the semiconductor. Our new technologies will put it under extreme pressure, no less than the war we face with a violent Network Army.

Still, I believe that people are at their best when things are at their worst, and people, so I'm told and so I believe, are essentially good. Imagine if it were otherwise in a World Without Secrets.

Notes

Chapter One

1. Visa USA, "About Visa USA," http://www.usa.visa.com/personal /about_visa/?it=ft_/index.html.

2. Amazon.com Privacy Policy, http://www.amazon.com/exec/obidos /tg/browse/-/468496/rcf=hp_hp_ct_4_2/t/002–7876889-6588044.

3. Victor A. Kovner, interview by Richard Hunter, October 11, 2001.

Chapter Two

1. Associated Press, "Tampa Uses Cameras to Scan for Wanted Faces," July 2, 2001. Reprinted with permission of The Associated Press.

2. "Technology Analysis: Biometric Technology," by Andrew Phillips, Gartner Dataquest, June 2001, p. 1.

3. Detective Bill Todd, interview by Richard Hunter, September 27, 2001.

4. "Super Bowl surveillance: facing up to biometrics," by John D. Woodward. Copyright 2001 by RAND Corporation. Reprinted with permission of RAND Corp.

5. C. S. Lewis, *The Four Loves,* Harcourt Brace Janovich, 1960.

6. Frances Zelazny, Visionics Director of Corporate Communications, interviews by Richard Hunter, September 14 and October 3, 2001.

7. "Violent Times: A Case Study of the Ybor City Historic District," by Dr. Terry A. Danner, St. Leo University (draft, 2001).

8. Terry Danner, interview by Richard Hunter, October 11, 2001.

9. Victor A. Kovner, interview by Richard Hunter, October 11, 2001.

10. Visionics Corporation Privacy Protection Principles, http://www
.visionics.com/newsroom/biometrics/privacy.html.

11. Testimony of Jeffrey C. Steinhoff, Assistant Comptroller General, Accounting and Information Management Programs, U.S. General Accounting Office, before a hearing of the Subcommittee on Government Management, Information, and Technology, June 6, 2000, http://www.house .gov/reform/gmit/hearings/2000hearings/000606.ffmia/000606js.htm.

12. "Business Goes to War," Richard Behar, *Fortune,* Vol. 144, No. 7, p. 145. © 2001. Time, Inc. All rights reserved.

13. Gramm-Leach-Bliley Act, 15 USC, Subchapter I, Sec. 6801–6810, Disclosure of Nonpublic Personal Information, http://www.ftc.gov/privacy /glbact/glbsub1.htm.

14. Federal Trade Commission Privacy Agenda, http://www.ftc.gov /opa/2001/10/privacyagenda.htm.

15. Sun Microsystems CEO Scott McNealy, press conference, January 24, 1999.

CHAPTER THREE

1. Neil Scott, Leader and Chief Engineer, Archimedes Project, Stanford University Center for the Study of Language and Information, interviews by Richard Hunter, September 13 and September 21, 2001.

2. Dr. Egil Juliussen, Telematics Research Group, www.telematicsresearch.com, interview by Richard Hunter, September 19, 2001.

3. Nicos Peonides, Arup, interview by Richard Hunter, September 18, 2001.

4. X10.com, http://www.x10.com/products/x10_ms13a.htm.

5. X10.com, http://www.x10.com/products/x10_sw21a.htm.

6. X10.com, http://www.x10.com/products/sk10a_deal.htm.

7. X10.com, "A Cynic's Demise," http://www.x10.com/news/articles /1012_cynic.htm.

8. *Katz v. United States,* 389 U.S. 347 (1967).

9. *Commonwealth v. Rekasie,* 778 A.2d 624 (Pa. 2001).

CHAPTER FOUR

1. David Reid, Motorola, interview by Richard Hunter, September 21 and September 27, 2001.

2. Telematics Research Group, Telematics: Technologies, Trends and Markets, September 2001; Executive Summary, http://www.telematicsresearch.com.

3. Steve Millstein, ATX, interview by Richard Hunter, October 2, 2001.

4. Dr. Egil Juliussen, Telematics Research Group, interview by Richard Hunter, September 19, 2001.

5. "Rental driver finds Big Brother over shoulder" by Richard Stenger, June 22, 2001. © Cable News Network LP, LLLP.

6. AirIQ Web site, http://www.airiq.com/text/about_main.html.

7. Don Simmonds, AirIQ, interview with Richard Hunter, October 5, 2001.

8. ATX Privacy Policy, http://www.atxtechnologies.com/aboutatx/legalpriv.asp#privacy.

9. ATX, A Vision for Telematics, http://www.atxtechnologies.com/telematics/future.asp.

10. SAS Website, Professions in SAS—Pilot, http://www.scandinavian.net/company/career/professions/pilot.asp.

CHAPTER FIVE

1. Global Business Network, http://www.gbn.com.

2. Pornography industry revenues from "Naked Capitalists: There's No Business Like Porn Business," by Frank Rich, New York Times, May 20, 2001.

3. U.S. Department of Justice National Drug Intelligence Center, http://www.usdoj.gov/ndic/pubs/716/marijuan.htm#Demand.

4. "Instant Company" by Po Bronson, July 11, 1999, Page 44, Section 6, Column 1 of Magazine Desk. Copyright © 1999 by the New York Times Co. Reprinted by permission.

5. For further discussion, see "Modernization's Challenge to Traditional Values: Who's Afraid of Ronald McDonald?" by Ronald Inglehart and Wayne E. Baker, The Futurist, March 2001, Vol. 35, No. 2, Page 16.

CHAPTER SIX

1. Reprinted by permission of Harvard Business School Press. From The Innovator's Dilemma by Clayton M. Christensen. Boston, MA, 2001.

Copyright © 2000 by the Harvard Business School Publishing Corporation; all rights reserved.

2. Eric Raymond, interviews by Richard Hunter, September 7 and September 9, 2001.

3. "The Cathedral and the Bazaar" by Eric Raymond, first official presentation May 21, 1997, http://www.tuxedo.org/~esr/writings/cathedral-bazaar.

4. The Halloween Papers, http://www.opensource.org/halloween.

5. Halloween Document VI, http://www.opensource.org/halloween/halloween6.html.

6. Robert Heinlein, *The Moon Is a Harsh Mistress,* Berkley Press, CA, 1966.

7. *Beware! Some of Your Co-Workers Could Be Hackers, IBM Says.* Copyright Reuters 2001. http://biz.yahoo.com/rf/010906/106543360.html.

8. Eric Raymond, How to Become a Hacker, http://www.tuxedo.org/~esr/faqs/hacker-howto.html.

9. From *Organizing Genius* by Warren Bennis and Patricia Ward Biederman. Copyright 1997 by Warren Bennis and Patricia Ward Biederman. Reprinted by permission of Perseus Books Publishers, a member of Perseus Books, L.L.C.

10. "Open Source Software: A (New?) Development Methodology," Microsoft internal memo by Vinod Valloppillil, August 11, 1998, http://opensource.org/halloween/halloween1.html.

11. Prepared Text of Remarks by Craig Mundie, Microsoft Senior Vice President; The Commercial Software Model; The New York University Stern School of Business, May 3, 2001, http://www.microsoft.com/presspass/exec/craig/05–03sharedsource.asp.

12. "Is Microsoft Secretly Using Open Source?" by Lee Gomes, Wall Street Journal Online, June 18, 2001. Copyright 2001 by Wall Street Journal Online. Reprinted by permission of Wall Street Journal Online via the Copyright Clearance Center.

CHAPTER SEVEN

1. Excerpt of the http://www.searchenginewatch.com/sereport/00/08-deepweb.html. Reprinted with permission from http://www.internet.com. Copyright 2001 INT Media Group, Incorporated. All rights reserved. Datamation and internet.com are the exclusive Trademarks of INT Media Group, Incorporated.

2. From Chris Wallace's Internet Expose, People on the Fringe, "Identity Theft." Copyright © 2001 ABC News Internet Ventures. Permission granted by ABCNEWS.com.

3. The Drudge Report, http://www.drudgereport.com.

4. As described in "CNN-er blasts King for sucking up to George W.," http://www.medialifemagazine.com/news2001/mar01/mar05/4_thurs/news7thursday.htm.

CHAPTER EIGHT

1. "A Two-Bit Conspiracy," by Patrick E. Cole and Elaine Shannon, *Time,* August 21, 1995. © 1995 Time Inc., reprinted by permission.

2. "Playing for a Stay," by Viveca Novak and Elaine Shannon, *Time,* June 11, 2001. © 2001 Time Inc., reprinted by permission.

3. Letter from Gen. Partin to U.S. Sen. Trent Lott, July 30, 1995, http://www.whatreallyhappened.com/RANCHO/POLITICS/OK/PARTIN/ok8.htm. See also interview with Samuel Cohen at http://www.constitution.org/ocbpt/ocbpt_01.htm. (*Note:* The author appreciates that the sources listed are not mainstream press, but the theories involved are not mainstream. The reader is advised to approach with caution.)

CHAPTER NINE

1. This article is excerpted from Andreas Florissen, Boris Maurer, Bernhard Schmidt, and Thomas Vahlenkamp, "The race to the bottom," *The McKinsey Quarterly,* 2001, Number 3, and can be found on the publication's Web site, www.mckinseyquarterly.com. Copyright © 2001 McKinsey & Company. All rights reserved. Used by permission.

2. Marco Alpert, interview with Richard Hunter, September 20, 2001.

3. "Bottled Water Ads Barely Make a Splash" by Theresa Howard, *USA TODAY,* October 8, 2001. Copyright 2001, *USA TODAY,* Reprinted with permission.

CHAPTER TEN

1. Sales data from Recording Industry of America reports at "A Chronological Index of RIAA/Market Data," http://www.riaa.org/MD-Index.cfm.

2. Miles Copeland, interview with Richard Hunter, August 15, 2001.

3. "O.A.R. Evolution of a Revolution" by Clay Steakley, *Performing Songwriter,* Vol. 8, Issue 54, Page 68, June 2001. Reprinted with permission of *Performing Songwriter.*

4. "Sound Bites" by Russell Hall, *Performing Songwriter,* Vol. 8, Issue 54, Page 16, June 2001. Reprinted with permission of *Performing Songwriter.*

5. "Napster Signs Deal with European Indie Labels," by James Ledbetter, *Industry Standard,* June 26, 2001.

6. "RIAA Wants to Hack Your PC," by Declan McCullagh, *Wired News,* October 15, 2001, http://www.wired.com. Copyright © 2001 Wired Digital Inc., a Lycos Network site. All rights reserved.

CHAPTER ELEVEN

1. "Technology Collection Trends in the U.S. Defense Industry," Volume VII, 2001, Defense Security Service, http://www.dss.mil /cithreats/2001_trend.pdf.

2. Laura Behrens, "Privacy and Security: The Secret Growth Strategy," Gartner G2 research, June 21, 2001.

3. U.S. Immigration and Naturalization Service, "Colombia: Kidnapping and extortion by armed groups in urban and suburban areas," January 3, 2000, http://www.ins.usdoj.gov/graphics/services/asylum /ric/documentation/COL00001.htm.

CHAPTER TWELVE

1. Reprinted from U.S. Naval Institute *Proceedings* with permission; Copyright © (1998) U.S. Naval Institute.

2. Ken Watman, interview with Richard Hunter, September 12, 2001.

3. James A. Savage, Jr. testimony to the Senate Committee on the Judiciary, Subcommittee on Technology, Terrorism, and Government Information, July 25, 2001, http://judiciary.senate.gov/te072501st-savage.htm.

4. "Cyber Attacks During the War on Terrorism: A Predictive Analysis" from Dartmouth's Institute for Security Technology Studies. Copyright 2001, Trustees of Dartmouth College. Reprinted with permission.

5. "Technology Collection Trends in the U.S. Defense Industry," Volume VII, 2001, Defense Security Service, http://www.dss.mil/cithreats/2001_trend.pdf.

6. "Cyber Threats and the U.S. Economy," testimony of Stephen E. Cross, Director, Software Engineering Institute, Carnegie Mellon University, before the Joint Economic Committee, U.S. Congress, February 23, 2000. http://www.cert.org/congressional_testimony/Cross_testimony_Feb2000.html#Vulnerability.

7. John Keegan, *A History of Warfare*. Random House, Inc./Knopf Publishing Group, 1994.

8. Len Hynds, interview with Richard Hunter, September 27, 2001.

9. Ellie Padgett, Testimony to the U.S. Senate Subcommittee on Technology, Terrorism and Government Information, June 10, 1998, Federal Document Clearing House, Inc.

10. "It's Time to Take Steps to Foil a Cyber Pearl Harbor," by James Pinkerton, © 2000 Newsday, Inc., May 2, 2000.

11. Congressman Rob Andrews, interview with Richard Hunter, September 28, 2001.

12. John Pescatore, "Web Server Security Hierarchy," Gartner Research Tactical Guideline, September 28, 2001.

13. Ibid.

CHAPTER THIRTEEN

1. Associated Press, "Security Adviser Warns of Cyberterrorism," December 8, 2000. Reprinted with permission of The Associated Press.

2. Dorothy E. Denning, "Cyberterrorism," testimony before the Special Oversight Panel on Terrorism, Committee on Armed Services, U.S. House of Representatives, May 23, 2000, http://www.cs.georgetown.edu/~denning/infosec/cyberterror.html.

3. "Technology's Role to Grow in a New World of Security" by William Glaberson, September 19, 2001, Page 1, Section B, Column 5 of National Desk. Copyright © 2001 by the New York Times Co. Reprinted by permission.

4. Susan Anderson, interview with Richard Hunter, August 30, 2001.

5. "After the Attack; Spreading Hate; The Terrorists Are Winning the War" by Charles Piller and Dave Wilson. September 19, 2001. Copyright 2001, Los Angeles Times. Reprinted by permission.

6. SA 1562, "Combating Terrorism Act of 2001," Sec. 832.

7. Bill Spernow, e-mails to Richard Hunter, August 16, 2001.

8. Ken Watman, interview with Richard Hunter, September 12, 2001.

9. "Technology's Role to Grow in a New World of Security" by William Glaberson, September 19, 2001, Page 1, Section B, Column 5 of National Desk. Copyright © 2001 by the New York Times Co. Reprinted by permission.

INDEX